Perennial
Combinations

Stunning Combinations That Make Your Garden Look Fantastic Right from the Start

C. Colston Burrell

Coauthor of *Hellebores—A Comprehensive Guide,*
Winner of the American Horticultural Society Book Award

RODALE

Book Design by Diane Ness Shaw
Illustrations by Sue Gettlin, Dale Mack, Elayne Sears, Mavis Augustine Torke, and Leslie Watkins

Library of Congress Cataloging-in-Publication Data

Burrell, C. Colston.
    Perennial combinations : stunning combinations that make your garden look fantastic right from the start / C. Colston Burrell—Rev. and updates pbk. ed.
        p.   cm.
    Includes bibliographical references and index.
    ISBN-13 978–1–59486–853–5   paperback
    ISBN-10 1–59486–853–0   paperback
    1. Perennials.   2. Planting design.   3. Gardens—Design.   I. Title.
    635.9'32—dc22   2007038202

Distributed to the trade by Holtzbrinck Publishers

2   4   6   8   10   9   7   5   3   1   paperback

On the cover: Coreopsis, salvia, and catmint highlight this combination of sun-loving perennials in a Santa Fe, New Mexico, garden designed by Julia Berman. (For more information about this perennial combination, turn to page 156).

We inspire and enable people to improve their lives and the world around them
For more of our products visit **rodalestore.com** or call 800-848-4735

To Carol M. Hegre, who urged me to write a book
about designing combinations of great plants,
and to Ellen Phillips, who gave form
to a good idea and made
this book a reality.

Contents

COMBINATIONS ON THE WILD SIDE

COMBINATIONS FOR EXTRA FUN

NEW COMBINATIONS FOR DRAMATIC EFFECT

A World of Change

The world of horticulture is never static. Things are always changing, from proper planting practices to botanical nomenclature. Since initial publication of *Perennial Combinations* in 1999, many botanical names have changed. These changes reflect both revisions in nomenclature based on historical precedents and discovery of new relationships between plants through gene mapping. Some large genera containing familiar garden plants are now placed in new genera based on a combination of factors. For ease of identification, I decided not to incorporate the changes in the text. Below is a list of some plants with new names not reflected in the text.

Aster cordifolius, now *Symphyotrichum cordifolium*
A. laevis, now *S. laeve*
A. novae-angliae, now *S. novae-angliae*
A. novi-belgii, now *S. novi-belgii*
A. oolentangiensis, now *S. oolentangiense*
A. spectablis, now *Eurybia spectabilis*
A. umbellatus, now *Doellingaria umbellata*

Eupatorium coelestinum, now *Conoclinium coelestinum*
E. maculatum, now *Eupatoriadelphus maculatus*
E. rugosum, now *Ageratina altissima*
Sedum 'Autumn Joy', now *Hylotelephium* 'Autumn Joy'
S. sieboldii, now *H. sieboldii*
S. spectabile, now *H. spectabile*

INVASIVE PLANTS ARE A REAL DANGER

Most of the plants we introduce into our gardens are well behaved, but from time to time a plant adapts too well and spreads beyond the garden. These invasive exotic species compete with native plants, altering the structure and function of the ecosystems they invade. An invasive plant is very different from an aggressive garden plant like bee balm, but some aggressive garden plants like goutweed can also be invasive. Not every invasive species acts the same in all parts of the country, or in all ecosystems within a region. Because invasive plants are regionally and ecosystem specific, find out which plants are invasive in your region or state. The way to stop the spread of an invasive plant is not to buy it. Be alert to any plants thriving beyond the confines of garden beds in your own yard and around your neighborhood. If you want more information on invasive alien plants, including a list of the worst offenders, contact the Plant Conservation Alliance at: http://weedsgonewild.org/. Plants featured in this book that are locally, regionally, or nationally invasive include:

Japanese maple (*Acer palmatum*)
Goutweed (*Aegopodium podagraria*)
Common wormwood (*Artemisia absinthium*)
Beach wormwood (*A. stelleriana*)
Butterfly bush (*Buddleja davidii*)
Red valerian (*Centranthus ruber*)
Foxglove (*Digitalis purpurea*)
Cypress spurge (*Euphorbia cyparissias*)
Fennel (*Foeniculum vulgare*)
Baby's breath (*Gypsophila paniculata*)

English ivy (*Hedera helix*)
Dame's rocket (*Hesperis matronalis*)
Goat's rue (*Galega officinalis*)
Genista (*Genista tinctoria*)
Yellow flag (*Iris pseudocorus*)
Japanese silver grass (*Miscanthus sinensis*)
Fountain grass (*Pennisetum alopecuroides*)
Lesser celandine (*Ranunculus ficaria*)
Brazilian verbena (*Verbena bonariensis*)
Periwinkle (*Vinca minor*)

Acknowledgments

This book is the product of many teachers, and I hope that, in turn, it will be used as a teaching tool. Thanks to all the people who have shared information with me during a lifetime of gardening endeavors. Special thanks go to Fern Marshall Bradley and Barbara Ellis for their gentle editing; to Jim Gallucci, who tirelessly sought the best photos from the most talented garden photographers; and to Ellen Phillips, who always turned a critical eye to photos and text whenever she was needed. Heartfelt thanks to Bruce, Farrand, and Ginny, who offered endless encouragement during my many months spent writing. A lifetime of love and encouragement from my father made the writing of this book possible. I wish he had lived to see it published.

I would like to thank all the readers who helped make the first edition of *Perennial Combinations* a best-selling title. Your encouragement and enthusiasm for this volume are greatly appreciated. For this paperback edition, I have added a completely new chapter filled with beautiful photographs and useful design and maintenance tips. One thing I really missed in the original book was a place to showcase garden art and ornamentation. Now, along with chapters on bold plants and bold colors, including tropical treasures and oversize foliage, bold accents are included to help you personalize your garden. Thanks to Karen Bolesta for spearheading as well as editing this project, Marc Sirinsky for selecting the photos, and Tara Long for her skillful layout. Special thanks go to Lucy Hardiman for reviewing the manuscript. Mary Jane Baker, Linda Cochran, Dan Corson and Derndt Stugger, Tina Dixon, Kevin Doyle, Linda Ernst, Marco Henry, Dan and Darlene Huntington, Dulcy Mahar, Patti McGee, Ernie and Marietta O'Byrne, and Rick Sarenson generously opened their gardens to me and my camera—thank you. I hope this book continues to inspire gardeners, designers, and all who love beauty.

How to Use This Book

Perennial Combinations is a unique guide to making foolproof choices for great-looking perennial gardens that will be perfect for your conditions. If you've ever felt overwhelmed by the tremendous variety of perennials available, or if you've struggled to find a group of congenial perennials that needs the same soil and light, *Perennial Combinations* will end your frustrations. I've taken the guesswork out of perennial gardening by profiling more than 100 beautiful small groups of perennials that will grow well and look great together.

If you're an experienced perennial gardener, you'll find these combinations to be a rich source of inspiration and new ideas. And whether you're a beginner or an expert, you'll love the special garden designs that blend several perennial combinations into a single flowerbed or border.

To start out, I've explained the simple but important principles for successfully combining perennials. If you're new to perennial gardening, be sure to read "Creating Great-Looking Combinations," starting on page 12.

Once you're familiar with the basics, explore the book as you will, starting with the topics you like the best. I've grouped combinations by theme, starting with "Combinations by Color" and "Combinations for All Seasons." There's also a section on "Combinations for Special Sites," including shady sites, clay soil, and wet soil.

Featured combination.
See a detailed view of each combination in a garden setting.

PHOTO KEY
1. 'General Sikorski' clematis (*Clematis* 'General Sikorski'); Zones 4 to 9
2. Delphinium (*Delphinium* hybrid); Zones 3 to 7
3. 'Ruby Regis' herb tree mallow (*Lavatera trimestris* 'Ruby Regis'); annual

A Mixed Planting for Beautiful Bloom

Mixed plantings of perennials, annuals, and vines, like this grouping of delphinium, herb tree mallow, and clematis, have decided advantages for small gardens. While most perennials have limited bloom seasons, annuals like the mallow commonly flower all season, giving the garden long-lasting color. Vines add height and color to a combination without taking up much space. Here, the clematis climbs a pillar, creating a column of color that towers over the stately spires of delphiniums. The clematis will flower for a month or more, and some varieties reflower throughout the season.

102

Combination description.
Read this to learn what features make the combination effective and how it will change with the seasons.

Photo key.
Refer to the key to learn the common and botanical names of the plants in the combination.

Secrets for Beautiful Summer Bloom

≈ Get the most from clematis. Clematis prefer rich, well-drained soil and a shady, well-mulched area to spread their roots. For best growth, be sure the soil pH is neutral to slightly acidic. The vines bloom best in sunlight, so train them up a trellis or pillar. Or, make shrubs do double duty as vine supports. Plant the clematis a foot or so from the shrub's crown. Then train its stems up through the shrub's branches, tying them loosely until the plants are large enough to ramble at will.

≈ Stake delphiniums for dramatic results. Delphiniums need staking or they'll topple over or break off in wind and rain. Provide each stem with a tall, thin, sturdy stake. Tie stems to the stakes with soft string or yarn.

≈ Use a delphinium substitute in the South. Delphiniums grow best in areas with low humidity and cool nights. In warm areas, like the humid South, substitute mulleins (*Verbascum* spp.), which have tall flowering spires in shades of yellow and pink.

≈ Start mallow from transplants. The saucer-shaped flowers of herb tree mallow look like miniature hibiscus flowers. The pink flowers of 'Ruby Regis' look perfect in this combination of pinks and purples, but there's also a lovely white cultivar called 'Mont Blanc' that would combine well with white clematis and delphiniums. If you live in a region with cool summers, you may find that these free-blooming annuals will self sow in light soil. For best results in other regions, set out established transplants each spring after danger of frost is past. If you're designing combinations of your own and want to include herb tree mallow, keep in mind that it can grow as tall as 6 feet by season's end!

Larkspur (*Consolida ajacis*) is a self-sowing annual that makes a great substitute for perennial delphiniums, which can be tricky to grow, especially in warm climates. Here, pink larkspur makes a great companion for perennial pinks (*Dianthus*).

103

Planting perennials is a pleasure, and I've included plenty of combinations for pleasure gardens, too, including "Soothing Woodland Wildflowers," "Perennial Companions for Water Gardens," "Combinations for Hummingbirds and Butterflies," and more.

For each combination in the book, there are several special features to help you understand where to plant it and how to care for the plants to keep them looking their best, as shown at left.

I was so excited by this great collection of perennial combinations that I was inspired to create garden designs that would show off their beauty—25 in all! You'll find illustrations of these gardens throughout the book, along with information about plant bloom time and color, size, and hardiness. If you'd like to try planting one of these gardens, check the "Garden Plot Plans" beginning on page 350, where you'll find plan drawings of the garden layouts plus a plant list and information on how many plants of each type to buy. These plan drawings are a helpful reference whether you're planting the garden exactly as I've designed it or adapting the garden to a special site in your yard or to substitute a few of your favorite plants.

To help you with plant shopping, I've included information for contacting some excellent mail-order nurseries. And to help you find information on specific plants quickly and easily, check the index beginning on page 367.

Creating and planting perennial combinations is a wonderfully rewarding experience, and with *Perennial Combinations* to guide you, you're sure to have a garden that's beautiful and successful in every season.

Creating Great-Looking Combinations

America is mad about perennials. And that's no surprise, since they offer gardeners an infinite variety of color, form, and texture. You can use them alone or combine them with annuals, bulbs, ornamental grasses, shrubs, and trees. There truly is a perennial for every place and purpose—when you count all the cultivars of every perennial species, there are literally thousands to choose from.

Because of their beauty and versatility, perennials form the backbone of most beds and borders. But with such a vast array of plants available, how do you decide which perennials to choose for your garden? And once you make your plant choices, how do you put them together to create thriving, beautiful gardens?

MATCHING PLANTS TO YOUR SITE

Before you start mixing and matching perennials in combinations, you need to examine the soil, light, and moisture conditions in your garden. A thorough understanding of your site will help you choose the best spot for the garden, pick plants that will thrive in your area's conditions, and ultimately make the most successful combinations.

Light, soil, and moisture are the three key factors to keep in mind when choosing perennials for combinations. These factors determine which plants will grow best in your garden. They can also help determine where you place your garden. Understanding your site conditions will ensure that you keep to the gardener's golden rule: "Match the plant to the site."

A successful combination can be as simple as this lively planting of two spring-blooming perennials: Grecian windflowers and lesser celandine.

There are two ways you can use this strategy to approach plant selection. The safest is to study your light, soil, and moisture conditions before you compile a list of plants you hope to grow. Once you know your conditions, you can choose plants that are sure to thrive where you plant them. An alternate approach is to dream up a list of horticultural hopefuls, and then pare it down based on the conditions of your site. Either way, the end result is the same—a solid list of the most adaptable perennials for your garden. Armed with the list, you can arrange the chosen plants in stunning, easy-care combinations.

Light Levels in Your Garden

Successful gardening depends on mastering light. I divide light levels into five categories based on intensity and duration: full sun, light shade, partial shade, full shade, and deep shade. These designations are based on the duration of time with or without sun, coupled with the density of the shade. (As you can see, all shade is not the same. My designations for types of shade are based on a lot of variables, including season, time of day, and the type and density of overhead foliage.)

Full Sun

To understand light and the requirements of perennials and other plants, I look to nature for help. In nature, full sun is found in meadow and prairie ecosystems. Plants grown in our gardens that require a full day's sun, such as yarrows and sunflowers, were native to these places. Full sun translates to 10 or more hours of uninterrupted direct sun each day.

Light Shade and Partial Shade

Light shade occurs where there is shade for up to half a day, such as along the edges of

You can create a full-scale perennial garden by combining several combinations that share common colors, like the whites, pinks, and yellows in this border. To tie the combinations together, you can interplant perennials that have attractive foliage all season long.

woodlands and in savannas, where trees make up as much as 25 percent of the plant population. Plants in a lightly shaded situation receive five to ten hours of direct sun a day. Partial shade occurs in open woods, glades, and forest clearings, where there is shade for more than half a day. Plants in a partially shaded situation receive one to five hours of direct sun a day.

Full Shade and Deep Shade

Full shade is found in woodlands and forests where the trees provide a full, sheltering canopy. Here plants receive less than an hour of direct sun a day, though they often benefit from filtered sun during part of the day. It's possible to have a gorgeous garden in full shade by choosing shade-tolerant plants like hostas, bleeding hearts, and other perennials featured in the combinations beginning on page 170.

Deep shade, on the other hand, is the bane of gardeners. In nature, look for deep shade in coniferous forests where direct sunlight seldom if ever reaches the ground. In the garden, deep shade occurs where walls and other solid structures completely block out the sun.

Light Intensity

The amount of light (or shade) a plant gets isn't the only light-related factor, however. The intensity of sunlight is just as important as the sun-to-shade ratio. Intensity refers to the strength of the sun's rays, which varies with the distance from the equator, the time of day, and the season. Afternoon sun is more intense—hotter—than morning sun. Since summer is the hottest season, that's when the sun's intensity is greatest. The sun is more intense at high elevations, too.

Shade plants aren't well-adapted to coping with intense sun and the resulting heat, so their leaves may be "sunburned" if they're exposed to hot afternoon sun. But sun-adapted prairie perennials, like sunflowers and Joe-Pye weed, love these seemingly adverse conditions.

Sun-loving yarrow, salvia, lady's-mantle, and veronica enjoy the sunny foreground of the garden, while shade-tolerant hostas and bleeding heart fill up the shady background.

Whether you live in the cool North or hot South plays a role, too. Some perennials, like Solomon's seal and cranesbills, that thrive in light shade in the North may need partial or full shade in the South.

Learning about Your Soil

Soil serves many functions in the garden. It supports the plants, provides nutrition and water, and buffers the roots from rapid temperature changes. Soil has two major components—minerals and organic matter. The mineral components are classified by their particle size as sand, silt, or clay.

Sand, Silt, and Clay

Sand is the coarsest mineral component. Particle size varies depending on the type of sand: For example, beach sand is very fine sand, whereas builder's sand (used for home construction projects and sometimes for soil preparation) is coarse. Sand offers good drainage and air circulation, but it dries out quickly and is not good for holding nutrients.

Silt is the next particle size, smaller than sand but much larger than clay. Silt is rough to the touch when rubbed through the fingers, but you don't notice individual particles as you do with sand. Silt is fairly good at holding both water and nutrients, but it's prone to drying out, especially in windy areas.

The finest mineral soil is clay. Clay feels smooth to the touch because the particles are so small. Clay soils are very fertile, and they are good at holding water. On the down side, they are heavy and difficult to work, and they may be slow to drain. When it's dry, clay soil shrinks and cracks, which can tear plant roots and expose them to drying light and wind.

Organic Matter

Organic matter is what gives life to the soil. As its name implies, it's made up of organic materials—dead and decaying leaves, roots, and

Silvery 'Valerie Finnis' artemisia and 'Orange Queen' yarrow are a good combination for sandy soil that doesn't retain much moisture, because they're both drought tolerant.

other plant and animal debris. Organic matter builds up naturally in the soil from the seasonal decay of those materials. Thoroughly decayed organic matter is called humus. Humus provides nutrients and holds lots of moisture, so it's a critical component of healthy soil.

Soil Texture and Structure

Virtually all garden soils are made up of all three types of mineral particles, as well as organic matter. Gardeners describe soil in terms of its texture: the relative amounts of sand, silt, and clay. Soil structure—the arrangement of the particles in the soil—is also important for plant growth. A soil that has good structure has lots of small spaces between the particles that can hold air and water.

Japanese primrose, Japanese iris, and bigleaf ligularia are a lush combination that's well-suited to wet soil. The iris foliage makes an attractive backdrop for the primroses.

When sand, silt, clay, and organic matter are combined in the right amounts, loam results. (The ideal loam is 40 percent sand, 40 percent silt, and 20 percent clay, but loams can vary in composition.) Loam is very friable, with about 50 percent solid space and 50 percent pore space for air, water, and nutrient movement. Few gardeners are lucky enough to have a perfect loam, but many of us do garden in somewhat loamy soil. There are few soils that can't be improved with good management and lots of added organic matter. Soil preparation—especially the addition of organic matter—will also improve your soil's ability to hold water.

To determine your soil type, you can send a sample to your county extension agent for analysis, or you can conduct a simple test with a scoop of soil and a jar of water. Place a scoop full of garden soil in a Mason jar that's been filled with water, and add a drop of dishwashing liquid. Shake the jar vigorously and let it sit while the particles settle out. Sand settles first, followed by silt, then clay and organic mater. The relative proportions of each component will tell you if you have a sandy loam, a clay loam, or another type of soil.

CHOOSING PLANTS FOR YOUR COMBINATIONS

Once you've analyzed your site, you're ready for my favorite part of designing a combination—choosing the plants. The best way to start is to make a list of all the plants you like that you know you can grow. Choose only the plants that thrive in your soil, moisture, and light conditions. After you've finished listing their names, look up the color, bloom time, height, and spread of every plant, and note them by each plant's name. This takes some time, but you'll be able to use this information throughout your design process.

Narrowing the List

To help you focus on the right plants for your garden, think in practical terms. Your own garden will make the first cuts for you. As I've explained, your soil will be too wet, too dry, too rich, or too infertile for many plants. You will have too much sun for some plants, too little for others. Some will not be hardy in your zone, and others will be too weedy or aggressive for the size of your garden.

Taste also figures prominently in plant choice. Some plants simply look good together, while others, though beautiful by themselves, just don't mix attractively. Some plants will bloom in colors you don't like. Many people have likes and dislikes they can't explain— some plants are too stiff, too bold, or too fussy. There's an inherent limitation, too: All plants have their unique growth cycle and season of bloom. You need to choose plants that provide color, form, and texture when and where you need it in the garden. Plants that don't meet your schedule or design criteria should be left off the list.

Another important clue to plant selection lies hidden underground. Different plants have

Pursuing Perfect Combinations

It's true what they say: Imitation *is* the sincerest form of flattery. If you see a combination you like, copy it. I can point to half a dozen combinations in my garden that I have recreated as I saw them in books, magazine articles, or gardens. I've altered a dozen more by substituting a blue-leaved hosta for a gold-leaved form or switching a pink bleeding heart with a white one.

You can start with the photographs in this book. Photographs are an easy-to-use and enjoyable way to learn which perennials grow well together and how to create plant combinations. Refer to "Recommended Reading," on page 332, for more great books filled with information, ideas, and inspiration.

You can also observe perennial combinations at botanical gardens, at display gardens at nurseries, in your friends' gardens, and in nature. For me, nature is a great source of inspiration. You know you'll get it right if you copy a grouping of woodland wildflowers or a gorgeous combination in an autumn meadow. In nature, only plants that share the same needs will be found growing together. You can't go wrong by imitating.

In someone else's garden, be sure the combinations that you admire are time-tested. Check the growth requirements of any new plants to make sure the designer followed the golden rule: Match the plant to the site.

different kinds of root systems, and you don't want your perennials' roots competing for the same space. Bulbs such as tulips and daffodils are compact, so they're great partners for shallow-rooted plants like rock cress and pansies, which can grow right over the bulbs. To maximize the potential of plants like bee balm and yarrow, which have creeping stems and shallow fibrous roots, grow them with early bulbs or tall, late-season plants with taproots, like purple coneflowers.

DESIGN BASICS

Once you've settled on which plants to grow and where you want to plant them, it's important to consider plant size and shape, flower and foliage color, and bloom time when you match up perennial combinations.

Plant Size and Shape

When I begin to create combinations, I make simple sketches to show how the plants might look next to each other once they reach mature size. That's because the mature plant size determines how much room your combination needs. Keep in mind that the height of the perennials is just as important as their spread. You wouldn't want a garden of plants that were all the same size and shape, but you don't want a random mix of tall and short plants, either. And a combination won't work if one plant is a vigorous spreader that will end up engulfing the other perennials with which you've combined it.

Here's how to make sure the perennials in your combinations work well together: Choose plants with similar or complementary growth habits for best results. For example, place rapid spreaders such as bee balm and yarrow together, so one doesn't swamp the other. You can also combine fast growers with tough plants like yuccas or baptisia—they can take the competition. Don't plant bee balm next to a delicate plant like an allium.

Repeating shapes makes a combination more interesting. Here, the ferny foliage of yarrow in the background echoes the shape of the purple flower spikes of salvia, while the pink chive blossoms repeat the shape of the deeper pink alliums.

Flower and Foliage Color

As you remember from grade school, the primary colors are red, blue, and yellow. They are the building blocks of all other colors. Secondary colors are created by combining primary colors in various ways. Red and yellow make orange, red and blue make purple, and blue and yellow combine to make green.

Primary and secondary colors are called hues. When you add white to a pure hue, you get a tint of that hue. When you add black to a pure hue, you create a shade. Tints and shades of the six basic hues produce all the colors of the garden.

Most flowers come in shades and tints rather than in pure hues. Shades and tints of purples, blues, and greens, as well as pale pinks and pale yellows, are referred to as cool colors. Bright yellows, oranges, reds, and deep magentas are called hot colors.

Hot colors are the festive colors of summer. Use them to create excitement in the garden. Contrast this excitement with cool colors, which create a restful effect that is visually soothing. Cool colors also look farther away from you than they are. This is especially true of blues and purples, which show up best against a bright background.

If you want to combine peach and purple, you could plant peachy daylilies with lavender or soft peach hollyhocks with bluebeard (*Caryopteris clandonensis*), a flowering shrub.

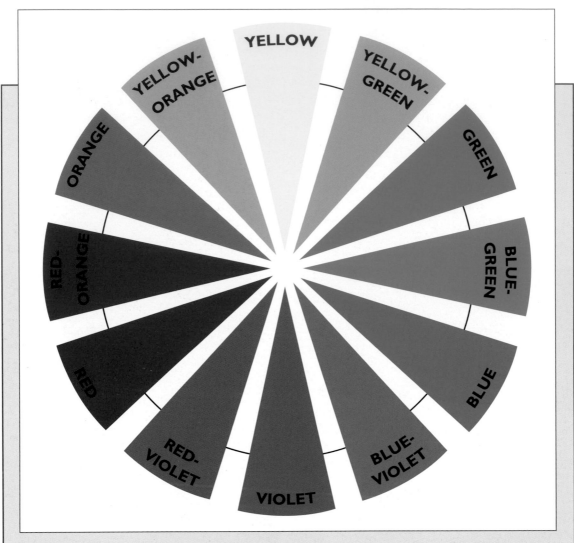

Using the Color Wheel

It's easy to make great-looking combinations by using the color wheel. Adjacent colors on the color wheel are related to one another by a shared pigment. Together, they form color harmonies. When you combine adjacent colors, you get a pleasing plant composition. An example of this is combining the related colors blue, violet, and red to produce a restful perennial combination. Combine red, orange, and yellow, and the flower colors will scream for attention.

Opposite colors on the color wheel are called complementary colors. Combining complementary colors creates a bright, dazzling effect. One complementary color makes the other seem brighter, such as yellow with violet or blue with orange. If you can picture a field of bright orange poppies and blue bachelor's buttons, you'll get the idea.

Brilliant red dahlias and purple cone-flowers make a striking summer show in this hot-color combination.

Designers' Color Secret

If your color scheme starts to look boring, jazz things up with a splash of a complementary color. In a blue, purple, and soft pink scheme, add a spot of bright yellow, cherry red, or scarlet. In a red, purple, and yellow combination, add some deep orange flowers.

Don't Forget Foliage

Foliage color plays a major role in the garden. After all, green is a color, too. In fact, it's a myriad of colors, including kelly, beryl, olive, sea, and forest. Foliage can also be red, purple, yellow, gold, gray, white, blue, orange, pink, or any variation or mix of these, as well as green. So beware: Because there are so many foliage colors, the foliage of one plant can clash with the flowers or foliage of its neighbors.

Form and Texture

When you're making combinations, the forms or shapes of your plants are also important considerations. Plants have three basic forms: spiky or spear-shaped, rounded or mounded, and flat or prostrate.

Spiky plants stand stiffly upright, with pointed or conical leaves or flowerheads. Spiky or strap-leaved plants such as Siberian iris and crocosmia provide a vertical accent that gives a break to the horizontal lines of the garden. Conical flower spikes, such as those of foxgloves, hollyhocks, and salvias, give a bit of lift to the garden's profile, while narrow spears, such as those of black snakeroot, add height to the border and carry your eye upward.

Use the soothing look of rounded or mounding plants to provide continuity to your garden. Fluffy mounds of baby's-breath, garden phlox, and showy stonecrop create waves of color at different heights. Add flat or ground-hugging plants to fill in the gaps in your beds and borders. They're also great for edges, especially low, spreading plants such as hardy cranesbills and wild ginger. Another one of my designer tricks is to use creeping plants as weavers to tie clumps of plants together at the front of the border. This trick gives a full and finished look to even the newest gardens.

Keep in mind that some perennials change their form during the season. For example,

Siberian irises appear rounded when in bloom, but are spiky after the flowers fade. Plants such as bleeding hearts and oriental poppies form huge mounds of foliage and flowers early in the season and then disappear entirely as the summer progresses. Give them a special spot in the garden where other plants will fill the space they leave behind.

Talking Texture

Texture refers to how foliage and flowers look to us: Are they fine, medium, or coarse? Ferns are fine-textured plants, as are ornamental grasses, airy baby's-breath, and the whirling butterfly-like flowers of white gaura. Fine textures melt into a dreamy haze

Not all combinations have to include flowers. This dynamic duo of spotted pulmonaria and deep purple smokebush (*Cotinus coggygria*) relies on rich foliage color alone.

at a distance, and they only show their intricacies on close inspection.

Medium-textured perennials like cranesbills and phlox offer visual detail even at a distance. So many perennials have a medium texture that you need to be sure to add plants with fine and coarse textures to keep your combinations lively.

Coarse or bold textures are the perfect antidote to a dull, uninspired combination. Who can resist a clump of showy 'Frances Williams' hosta growing among delicate ferns? The dinner-plate-size flowers of hybrid hibiscus are sure to demand attention.

Some plants have a combination of textures. Lady's mantle is fine-textured when smothered in a sea of chartreuse foamy flowers, but has medium- to slightly coarse-textured leaves when not in bloom. Yarrow has coarse-textured flowers but fine-textured foliage.

Bloom Time

Providing year-round bloom is a difficult task for even the most experienced garden designer. If you're combining two plants because you think the flowers would look gorgeous together, make sure they'll actually bloom at the same time. Bloom sequence is dependent on where you live, how hot or cool it is, and the type of soil you have.

An iris growing in North Carolina in sandy soil will bloom about one month earlier than the same iris growing in a moist clay soil in Minnesota. Also, because of the shorter season in Minnesota, certain plants that bloom with the iris in Minnesota will have already finished blooming in North Carolina by the time the iris blooms. To get the bloom sequence right in your own garden, observe when plants bloom in your area and keep a record so you can check it when planning combinations.

MAKING GREAT GARDENS FROM COMBINATIONS

Once you've created a beautiful combination, you can compose another one that looks nice with the first combination…and then a third to complement the first two. Before you know it, you'll have designed a beautiful garden bed, one combination at a time.

As a test, I like to draw my designs before I plant them. You don't need to be a great artist to do this. Just draw the plants roughly to scale, and try to show their overall shape, whether it's mounded, spiky, or prostrate. Drawing shows me whether the forms are too similar and where I need to add some excitement by including a plant with bold texture or a spiky form.

To make your garden as effective as possible, be sure to repeat one plant, key color, or strong form throughout the garden. This will draw the design together and make the garden look and feel right.

To create season-long interest, include two or three good combinations that bloom in different seasons. For larger beds, use a set of combinations as the basis for the garden, and link them together with complementary plants,

Divine Inspiration

How can you tell whether the plants of your dreams would really make a successful combination? In the garden, you can check to see if two plants will look good together by cutting the flower of one and placing it next to a variety of possible companions.

Another easy way to make great combinations is to take an exploratory trip to your local nursery or garden center. Gather your favorite plants in a garden cart, and compose and test your combinations before you buy.

such as ornamental grasses or gray-leaved perennials.

When you start to put together your own combinations and gardens, be bold and experiment. Since everyone's taste is different, there are no right or wrong combinations. What's the real secret of successful garden design? Just this: Make your garden something you'll enjoy every time you see it.

A simple combination of wild blue phlox and maidenhair fern can become the basis for an entire woodland garden—just plant a large mass of each plant.

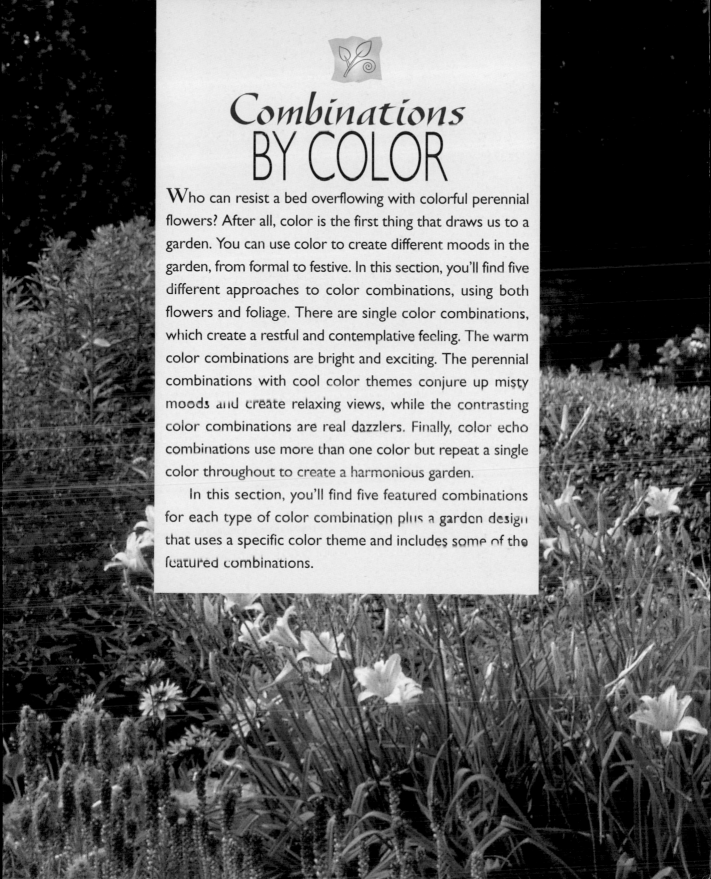

Combinations
BY COLOR

Who can resist a bed overflowing with colorful perennial flowers? After all, color is the first thing that draws us to a garden. You can use color to create different moods in the garden, from formal to festive. In this section, you'll find five different approaches to color combinations, using both flowers and foliage. There are single color combinations, which create a restful and contemplative feeling. The warm color combinations are bright and exciting. The perennial combinations with cool color themes conjure up misty moods and create relaxing views, while the contrasting color combinations are real dazzlers. Finally, color echo combinations use more than one color but repeat a single color throughout to create a harmonious garden.

In this section, you'll find five featured combinations for each type of color combination plus a garden design that uses a specific color theme and includes some of the featured combinations.

PHOTO KEY
1. **'Kashmir White' Clark's geranium (*Geranium clarkei* 'Kashmir White');** Zones 4 to 8
2. **'Janet Fisk' Bethlehem sage (*Pulmonaria saccharata* 'Janet Fisk');** Zones 3 to 8

A Shimmering Duo in Silver and White

Light up a shady corner of your garden with this duo of snowy white geranium flowers and silver-mottled Bethlehem sage foliage. White flowers and silver or gray foliage reflect light and seem to glow in the garden, especially in the late afternoon when the sun is low or in the evening when there's a full moon. Contrast between the foliage of these two plants keeps this combination interesting: The deeply cut,

rich green leaves of the geranium look soft and airy compared to the bold, splashy leaves of the Bethlehem sage. Dainty white flowers floating above the foliage echo the color of the silver-speckled leaves, but the difference in size and texture between the two keeps the combination intriguing. You can turn this silvery duo into a trio by adding 'White Swirl' Siberian iris. To extend the bloom season beyond early summer, also plant a white astilbe such as *Astilbe thunbergii* 'Professor van der Weilen'. To get the best from this combination, plant it in partial shade and rich, well-drained soil that never dries out.

26

Secrets for Silvers and Whites that Shimmer

❧ **Cut back Clark's geranium for longer bloom.** Clark's geranium blooms for a month or more in early summer. Grow it in rich, moist soil in either full sun or partial shade, but keep in mind that plants grown in shade will bloom for a shorter period of time than those in sun. To prolong bloom in sun or shade, cut the stalks to the ground as they fade. To add more color to this combination, substitute purple-flowered 'Kashmir Purple'.

❧ **Enjoy great foliage and flowers, too.** Bethlehem sage and other pulmonarias are valuable foliage plants with showy leaves that remain attractive all season long, but their early-spring flowers are an added bonus that shouldn't be overlooked. The flowers appear before the foliage, around the time that early daffodils and forsythia bloom. 'Janet Fisk' bears pink flowers that fade to lavender-blue, but there are other pulmonaria cultivars with white, rose, red-violet, or blue-purple blooms.

❧ **Brighten the shade with silver and white.** Shade-loving plants that are variegated with silver or white are especially useful because they brighten up spots in partial to full shade all season long. Variegated plants also make attractive accents for the deeper greens of most shade-loving perennials, such as ferns, European wild ginger (*Asarum europaeum*), and solid green hostas.

❧ **Avoid powdery mildew on pulmonarias.** To help keep powdery mildew from getting a foothold among your Bethlehem sage and other pulmonarias, keep the soil evenly moist and don't let the plants wilt. That's because wilting allows the fungus to take hold on the leaves. Trim off any leaves that do become infected, and dispose of them to prevent the mildew from spreading to uninfected leaves. New leaves will soon appear. Pulmonaria cultivars with more silver on the leaf are less likely to suffer from powdery mildew than those with greener leaves.

This pink-flowered duo of 'Montreaux' Asiatic lilies and spires of 'Montgomery' astilbe is set off beautifully by purplish smokebush leaves. This combo will grow well in light to partial shade and moist soil.

A Lovely Trio in Silver and Gray

Dramatic foliage contrasts make this perennial combination breathtakingly beautiful. Even though all the foliage is the same color, this trio has wonderful variety in leaf size, shape, and texture. The coarsely textured, woolly leaves of lamb's-ears highlight the fernlike foliage of 'Powis Castle' artemisia. Small leaves of a young catmint plant creep through the leaves of the other two perennials. In late spring, the lamb's-ears will send up woolly flower stalks that sport small purple flowers. Cut back the flower stalks after blooms die, and this combination of long-lasting foliage plants will continue to shine through the fall.

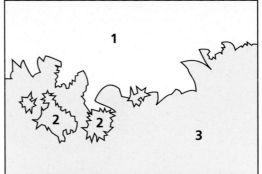

PHOTO KEY
1. **'Powis Castle' artemisia (*Artemisia* 'Powis Castle');** Zone 4 (with winter protection) or Zones 5 to 8
2. **'Six Hills Giant' catmint (*Nepeta* × *faassenii* 'Six Hills Giant');** Zones 3 to 8
3. **Lamb's-ears (*Stachys byzantina*, also offered as *S. lanata*);** Zones 4 to 8

Tips for Silver- and Gray-Leaved Perennials

❧ Plant silver and gray for drought tolerance. Most silver- or gray-leaved plants are drought-tolerant, and lamb's-ears and artemisia are no exceptions. They thrive in full sun and well-drained soil. Water regularly until plants are established; after that, they need minimal care.

❧ Keep this shrubby perennial in top-notch form. 'Powis Castle' artemisia is a woody-stemmed shrub that most gardeners cut back by one-half to two-thirds in fall or in early spring before new growth begins. (In the northern part of its range, the plant's stems are usually killed to the ground in winter.) This annual renewal pruning encourages vigorous new growth and keeps the plants compact. Unpruned plants tend to become rangier and less attractive because they sprout higher up on the branches.

❧ Consider planting for foliage only. Lamb's-ears sends up woolly spikes with tiny purple flowers in early summer, and 'Powis Castle' artemisia may bear clusters of small, yellow-tinged flowers in late summer. In both cases, many gardeners believe the flowers detract from the foliage and remove them as they appear. Caution: Some catalogs describe 'Silver Carpet' lamb's-ears as nonflowering, but in my experience, it does produce flowers.

❧ Protect aromatic foliage that's good enough to eat. Both artemisia and lamb's-ears have leaves that emit a strong, pleasant, somewhat musty aroma when crushed. While foliage fragrance deters insects that might eat the leaves, in my garden it seems to attract rabbits and other wild creatures. Protect the young shoots with wire cages until the plants get established.

The silver leaves of *Pulmonaria* 'British Sterling' add drama to any shady garden. Here, they're paired with variegated broad-leaved sedge (*Carex siderosticha* 'Variegata'), whose smartly striped blades provide maximum contrast.

PHOTO KEY
1. **Blue false indigo (***Baptisia australis***); Zones 3 to 9**
2. **'May Night' salvia (***Salvia* × *sylvestris* **'May Night');** **Zones 5 to 9**
3. **Meadow sage (***Salvia pratensis***); Zones 3 to 9**

A Mix of Cool Colors That Takes the Heat

Dreamy blue flowers and misty, gray-green foliage create a soft, cool picture in this early-summer combination. Distinctive shades of blue and variety in flower size keep this combination from being ordinary. And after the flowers fade, the foliage of the blue false indigo forms a broad, rounded mound that contrasts with the spiky seedheads of the salvias.

These plants are as tough as they are beautiful. They take full summer sun, heat, and drought in stride, remaining fresh and blooming strongly when other plants would shrivel.

Salvias and false indigos thrive in well-drained soil. They are perfect for well-drained spots with sandy soil and do well in seaside gardens. They both tolerate dry clay soil, and false indigos will thrive in moist clay as well. For a month of late-season color, add *Aster* × *frikartii* 'Monch' to this combination. It flowers from midsummer to fall.

Growing Perennials That Can Take the Heat

❧ **Wool coats keep plants cool.** You would never think of wearing a wool sweater to stay cool, but plants do. Salvias and many other plants from hot, dry areas have soft hairs that cover the stems and leaves. The hairs form a barrier layer that traps moisture given off by the plant, thus keeping the humidity high near the leaf surface. The result is that the plants stay cooler and lose less moisture.

❧ **Deep roots form a water reservoir.** Blue false indigo is a native prairie plant with thick tap roots that plunge deep into the ground in search of moisture. The fleshy roots can store precious water, and as a result, these easy-care plants can survive heat and drought without so much as a wilted leaf. Because of their deep roots, they do resent being transplanted, however. Space them 3 feet apart at planting time to accommodate their eventual mature spread.

❧ **Side shoots produce a second show.** You can induce salvias to rebloom from side shoots by cutting off the top of the flower spikes after the flowers fade. In southern gardens, where the growing season is long enough, you can cut the plants to the ground after flowering and they will produce new flowering stems.

Clary sage (*Salvia sclarea* var. *turkistanica*) combined with bold spikes of foxglove provide early summer color in this pink theme planting. The rounded flowers of 'Gloire de Dijon' roses add a pleasing note of contrast, plus wonderful fragrance.

PHOTO KEY
1. Yellow flag (*Iris pseudacorus*); Zones 4 to 9
2. Genista (*Genista
   tinctoria*); Zones 2 to 8
3. Lady's-mantle (*Alchemilla
   mollis*); Zones 3 to 8
4. 'Overdam' feather reed
   grass (*Calamagrostis* ×
   acutiflora 'Overdam');
   Zones 4 to 9

A Yellow Combo with Rich Texture

F lowers in shades from bright yellow to
chartreuse add glowing accents to this
richly textured early-summer combination.
The bold, strap-shaped iris foliage and the
fine-textured variegated grass jut up strongly
over the low, rounded clump of lady's-mantle
planted at their feet. While the spiky clusters
of genista flowers echo the upright form of
the iris and grass leaves, they complement
the rounded chartreuse clusters of lady's-
mantle flowers. When the genista flowers
have faded, the form of the plant will change
from spiky to round, creating a noticeable
shift in the look of the combination. Another
change will happen after the early summer
flowers fade: The grass will come into bloom.
Its stunningly variegated leaves and red-
brown, plumelike flower clusters will add an
airy exclamation point to this splendid mix
of foliage right through fall.

Secrets for Bold Color and Texture

❧ Give flags room at planting time.

Keep in mind that even small, pot-grown yellow flags are giants in the making. In rich, moist to wet soil, this type of iris can spread to form bold clumps 3 to 4 feet across and up to 4 feet tall. They also thrive in the well-drained soil of the average perennial border, but the slightly drier conditions contain their spread a bit. When setting out young plants, give them a minimum of 1½ to 2 feet on all sides, or be prepared to move smaller plants out of the way as the iris spreads.

❧ Know your plants and your site.

Genista, or Dyer's broom, is something of a surprise in this planting of moisture-loving perennials. Usually found in dry-soil gardens, genista is extremely drought and heat tolerant once established. This combination works because the other plants, which all require rich soil, can tolerate moist but well-drained conditions, and the well drained site here seem to satisfy the genista as well. Knowing your site also can help you combine plants with slightly different needs. For example, siting a dry-soil plant, such as genista, on a slightly higher, drier spot in a bed or border can make the difference between success and failure.

❧ Add a stunning ornamental grass.

Feather reed grass produces clumps of arching leaves that normally reach 2 to 3 feet in height, but in cool climates and moist soil, plants can reach 3 to 4 feet. In the South, the variegated cultivar 'Overdam', featured in this combination, requires partial shade to look its best.

❧ Give lady's-mantle a summer trim.

Lady's-mantles are lovely in bloom, but as the flowers fade to brown, the plants begin to look past their prime, especially because the foliage begins to turn brown at the same time. Cut them to the ground as flowers fade and they quickly produce a fresh crop of leaves.

A long view shows a broad clump of 'Moonshine' yarrow growing next to the combination shown in detail on the opposite page.

A White Garden with Color Accents

Soft gray-blue hosta leaves are the special accent in this white spring garden. If you want to dabble with adding secondary colors in a single-color combination, the secret is using a pale shade of a color that complements the main flowers in the combination. Use it sparingly, or you'll distract too much from your chosen color theme. In this combination, the variations on the color theme change with the seasons. By early summer, creamy white flowering wands of black cohosh wave above its mounds of fernlike foliage and rich purple-blue Siberian iris add an even brighter contrast. Pale lilac hosta flowers accent the garden in summer, followed by the yellow-orange blooms of ligularia. The ligularia blooms change to tufted brown seedheads for fall interest.

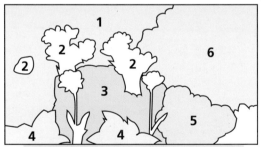

PHOTO KEY
1. Black cohosh (*Actaea [Cimicifuga] racemosa*); Zones 3 to 8
2. 'Mount Tacoma' tulip (*Tulipa* 'Mount Tacoma'); Zones 3 to 8
3. 'Desdemona' bigleaf ligularia (*Ligularia dentata* 'Desdemona'); Zones 3 to 8
4. 'Halcyon' hosta (*Hosta × tardiana* 'Halcyon'); Zones 3 to 8
5. 'Dale's Strain' heuchera (*Heuchera americana* 'Dale's Strain'); Zones 4 to 9
6. White old-fashioned bleeding heart (*Dicentra spectabilis* 'Alba'); Zones 3 to 9

Tips for Using Color Accents

Grow tulips as annuals or perennials. In well-drained soil and full sun, tulips can perform as perennials, but in this semi-shaded garden, the peony-flowered tulips don't get enough direct sun to store the energy they need to flower again next year. To ensure that this lovely combination continues from year to year, carefully plant new tulip bulbs around the crowns of the perennials each fall. Species tulips and some hybrids, such as Darwins and lily-flowered, are the most long-lasting tulips.

Fill spots left by fading foliage. As the tulips go dormant in this combination, the rounded leaves of ligularia will quickly fill the void. In the North, the fernlike foliage of bleeding heart often lasts until fall, but in the South, the plants go dormant in summer. To fill the gap left by the bleeding heart, you can plant shallow-rooted annuals in the space.

Just be careful not to damage the crown of the bleeding heart when you plant.

Plan a pleasing mix of foliage. Keep in mind that flowers are fleeting, but foliage fills the garden all season. This combination features plants with striking leaves that look great right through fall. The black cohosh foliage forms a fine-textured background for the bold heuchera, hosta, and ligularia.

Try a combo that's pretty in pink. If you prefer pink to white, plant old-fashioned pink-flowered bleeding heart with the pink peony-flowered tulip called 'Angelique'.

Pick the right site for ligularia. In the right site, ligularia is a dramatic plant with enormous leaves and showy flowers. Without constant soil moisture and light to partial shade, however, plants wilt dramatically and gradually decline.

The touch of yellow in these 'Spring Green' tulips makes them the perfect complement to primrose yellow *Saruma henryi*, an unusual woodland plant native to China that blooms for over a month in spring.

A Combination in Sunset Shades

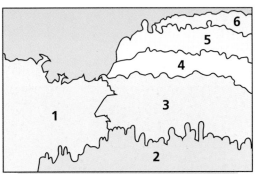

Brilliant yellow daylilies and heliopsis combined with violet and purple echo the rich colors of a tropical sunset in this garden. The perennials are planted in large drifts of color that suggest waves running down the length of this unusually wide border. Each drift is taller than the one in front of it, building toward the back.

By looking carefully at this combination of colorful flowers, you can learn a great deal about how to strike a balance between variety, which makes a garden interesting, and repetition, which keeps a garden from looking too jumbled. Notice how this design repeats certain colors—such as the drifts of yellow flowers—at regular intervals down the border. This designer's trick helps to draw a large planting together.

PHOTO KEY
1. Daylily (*Hemerocallis* hybrid); Zones 3 to 9
2. 'Kobold' dense blazing-star (*Liatris spicata* 'Kobold'); Zones 3 to 9
3. 'The King' garden phlox (*Phlox paniculata* 'The King'); Zones 4 to 8
4. Fernleaf yarrow (*Achillea filipendulina*); Zones 3 to 9
5. Globe thistle (*Echinops ritro*); Zones 3 to 8
6. Sunflower heliopsis (*Heliopsis helianthoides*); Zones 3 to 9

Techniques for Drifts of Sunset Colors

❧ **Get maximum impact from your combinations.** Mass plantings of perennials create a striking show, especially when all plants bloom at the same time. This style is not for everyone, however. Peak bloom in this combination lasts for a month or so in summer, and the garden is green for the rest of the season. A design like this one is a good choice if you have a vacation home you use most often in high summer, for example, or if you want to pack all the enjoyment of your garden into a few short weeks.

❧ **Bend the rules to suit your site.** While successful gardening depends on choosing plants with similar needs, if you know your climate, site, and soil well, you can get away with bending the rules a bit. Most of the plants in this combination thrive in light, well-drained soil, but there are two notable exceptions: daylilies and phlox. While daylilies grow and bloom best in rich, evenly moist, well-drained soil, they also grow in drier conditions because they have tuberous roots that store water. In most cases, garden phlox needs rich, moist soil to look its best. This garden works because it's located in the northern part of Zone 5, where summers are generally cool, and the phlox is able to withstand the drier conditions. In warmer zones, the phlox would need to be replaced with a more drought-tolerant plant such as centaurea, salvias, or *Knautia macedonica*.

❧ **Help plants adapt with organic matter.** If you're combining perennials that prefer light, well-drained soil with ones that prefer richer conditions, amending the soil at planting time can help the plants adapt. Dig an extra dose of compost or well-rotted manure into the soil before planting species that prefer richer, moister conditions. Keeping those plants mulched with compost or chopped leaves will also help keep your soil's levels of organic matter, and thus moisture, high.

For a dynamic hot-colored trio, combine rich pink garden phlox, the purple flower cones of drumstick chives (*Allium sphaerocephalun*), and the red pincushion flowers of *Knautia macedonica*.

A Sizzling Mix of Flowers and Foliage

Orange flowers and burgundy foliage seem like incompatible bedfellows, but they make a striking combination. The colors harmonize because they share a common pigment: red. And this combination makes good garden sense, too, because both the penstemon and the wallflower thrive in full sun to light shade and average to rich, well-drained soil. They also both tolerate some drought. 'Husker Red' penstemon is a great choice for many combinations because its burgundy foliage adds color all season long and contrasts with the green leaves of its neighbors.

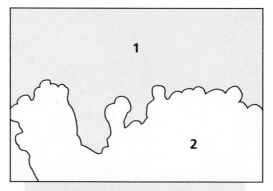

PHOTO KEY
1. **'Husker Red' foxglove penstemon** (*Penstemon digitalis* **'Husker Red'**); Zones 4 to 8
2. **'Orange Bedder' Siberian wallflower** (*Erysimum cheiri* **'Orange Bedder'**); Zones 3 to 7

Secrets for Long-Lasting Sizzle

🌿 **Add interest with decorative seedheads.** 'Husker Red' penstemon is lovely in flower, but like most perennials, it blooms for only a few weeks. I don't cut back the plants after they flower, because the seedheads are attractive and last through winter, when they add rich brown color and interesting texture to the landscape.

🌿 **Watch for red seedlings.** 'Husker Red' penstemon, featured in this combination, is a prolific self-seeder. If you leave the seedheads standing, you'll get lots of seedlings. Not all of them will have red leaves, however. Once seedlings have some leaves, you'll see which ones are red. Pull up any green-leaved seedlings to make room for their more striking siblings.

🌿 **Keep a clear path for seedlings.** Have you ever noticed how seedlings seem to pop up in garden paths? Pathways are a perfect place for seedlings because they are open and free of competition. Gravel, mulch, and other pathway materials make great seedbeds, because the seeds find an ideal environment for germination once they settle down into the crevices where there is extra moisture and fine soil. (This is also the reason weeds like pathways!) You can easily dig up the seedlings and move them to more convenient locations in beds and borders, or pot up the seedlings and share them with friends.

🌿 **Replace wallflowers every two years.** Wallflowers are short-lived perennials and are usually grown as biennials, meaning they are replaced every two years. That's because young, vigorous plants bloom much better than older ones do.

Rich red dahlia flowers really turn up the heat in this combination with orange *Crocosmia* 'Jackanapes' and yellow *Helenium* 'Garden Sun'. The purple foliage of the dahlia creates a dramatic counterpoint to the fiery flowers.

PHOTO KEY
1. **Golden wood millet** (*Milium effusum* **'Aureum'); Zones 6 to 9**
2. **Rock cress (*Aubrieta deltoidea*); Zones 4 to 8**

Glowing Color for Spring Gardens

Yellow and purple make a head-turning duo in this combination of a perennial and an ornamental grass. Rock cress is a popular perennial that produces a dense carpet of flowers in purple as well as white, rose-pink, and rosy purple. Plants bloom for a month in spring, and may rebloom in fall if sheared back. They usually range from 2 to 4 inches tall, but sometimes stretch to 8 inches, and

have evergreen leaves. Golden wood millet, an ornamental grass, adds a vertical accent to this simple combination. The contrast between the millet's airy stems of golden leaves and the dense, low-growing flowers is dynamic.

This combination works best in areas with cool summers. Rock cress will grow in full sun to light shade and prefers average to somewhat rich soil that is well drained, but it's short-lived in warmer zones. Golden millet is best in light shade and rich, well-drained soil, but it will tolerate full sun with steady soil moisture.

40

Expert Advice for Spring Color

❧ **Include grasses.** Grasses that begin growing early in the spring, as soon as the ground thaws and the sun warms the earth a bit, are called cool-season grasses. They grow best at temperatures between 60° and 75°F and grow actively in spring and fall, resting during the heat of summer. Depending on the species, they bloom from late spring to midsummer. The best-known cool-season grass is Kentucky bluegrass, the most popular lawn grass in the country, but there are several cool-season ornamental grasses suitable for garden beds and borders. Besides the golden wood millet featured in this combination, you can try feather reed grass (*Calamagrostis × acutiflora*), blue fescue (*Festuca glauca*), and blue oat grass (*Helictotrichon sempervirens*).

❧ **Add a blanket of gold.** If you want a blanket of yellow flowers rather than purple for your spring garden, consider basket-of-gold (*Aurinia saxatilis*). This ground-hugging species reaches 10 to 12 inches in height and produces masses of tiny yellow flowers over gray-green leaves in spring. Plant it in average well-drained soil and full sun. While it wouldn't combine well with golden wood millet, it would look lovely planted with candytuft (*Iberis sempervirens*) and sedums.

❧ **Propagate to keep rock cresses vigorous.** While rock cresses tend to be short-lived perennials, if you propagate them regularly, you can enjoy them year after year. Take cuttings in early summer after the flowers fade, or divide the clumps in fall, keeping the younger, more vigorous portions of the clump. They also are easy to grow from seeds, but remember: Seedlings from named cultivars won't look like the parent plants. It's best to propagate named cultivars only by division or cuttings.

For a midspring combination in yellow and purple, try 'Burgundy' lily-flowered tulips contrasted with brilliant yellow-green cushion spurge (*Euphorbia polychroma*).

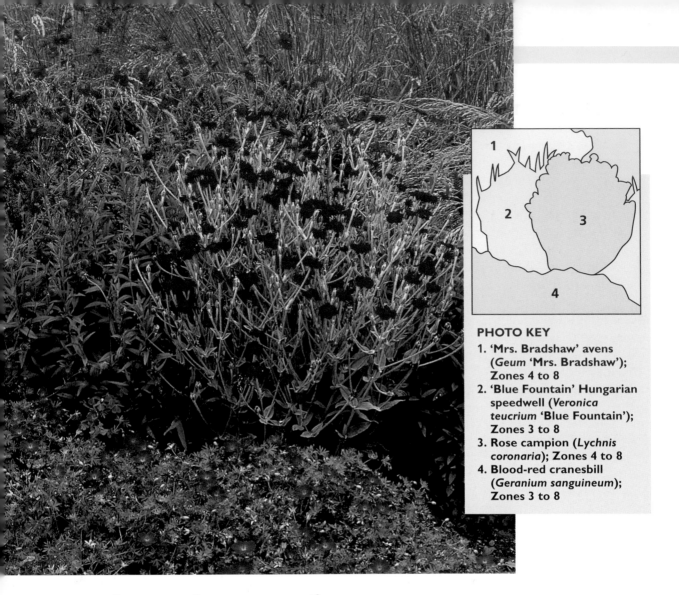

PHOTO KEY

1. 'Mrs. Bradshaw' avens (*Geum* 'Mrs. Bradshaw'); Zones 4 to 8
2. 'Blue Fountain' Hungarian speedwell (*Veronica teucrium* 'Blue Fountain'); Zones 3 to 8
3. Rose campion (*Lychnis coronaria*); Zones 4 to 8
4. Blood-red cranesbill (*Geranium sanguineum*); Zones 3 to 8

Colors That Knock Your Socks Off

If you're a daring gardener, this garden filled with brilliant shades of crimson-red, orange-red, and magenta will suit your style. In this combination, your eye travels first to the rose campion, because its flowers are so bright they almost vibrate. The impact is even greater because the flowers contrast so distinctly with the plant's silvery white, woolly stems and leaves. The airy-looking branched stems of orange-red geum and a low mound of magenta-flowered bloody cranesbills add to the clamor of colors in this summer garden. The combination works because the colors are variations on a red theme. The rounded shapes of the plants in this garden picture also help prevent it from looking too busy.

All of the plants in this combination thrive in full sun with rich, well-drained soil. Rose campion is a biennial or a short-lived perennial, but since it self-sows freely, you'll find seedlings popping up in unexpected places from year to year.

Plants for Knock-Your-Socks-Off Color

🍃 Try out some hot hues. Warm colors may be an acquired taste, but you won't regret experimenting with them because a dash of bright red or magenta can turn an ordinary combination into something extraordinary. If you've been timid about planting hot-colored flowers, an easy way to test them out is by planting annuals. That way, you've made only a one-season commitment. Try impatiens, dahlias, petunias, zonal geraniums, and zinnias, all of which come in shades from hot pink to magenta.

🍃 Use an old-fashioned favorite. The richly colored flowers and silver-gray stems and leaves of rose campion make it an eye-catching plant in any garden. If crimson isn't your color, try 'Alba', a pure white selection, or 'Angel's Blush', which has white flowers with pink centers.

🍃 Don't shun maligned magenta. The color magenta has been both in and out of fashion with gardeners. If it's one of your favorites, you have plenty of great perennials to choose from. Plants as diverse as cranesbills (*Geranium* spp.), pinks (*Dianthus* spp.), garden phlox (*Phlox paniculata*), and obedient plant (*Physostegia virginiana*) all come in shocking shades from pink to magenta.

🍃 Plant this nonstop bloomer. Blood-red cranesbill is one of the longest-blooming cranesbills available. Masses of flowers smother the plants for a month or more in early summer. Plants continue to bloom sporadically from midsummer to fall, even in partial shade. If plants get too big or lanky, cut them back by half and they will quickly leaf out again.

Set a moist spot in partial shade afire with this late-summer duo of burning red 'Lucifer' crocosmia and bright spikes of cardinal flower (*Lobelia cardinalis*).

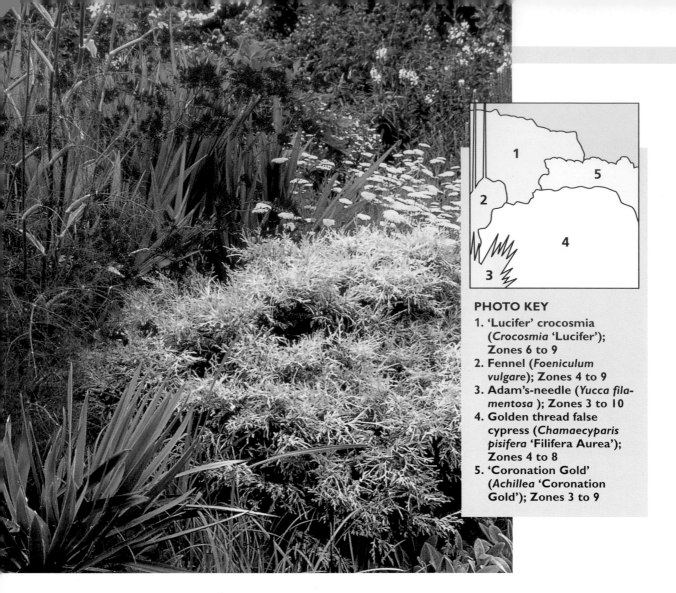

PHOTO KEY
1. 'Lucifer' crocosmia (*Crocosmia* 'Lucifer'); Zones 6 to 9
2. Fennel (*Foeniculum vulgare*); Zones 4 to 9
3. Adam's-needle (*Yucca filamentosa*); Zones 3 to 10
4. Golden thread false cypress (*Chamaecyparis pisifera* 'Filifera Aurea'); Zones 4 to 8
5. 'Coronation Gold' (*Achillea* 'Coronation Gold'); Zones 3 to 9

Hot Tones from a Mixed Planting

For a mix of color and texture that lasts all season, combine traditional perennials with herbs and shrubs that have handsome foliage. In this combination, the flattened flower clusters of yarrow echo the golden yellow false cypress. At the same time, they add bold texture. Sprays of rich red, trumpet-shaped crocosmia, borne above clumps of bronzy, strap-shaped leaves, provide strong contrast in both color and form. Lacy fennel leaves add a veil of green that partially screens the crocosmia. From mid- to late summer, the fennel produces showy, flat-topped clusters of tiny yellow flowers at the tops of its tall stems. Straplike Adam's-needle leaves also repeat the form of the crocosmia foliage. While the false cypress provides color in the garden all year long, this planting for full sun and well-drained soil really comes into its own from mid- to late summer, when the flowers are at peak bloom.

Tips for a Hot-Color Mixed Planting

Plant some incredible edibles. Edible plants like herbs and vegetables can make terrific ornamentals. The fennel in this combination is as wonderful in the garden as it is in the kitchen. Other handsome food plants to try combining with perennials include Swiss chard, parsley, sage, rhubarb, eggplant, and purple basil.

Add see-through plants for a veil of color. Plants like fennel that have airy stems of threadlike leaves or loose spikes of tiny flowers add depth and richness when planted at the front of a bed or border. There, they act like a translucent screen through which you can spot denser or brighter blocks of perennials planted behind.

Try flowers of fire. Crocosmias can add weeks of brilliant color to gardens from midsummer to fall. The plants, which grow from corms, are reliably hardy to Zone 6, but some cultivars will withstand Zone 5 winters with a protective layer of mulch. Mulch the plants after the ground freezes in fall. Where crocosmias are not hardy, plant the corms out in spring. Then, after the first frost, dig and store them in a cool, dry, frost-free place over the winter.

Give yuccas a second chance. All too often, yuccas like the Adam's needle in this combination are overlooked in favor of flashier, more exotic perennials. You may change your attitude about yuccas if you invite them into your beds and borders. Surround them with fine-textured plants and their stiff, swordlike leaves make exceptional accents. Or plant variegated cultivars such as 'Bright Edge' or 'Golden Sword'. Hint: You could substitute either one in this combination, and the yellow striping in their leaves would pick up the color theme.

Turn up the heat on subtle foliage with the seasonal blaze of hot colored tulips. Yellow- and red-streaked 'Triumph Tulips' make a hot combination with yellow-margined 'Wide Brim' hosta.

A Cool Combo with Contrast

Contrasting shapes and color echoes lend pizzazz to this cool color combination for a sunny garden. The clump of hakone grass forms the focal point, with its chartreuse- and green-striped leaves that contrast with the bold, pleated foliage of lady's-mantle. The frothy clusters of chartreuse lady's-mantle flowers will last through midsummer. While the color of the flowers echoes that of the grass, the rounded shape of the flowers adds contrast to the mix. Lilac-blue catmint keeps this combination lively by adding color contrast and a spiky shape.

PHOTO KEY
1. Lady's-mantle (*Alchemilla mollis*); Zones 3 to 8
2. Persian catmint (*Nepeta × faassenii* 'Blue Wonder'); Zones 3 to 8
3. Golden variegated hakone grass (*Hakonechloa macra* 'Aureola'); Zones 5 to 9
4. 'Morning Light' Japanese silver grass (*Miscanthus sinensis* 'Morning Light'); Zones 4 to 9

Secrets for Long-Lasting Contrast

❧ Guarantee good looks with a haircut.
After a month or more of flowering, lady's-mantle blooms will begin to fade to brown. Trim off the spent flowers so they won't detract from the combination. If the lady's-mantle leaves begin to brown out, cut the plants to the ground and fresh new leaves will appear. For best results and the longest-lasting leaves, keep the soil evenly moist.

❧ Shear catmint for continuous bloom.
After the first flush of early summer bloom, catmint may get floppy and shabby looking, especially in rich, moist soil. Shear the plants back by at least half and they'll quickly push out fresh new foliage and flowers. Continue shearing them as necessary throughout the summer.

❧ Strike the right soil balance. Catmint and lady's-mantle are long-blooming and adaptable to a wide range of soil and moisture conditions. Ideally, catmint prefers lean, dry soil and lady's-mantle likes it rich and moist, but you can grow them together successfully because lady's-mantle can take dry conditions with grace, and catmint will stand moist soil as long as it's well drained.

❧ Add movement and light with grasses. The fine-textured foliage of ornamental grasses is especially attractive when it sways in the wind, adding movement and gentle rustling sounds to the garden. Taller grasses, such as the Japanese silver grass in this combination, also glow when their foliage and fall flower spikes are lit from behind by the late afternoon sun—a fact to consider when you choose a site for this combination.

❧ Give hakone grass moist soil. Golden variegated hakone grass grows equally well in sun or shade, provided it has evenly moist, well-drained soil. In the South, plants appreciate protection from hot afternoon sun.

For a cool color combination on a dry site, try the lavender-blue spikes of 'Six Hills Giant' catmint with the cup-shaped, blue-violet blooms of *Geranium* × *magnificum*. Pink peonies, just beginning to bloom, create an attractive backdrop.

Beautiful Flowers and Foliage for Sun

In or out of bloom, this trio of perennials in soft, restful colors is sure to please. It features a wealth of flowers, a rich mix of foliage, plus fragrance, courtesy of both the flowers and foliage of the lavender. Endress cranesbill weaves through the planting, tying it together by filling open spaces with its sprawling stems and pale pink flowers. The fine-textured oat grass softens the combination, and its spiky, wandlike seedheads add an eyecatching vertical accent from midsummer to fall. This combination will do best in full sun to partial shade and rich but well-drained soil.

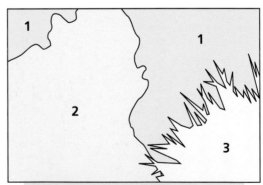

PHOTO KEY
1. Lavender (*Lavandula angustifolia*); Zones 5 to 9
2. Endress cranesbill (*Geranium endressii*); Zones 4 to 8
3. Variegated bulbous oat grass (*Arrhenatherum elatius* var. *bulbosum* 'Variegatum'); Zones 5 to 8

Tips for Beautiful Flowers and Foliage

🌿 **Enjoy tough, versatile lavender.** You can use lavender in beds and borders, as a low hedge or edging plant, in containers, or in the herb garden. Plants require full sun and average, well-drained soil. Add ground limestone to acid soil to raise the pH and bring it closer to neutral or slightly alkaline. Cut back the plants by one-third in spring, and remove any dead or damaged stems to keep them vigorous. Some gardeners replace old plants every five years or so to maximize flowering.

🌿 **Be choosy about cranesbills.** Consider flower color, height, and leaf texture when deciding which type of hardy cranesbill (also known as hardy geranium) to use in a combination. Colors range from subtle to bold, and include white, pale pink, lavender, violet, and magenta. This combination features endress cranesbill, which forms a low, spreading mound that's best at the front of a border,

where its lacy leaves and abundant flowers won't be hidden. *Geranium* 'Johnson's Blue', which bears 2-inch, purple-blue flowers on somewhat shrubbier plants, is a good choice for the front or the middle of the border. Tall species, especially those with bold foliage, such as Armenian cranesbill (*G. psilostemon*), which is 2 to 4 feet tall and bears magenta flowers with black eyes, belong in the back where they have room to spread.

🌿 **Control rust on bulbous oat grass.** Rust is a fungal disease that causes yellow-orange bumps to appear on oat grass leaves, which eventually become brown and disfigured. Rust is especially problematic in summer when conditions are damp, and selecting a site in full sun with good air circulation is the best prevention. If plants become infected, cut off diseased leaves at the base and discard them. New leaves appear quickly.

If traditional lilac-blue lavender flowers don't fit your color scheme, choose a pink-flowered cultivar like 'Rosea' instead. 'Jean Davis' and 'Loddon Pink' are two other good choices.

A Lush Planting for Moist Soil

A spot with moist soil, such as along the edge of a pond or stream, offers a terrific opportunity for combining plants with different growth requirements. In this stunning spring-blooming combination, Siberian iris and astilbes, both of which love wet feet, fill the dampest spots where rich soil and constant moisture ensure luxuriant growth. The strappy iris leaves and astilbe plumes contrast with mounds of fine-textured cranesbills and velvety lamb's-ears, which are growing on higher, drier ground. Bergenias, which thrive in rich, evenly moist soil, add a bold foliage accent.

PHOTO KEY
1. Siberian iris (*Iris sibirica*); Zones 2 to 9
2. Heartleaf bergenia (*Bergenia cordifolia*); Zones 3 to 9
3. 'Silver Carpet' lamb's-ears (*Stachys byzantina* 'Silver Carpet'); Zones 4 to 8
4. Astilbe (*Astilbe* × *arendsii*); Zones 3 to 9
5. 'Johnson's Blue' cranesbill (*Geranium* × 'Johnson's Blue'); Zones 4 to 8

Perennials for Moist Soils

⁊ Water-loving irises. There's an iris for nearly any variation on a wet site. Siberian irises like wet feet but won't survive long submerged in water. If you want to plant irises in standing water, try yellow flag (*Iris pseudacorus*) or one of the blue flags, either *I. versicolor* or *I. virginica*. Louisiana hybrid irises are another good choice for wet spots and are available in a rainbow of colors, including red. Japanese iris (*I. ensata*) needs wet soil in spring and summer, but drier conditions in winter.

⁊ A native astilbe. Commonly called false goat's beard, *Astilbe biternata* is a native woodland wildflower with creamy white flowers on 2-foot stems. Like other astilbes, it thrives in constantly moist, humus-rich soil and grows well in partial shade.

⁊ More plants for wet soil. A moist-soil site opens the door to growing many spectacular perennials that are difficult or impossible to accommodate in the well-drained conditions of the average perennial border. For example, you could extend this moist soil combination by adding southern blue flag (*Iris virginica*), which has blue-violet flowers on 2- to 3-foot plants, or great blue lobelia (*Lobelia siphilitica*), which bears spikes of deep blue flowers in midsummer.

⁊ Plants for wet or dry soil. Some plants are more adaptable to soil moisture than others. Most of the plants in this cool-color combination are adaptable. Siberian irises will grow in constantly moist soil, but they are equally happy in rich, evenly moist soil that has good drainage. Astilbes, on the other hand, demand constantly moist soil or their leaves will scorch, ruining their beauty. Berge-

Bergenias have cool green foliage in summer that turns gorgeous shades of crimson, burgundy, rose, or bronze when chilly fall nights arrive. The plants can remain colorful all winter, so they're a great choice for four-season garden interest.

nias thrive in rich, evenly moist soil, but don't tolerate wet feet. When in doubt, give them soil on the drier side—once established, bergenias even tolerate drought. Cranesbills prefer rich, moist, well-drained soil. Lamb's-ears is the exception in this garden: Plant it in well-drained sandy or loamy soil.

A Celebration of Texture and Color

Bold, contrasting textures and drifts of flowers make this combination a real eye-catcher. The spiky flowers of Miss Willmott's ghost (also called giant sea holly) pushing up through the bold green peony foliage grab your attention first. Fine-textured foliage and flowers surround Miss Willmott's ghost, accentuating its silvery clusters. A drift of milky bellflower adds a contrasting backdrop to the design. Although its individual flowers are small, the bellflower bears them in bold clusters that hold their own. Goat's rue adds a spiky accent and soft pink color.

PHOTO KEY
1. **'Pritchard's Variety' milky bellflower** (*Campanula lactiflora* **'Pritchard's Variety'**); Zones 3 to 7
2. **Miss Willmott's ghost** (*Eryngium giganteum*); Zones 4 to 8
3. **Peony** (*Paeonia*); Zones 3 to 8
4. **Goat's rue** (*Galega officinalis*); Zones 5 to 10

Perennials for Striking Textures

🍃 Look for Miss Willmott's ghost!

Eryngium giganteum was a favorite plant of English gardener Miss Ellen Ann Willmott (1858–1934). Tradition has it that she always carried seeds of it with her. If she chanced to visit a garden that lacked this dramatic plant, she simply sprinkled seeds about as she walked the garden paths. The next year, to the lucky gardener's surprise, a special calling card appeared—the large, silver-gray heads of Miss Willmott's ghost (the name has also been attributed to Miss Willmott's prickly personality). This perennial self-sows freely in open, well-drained soil. If seedlings pop up in spots where they're not wanted, they're easy to weed out. The flowers are ideal for dried arrangements.

🍃 Enjoy showy sea hollies.

Miss Willmott's ghost and other *Eryngium* species (collectively called sea hollies) have conelike clusters of small flowers that aren't too impressive. The real show comes from the petal-like structures called bracts that surround the flowers. These silvery bracts are actually modified leaves.

🍃 Get to know milky bellflower.

This underused perennial has lots to offer. It produces a profusion of deliciously fragrant flowers that last for weeks on 4- to 5-foot stalks in early summer. Cut back the stalks as the flowers fade, and plants will bloom again from side shoots. If you'd prefer pink flowers to purple in this combination, try 'Loddon Anne'.

🍃 Add a striking perennial.

Goat's rue produces shrubby, open clumps of 3- to 4-foot-tall stems clothed in fernlike leaves. The real treat of this outstanding plant is the spikes of rose-tinted blue flowers that cover the plant in summer. 'Alba' is a white-flowered form. 'Lady Wilson' is a widely available hybrid with lavender-blue and white flowers.

Silver flowers and foliage are supposed to tone down bright colors, but sometimes silver has the opposite effect, such as when this deep red daylily is accented by silvery Miss Willmott's ghost.

PHOTO KEY
1. Siberian iris (*Iris sibirica*); Zones 2 to 9
2. 'Kinsey Blue' pinks (*Dianthus* 'Kinsey Blue'); Zones 3 to 8
3. Variegated garden phlox (*Phlox paniculata* 'Norah Leigh'); Zones 3 to 8
4. Peony (*Paeonia* hybrid); Zones 3 to 8
5. Common foxglove (*Digitalis purpurea*); Zones 4 to 8
6. Catmint (*Nepeta* × *faassenii*); Zones 3 to 8

Cool Colors, Exciting Contrasts

The bold stems of bell-shaped foxgloves serve as exclamation points in this classic combination of early summer-blooming perennials. I like the mix of rounded and spikey flowers in this planting. Low, mounding catmint and pinks fill the foreground, and the showy flowers of peonies plus a large clump of white irises add bold notes to this garden. The 'Kinsey Blue' pinks (which have pink flowers and bluish foliage) create a vibrant contrast with purple-blue catmints. Foxgloves and peonies repeat their pink color. Overall, the garden is restful and calming—just what we expect from combinations of cool colors.

When the spring flush of bloom has passed, the clump of iris foliage will become a spiky accent for the mounds of catmint and pinks. Cut off the faded blooms of the irises, peonies, and pinks—and cut the catmint back by two-thirds—to keep them looking their best. Phlox, growing between the foxgloves and irises, will begin blooming in midsummer.

Fragrance is an added benefit of this sun-loving combination. Pinks have deliciously scented flowers, and you only have to walk near them to enjoy the aroma. Peonies, too, are known for their fragrance. Just brush against the catmint to release its rich, herbal scent.

Techniques for Constant Color

Plan for annual bloom from biennials. Foxgloves, along with many other biennials, make stunning, long-blooming additions to perennial gardens. They have one drawback, however: They die after they bloom. Although the plants generally reseed, it takes them two years to bloom. To make sure you will have foxgloves in bloom every year, set out year-old plants for two successive years. Once the seeding cycle is established two years running, you'll have foxgloves to enjoy every summer.

Mix in a variegated phlox. Phlox combines well with many favorite border perennials, including peonies, Siberian iris, bluestar (*Amsonia tabernaemontana*), and ornamental grasses. Using variegated garden phlox gives you the benefit of the white-variegated foliage, as well as fragrant, lilac-pink flowers in summer. If your style is more flamboyant, try 'Harlequin', which has hot pink flowers.

Start the season with bulbs. Low, ground-hugging perennials make the perfect covering for a planting of early-spring bulbs. To add early color and bloom to this early-summer combination, plant a mix of bulbs at the front of the bed, such as species crocuses, glory-of-the-snow, snowdrops, miniature daffodils such as 'Tête-à-Tête', and species tulips. The bulbs will relish the moist soil and full sun conditions in spring and will also benefit from the heat in summer as they lie dormant under the wealth of flowers that follow them. Plus, as the foliage of these minor bulbs dies back after bloom, they'll be hidden by the young, fresh foliage of the pinks and catmint.

Cool colors can be exciting when they're mixed with white in flowers with a dramatic form, like these hybrid lupines. Lupines are a perfect choice for gardens with acid soil in areas that have cool summer nights.

A Rich Mix of Yellow and Blue

Eye-catching contrast is the hallmark of plant combinations that feature complementary colors such as yellow and blue. The yellow of the coneflowers in this combination has a bit of orange in it, which deepens the color and makes the combination richer. The clusters of white yarrow flowers enhance the contrast between the blue lily-of-the-Nile and yellow-orange coneflowers, a trick you can try with many contrasting color combinations. These plants all do well in full sun and moist, well-drained soil, so they're a great starting point for a sunny perennial bed.

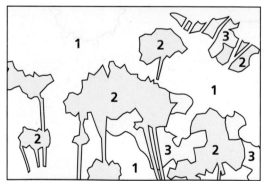

PHOTO KEY
1. **'Herbstsonne' shining cone-flower (***Rudbeckia nitida* **'Herbstsonne'); Zones 4 to 9**
2. **Lily-of-the-Nile (***Agapanthus* **Headbourne hybrids); Zones 7 to 9**
3. **Common yarrow (***Achillea millefolium***); Zones 3 to 9**

Tips for a Rich Mix of Colors

ಶ **Select sunny daisies for summer.** The cultivar name 'Herbstsonne' means "autumn sun," but this bold perennial begins blooming in high summer, not autumn. It produces daisylike flowers for weeks, easily lasting into late summer or early fall. The plants are shrub-size: They can reach 6 feet in height and spread to form 3- to 4-foot-wide clumps.

ಶ **Overwinter lily-of-the-Nile.** While lily-of-the-Nile is a popular garden plant in warm climates, many gardeners live in areas where it's too cold to grow it outdoors all year. The Headbourne hybrids are the hardiest, and, with protection, they've been grown as far north as southern New York, in Zone 7. To enjoy lily-of-the-Nile in colder zones, plant them out in spring in a sunny site with rich, well-drained soil, then dig the plants each fall before cold weather sets in. Store them in a cool, dry place, watering them about once a month so they don't dry out completely. Better yet, grow them in large pots. Either sink the pots in the soil in late spring or set them on a patio. Bring the pots indoors in fall and keep them in a sunny window over the winter.

ಶ **Extend the season.** This high summer combination will look best if you add some companions to spruce it up at the beginning and end of the season. For lively spring color, use species tulips such as yellow and white *Tulipa turda* or magenta *Tulipa pulchella*. For early summer, count on penstemons such as *Penstemon barbatus* in shades of pink and red. For bold texture, try oriental poppies (*Papaver orientale*). For fall color, add Russian sage (*Perovskia atriplicifolia*) and asters.

'Moonshine' yarrow flowers sometimes topple under their own weight. Here, the sprawling yellow flowers landed among the true-blue blossoms of annual 'Cambridge Blue' edging lobelia, creating a vibrant contrast.

A Bold Duo Starring Magenta and Yellow

Soft yellow yarrow flowers make magenta cranesbills seem to vibrate in this simple planting. The contrast in shape and size between the flat-topped yarrow flower clusters and the cup-shaped cranesbill blossoms add even more excitement. Foliage contrast keeps the combination interesting even when it's not in bloom: The yarrow leaves are soft and fernlike, while the deeply cut cranesbill leaves are stiff and angular. The foliage of both plants is similar in color, which adds a pleasing harmony among all the contrasts of this bold duo.

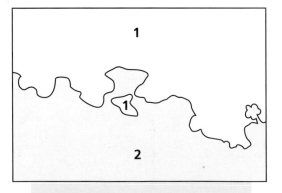

PHOTO KEY
1. 'Moonshine' yarrow (*Achillea* 'Moonshine'); Zones 3 to 8
2. Hardy cranesbill (*Geranium* × *riversleaianum*); Zones 6 to 9

Secrets for Magenta-and-Yellow Duos

❧ Put this cranesbill at the front of the border. The *Geranium* × *riversleaianum* featured in this combination is a low, spreading species that blooms all summer long as the new growth spreads outward. By midsummer, plants may reach 2 feet or more across. Because this cranesbill is a hybrid between popular Endress cranesbill (*G. endressii*) and a tender species, it may not grow well in cold climate gardens. North of Zone 6, substitute blood-red cranesbill (*G. sanguineum*), or 'Ann Folkard' cranesbill, which has deep magenta flowers with black centers.

❧ Divide yarrow to conquer it. Yarrow thrives on neglect, but plants need dividing occasionally to prevent them from taking over the entire garden. Dividing will also reinvigorate aged plants. Lift the plants in early spring, as the fresh growth is emerging, or in fall. Pull or cut the clumps apart, and remove and discard the dead and woody portions. While you have the plants out of the ground, loosen and enrich the soil where the clump grew. Replant the divided yarrow, and water it well.

❧ Try these great combinations. If yellow and magenta combinations appeal to you, try planting moss phlox (*Phlox subulata*) with basket-of-gold (*Aurinia saxatilis*) on a dry bank or in a stone wall for early spring color. For summer color in a well-drained site with lean soil, combine winecups (*Callirhoe digitata*) with yellow evening primroses (*Oenothera* spp.). In a moist to wet partly shaded spot, plant Japanese primroses (*Primula japonica*) with marsh marigolds (*Caltha palustris*) for spring bloom, and ligularias (*Ligularia* spp.) with a rosy lobelia, such as *Lobelia* 'Ruby Slippers', for summer.

Create a magenta and yellow contrast in a large garden by pairing yellow-flowered dusty meadow rue (*Thalictrum flavum* ssp. *glaucum*) with Armenian cranesbill (*Geranium psilostemon*), which can reach 2 to 4 feet tall.

PHOTO KEY
1. Dahlia (*Dahlia hybrid*); Zones 9 to 10
2. 'Laurin' goldenrod (*Solidago* 'Laurin'); Zones 3 to 9
3. Helenium (*Helenium autumnale*); Zones 3 to 8
4. 'Lucifer' crocosmia (*Crocosmia* 'Lucifer'); Zones 5 to 9
5. Garden phlox (*Phlox paniculata*); Zones 3 to 8

A Border with Flaming Flowers

Fiery hot-colored flowers arranged in bold drifts of contrasting yellow and red work together to create an eye-catching border. The color yellow is repeated throughout the garden to help unify it, but there's a pleasing variety because several different yellow-flowered perennials were used. The differences in shapes, sizes, colors, and textures keep the planting lively. For example, the low, mounding phlox and helenium are punctuated by clumps of spiky daylily foliage and tall flowering stems of goldenrod. Drifts of red flowers also add bold exclamation points, and foliage color adds excitement, too. The purple foliage of the dahlias intensifies the color of the rich red flowers around it and makes a good backdrop for the bright yellows.

Notice the irregular stair-stepped pattern in this combination, with the shortest plants near the front and taller plants behind, so each shows to best advantage. If you plan a combination like this, bring a few taller plants toward the middle to avoid a rigid pattern. All the plants in this garden thrive in full sun and well-drained soil that's rich in organic matter.

Techniques for Fiery Contrast

Protect crocosmias in the North.
Crocosmias add brilliant spots of hot red, orange, and yellow to the garden from mid-summer into fall. Their narrow, lance-shaped leaves emerge early in the season from a flattened underground stem called a corm. Although crocosmias are hardy in warmer zones and can be left in the garden year-round, gardeners north of Zone 6 should dig up the corms and bring them indoors over winter. Dig the corms after the first frost. Store them in a net sack or a paper bag in a cool, dry place where they will stay dry. Plant the corms back in the garden in spring. They can withstand light frost, so you can set them out early—a week or so before the last frost date in your area.

Overwinter dahlias indoors. Like crocosmias, dahlias must be dug in the fall and stored indoors over the winter. Lift dahlia tubers after first frost, rinse them clean, and store them in peat moss or vermiculite to keep them from drying out. The storage medium should be kept slightly moist but never wet. Check the tubers frequently to make sure they're not rotting or drying out. In spring, you can divide the clumps of fleshy roots, pot them up, and give them a headstart under lights or in a sunny windowsill, then move them to the garden after all danger of frost has passed. Or, set the roots out in the garden once the soil warms up.

Grow more great goldenrods. Goldenrods have two growth habits, creeping and clump forming. Creepers can spread rapidly in the rich soil of a flowerbed. I prefer to use the less well-known clump-formers, such as 3- to 4-foot stiff goldenrod (*Solidago rigida*), with wide flattened flower clusters and fuzzy oval leaves. It combines well with New England aster and culver's root (*Veronicastrum virginicum*).

To add fiery color to combinations, try hot-colored annuals, like red zonal geraniums, and tender perennials, like violet-purple *Verbena rigida*. They look great with bright yellow perennial 'Early Sunrise' coreopsis flowers popping through.

PHOTO KEY
1. 'East Friesland' salvia (*Salvia* × *sylvestris* 'East Friesland'); Zones 4 to 7
2. 'Golden Queen' hybrid globeflower (*Trollius* × *cultorum* 'Golden Queen'); Zones 3 to 6

A Stunning Orange-and-Purple Planting

Rich yellow-orange globeflowers seem to jump out of this combination. That's because their coarse texture and warm color make them seem closer to you. Deep, cool colors, such as the purple flowers of the salvia, have the opposite effect—they seem to recede from the eye. Fine textures also drop back. This combination succeeds because it combines both warm and cool colors and coarse and fine textures.

Globeflowers bloom early in the season and often go dormant by midsummer. Plant a billowing fern or a bold-leaved rodgersia (*Rodgersia* spp.) to fill the empty space. If you want more flowers instead, consider daylilies or turtlehead (*Chelone* spp).

Secrets for Orange-and-Purple Mixes

🌺 Find the right site. A spot in a cool northern garden makes this combination possible. Globeflowers are native to northern zones and don't grow well south of Zone 6. Plus, they prefer rich, constantly moist soil, while the salvia likes rich, moist soil with good drainage. This planting works because cool summer temperatures allow the globeflowers to get by with a little less moisture. In warmer zones, they would require constant moisture, which would cause the salvia to rot.

🌺 Try a drier-soil substitution. For an orange-and-violet planting in a drier spot, pair 'East Firesland' salvia with avens—either scarlet avens (*Geum coccineum*) or Chilean avens (*G. quellyon*) or butterfly weed (*Asclepias tuberosa*) instead of the globeflower. You could also substitute speedwells, such as *Veronica grandis*, for the salvia.

🌺 Encourage salvia to rebloom. Removing the spent flower stalks of the 'East Friesland' salvia in this combination will encourage the sideshoots to flower. Or, you can rejuvenate the entire clump by cutting it to the ground. New shoots and flowers will appear in just a few weeks.

🌺 Jazz up a container planting. Combinations with color contrasts make an especially bold statement in containers. In spring, use purple pansies with a rich orange tulip, such as 'Sunrise' or 'Orange Queen'. For summer, mix a perennial with tender plants: Try hardy, spiky salvias with tender, trailing orange lantana (*Lantana camara*) and a bright, bold variegated coleus for foliage contrast. Add a long-blooming purple annual, such as heliotrope, to take over when the salvia isn't blooming.

Annuals are perfect for bridging the gaps between clumps of perennials. Here, deep purple 'Marine' heliotrope (an annual), contrasts with biennial gloriosa daisies (*Rudbeckia hirta*).

PHOTO KEY
1. **'Lucifer' crocosmia**
   (*Crocosmia* **'Lucifer'**);
   Zones 5 to 9
2. **'Moerheim Beauty'**
   helenium (*Helenium*
   'Moerheim Beauty');
   Zones 3 to 8

Bright Reds and Greens for Late-Summer Sparks

When you're dreaming up colorful combinations of perennials, remember that green is a color worth considering, as this pairing of bright red flowers and vibrant green foliage demonstrates. Red and green are dynamic contrasting colors, as rich green seems to intensify the color of red flowers. Both crocosmia and helenium add a month or more of color to the late-summer garden. To create a garden that flowers all summer and into the fall, you could add 'Starfire' garden phlox, bright red 'Gardenview Scarlet' bee balm and cardinal flower (*Lobelia cardinalis*) for mid-summer color, and the bright foliage and berries of red chokeberry (*Aronia arbutifolia*), a native shrub, to carry the combination through the autumn. All of these plants will thrive in moist, rich soil in full sun or light shade.

Tips for Late-Summer Sparks

Try helenium of another color. Hybrid heleniums like the 'Moerheim Beauty' featured here have multicolored blossoms that are rich red and brown, so they match up beautifully with brilliant red 'Lucifer' crocosmia. To add more variety to this combination, you could try using the native form of helenium instead. It has clusters of bright yellow flowers in late summer and fall.

Give helenium a haircut in the South. If you want to grow hybrid heleniums south of Zone 7, make sure the soil stays evenly moist all season, or the lower leaves will shrivel. To keep the foliage full and healthy near the base of the plants, perennial expert Alan Armitage recommends cutting heleniums back by half in early July to encourage stronger, shorter leafy stems and abundant bloom. You can also try substituting *Helenium flexuosum*, which is native to warmer southern regions. This helenium has flowers with drooping yellow petals and dark brown centers, and it is available from nurseries that specialize in wildflowers.

Divide crocosmias to keep them blooming. Crocosmia produces fiery red, yellow, or orange flowers throughout much of the summer. The flowers stand up in a row on the wiry stems, and they make excellent, long-lasting cut flowers. Even when the plants aren't in bloom, the swordlike foliage is an attractive asset in a garden. Plants grow from flattened corms (underground stems). To keep crocosmia vigorous and blooming strongly, divide the clumps every few years. In the north, lift corms after the first frost, and store them indoors over the winter. Replant outdoors in spring.

Fall is full of contrasting colors in perennial gardens, and this duo of hot pink 'Bressingham Glow' Japanese anemone and bright red Italian asters (*Aster amellus*) offers startling contrast for a sunny garden.

A Perfect Pair of Pink Cranesbills

A red color echo and contrasting size work together to make this simple combination stunning. The magenta and pale pink flowers of the two cranesbills are said to "echo" one another because they share the same basic color—red. Pale pink is red with white added, while magenta consists of red combined with black and blue. Combinations like this one that use two plants with similar foliage, flowers, and form need contrast to keep them interesting. Although the foliage and flowers of these cranesbills are similar, their dramatic difference in size adds the essential contrast.

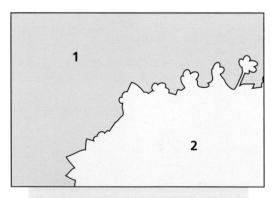

PHOTO KEY
1. Armenian cranesbill (*Geranium psilostemon*); Zones 4 to 8
2. 'Wargrave Pink' Endress cranesbill (*Geranium endressii* 'Wargrave Pink'); Zones 4 to 8

Techniques for Cranesbill Color Echoes

🐛 **Keep your cranesbills green and growing.** Cranesbills, also called hardy geraniums, thrive in rich, evenly moist soil in full sun to light shade. In areas with hot summers, afternoon shade is especially beneficial. Lift clumps and divide them every three to four years in early spring or fall.

🐛 **Consider magenta in a smaller package.** If you love magenta but have a small garden that won't accommodate Armenian cranesbill, cheer up. 'Ann Folkard' cranesbill bears flowers in the same vivid color on plants that are only a foot tall. It blooms all summer and may spread to 3 feet.

🐛 **Remember size when you plant.** Endress cranesbill is a low, mounding plant about 1 foot tall and 1½ feet across. When you plant Endress cranesbill, you can space plants about 1 foot apart. However, Armenian cranesbill is a bold-textured giant that can reach 3 feet tall and wide, or even larger in cool climates. Be sure to leave at least 2 feet of open space all around this Goliath at planting time, especially when combining it with smaller plants.

🐛 **Extend the season with companion plants.** To add early spring color to a planting of cranesbills, which bloom in late spring and early summer, underplant with daffodils, Grecian windflower (*Anemone blanda*), and crocuses. For late-season color, try asters, grasses, showy crocus (*Crocus speciosus*), and autumn crocuses (*Colchicum* spp.).

At the end of the season, when cranesbills are long past bloom, you can introduce new color echoes in your garden with pink- and purple-flowered Italian asters (*Aster amellus*). If you have trouble finding pink-flowered Italian asters, try 'Patricia Ballard' New York aster instead.

PHOTO KEY

1. **Yellow corydalis (***Corydalis lutea***); Zones 5 to 8**
2. **Christmas fern (***Polystichum acrostichoides***); Zones 3 to 8**
3. **'Kabitan' narrow-leaved hosta (***Hosta lancifolia* **'Kabitan'); Zones 3 to 8**

Yellow Echoes in Flowers and Foliage

With variegated foliage, it's easy to weave a single color through an entire planting, letting it echo in both flowers and foliage. In this shaded woodland planting, yellow corydalis flowers echo the yellow-, chartreuse-, and green-striped leaves of the hostas. The dark green Christmas fern fronds emphasize the startling color of the hosta foliage. Rich contrasts in foliage texture are at work here,

too. The fine-textured corydalis leaves make an attractive match for the strap-shaped hostas. Both appear delicate in contrast to the bold rocks in the background.

This handsome combination will last all summer long, because corydalis blooms continuously from spring right through fall if the soil stays evenly moist. In late summer, the hostas will send up spikes of violet flowers. And while the hostas will die back in fall, the corydalis leaves last well into winter, and the fern fronds are evergreen, adding rich green to the landscape all year.

Expert Advice
for a Foliage and Flower Echo

🌱 Try a carpet of corydalis. Yellow cory- dalis can be hard to find (try a mail-order com- pany that offers lots of woodland plants), but it's well worth the effort it takes to locate it. All you need is one established plant and you'll have corydalis to spare, because it's a prolific self-sower. Seedlings will pop up around other plants, in cracks and crevices, and along paths—they will carpet open areas if you let them. Pull up seedlings that appear in the wrong place, or dig them with a trowel and move them to new locations. Corydalis thrives in rich, well-drained soil that is evenly moist.

🌱 Cool down this combination with white. To recreate this combination in white, substitute 'Ginko Craig' hosta, which has deep green leaves with white edges, and white- flowered fringed bleeding heart (*Dicentra*

eximia 'Alba'), which will bloom intermit- tently into fall.

🌱 Enjoy ferns for the holidays. Christ- mas ferns were once gathered to make wreaths and other festive holiday decorations. Al- though collecting fronds from the wild isn't a good idea, you may want to harvest some from your garden to celebrate the holidays.

🌱 Add perennials to a rock wall. Cory- dalis and Christmas fern can be a great combi- nation for planting in an unmortared rock wall. An easy way to position plants in the wall is to use a chopstick. Use the chopstick to work some soil out of a crevice. Then, put the plant in place and use the chopstick again to gently push the roots into the opening. Fill in soil around the roots, and gently tamp it down.

The golden-edged leaves of a variegated form of garden sage (*Salvia officinalis*) echo the butter yellow cen- ters of the garden mums in this simple fall combination.

Late-Summer Echoes of Pink and White

Soothing pinks in a range of hues from red-violet to mauve and pale pink echo through the mounds of color in this showy garden that's perfect for a spot in full sun or light shade. Masses of Shasta daisies and baby's-breath seem to extend the range of colors from palest pink to pure white. Contrasts between the shapes and textures of the plants and flowers create added excitement. Pink Chinese anemones echo the shape of the classic white Shasta daisies, while prairie blazing-star adds a spiky accent.

PHOTO KEY
1. Bronze fennel (*Foeniculum vulgare* var. *purpureum*); Zones 4 to 9
2. Shasta daisy (*Chrysanthemum × superbum*); Zones 4 to 8
3. Garden phlox (*Phlox paniculata*); Zones 3 to 8
4. Baby's-breath (*Gypsophila paniculata*); Zones 3 to 9
5. Prairie blazing-star (*Liatris pycnostachya*); Zones 3 to 9
6. 'September Charm' Chinese anemone (*Anemone hupehensis* 'September Charm'); Zones 5 to 9

Secrets for a Late-Summer Color Echo

❧ Look for subtle secondary echoes.
Look closely and you'll see that Shasta daisies and Chinese anemones both have yellow at the centers of their flowers. The flat-topped clusters of the bronze fennel flowers provide a yellow color echo. The airy bronze-purple foliage of the fennel also sets off the pink flowers in this combination nicely.

❧ Adjust soil pH for this lime lover. The botanical name of baby's-breath, *Gypsophila*, means lime loving, because these plants are native to regions with alkaline soils. While baby's-breath performs best in the garden under alkaline conditions (pH above 7, or neutral), they'll tolerate neutral soil. In strongly acid soil, below pH 6, the plants are short-lived. The other perennials in this combination grow best in neutral to slightly acidic conditions, but they'll tolerate the slightly alkaline soil that's important for the baby's-breath.

❧ Grow a banquet for butterflies. This perennial combination offers a feast for more than just your eyes; it feeds butterflies, as well. Fennel is a good food source for swallowtail caterpillars. When the adult butterflies emerge from their cocoons, two favorite nectar plants, phlox and prairie blazingstar, await them.

❧ Consider pretty in all-pink. To create an all-pink version of this planting, substitute 'Pink Fairy' or 'Pink Star' baby's-breath. Instead of the Shasta daisies, use pyrethrum daisies (*Tanacetum coccineum*), which come in shades of pink, rose-pink, or red.

Understated color echoes add polish to a perennial combination. The rose blush stripes on lily-flowered 'Marilyn' tulips echo the rich pink flowers of old-fashioned bleeding heart (*Dicentra spectabilis*).

A Meadow Garden in Fiery Fall Hues

Large plants, bold flowers, and rich color echos abound in fall, especially in meadow-style gardens like this one. Masses of brightly colored daisies flow throughout the bed, with the orange and bronze heleniums echoing the yellow to golden orange black-eyed Susans. Clumps of pure yellow heleniums link the planting together by echoing the yellows of the black-eyed Susans. The tall Joe-Pye weed adds contrast when it's in full flower, but the dusty rose blooms soon fade to rusty brown. Once they do, they echo the rusts and oranges of the other flowers around them.

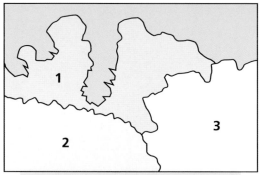

PHOTO KEY
1. 'Atropurpureum' Joe-Pye weed (*Eupatorium purpureum* 'Atropurpureum'); Zones 2 to 8
2. 'Goldsturm' black-eyed Susan (*Rudbeckia fulgida* var. *sullivantii* 'Goldsturm'); Zones 3 to 9
3. Helenium (*Helenium autumnale*); Zones 3 to 8

Expert Tips for Meadow-Style Plantings

🐛 **Choose colorful heleniums.** The brightly colored orange, burgundy, and yellow heleniums we grow in gardens today are hybrids that were developed in Germany. You may see helenium hybrids sold under either their German names or English translations. Some of the most colorful hybrids include: 'Bruno', with dark crimson or red-brown flowers on stems as tall as 4 feet; 'Dunklepracht' (also sold as 'Dark Beauty'), with rich red flowers; 'Moerheim Beauty', with burnt orange petals and dark centers; and 'Kugelsonne' (also sold as 'Sunball') with lemon yellow flowers.

🐛 **Create a meadow bouquet.** All the flowers in this combination make great, long-lasting cut flowers. Just cut them in the morning and put them straight into a vase to enjoy indoors or outdoors on a garden table.

🐛 **Plant winter seedheads for the birds.** Leave the stems and seedheads of Joe-Pye weeds and black-eyed Susans standing in your garden over winter to add interest to the winter landscape. They're especially pretty when they're topped with fresh white snow. The seedheads offer a winter smorgasbord for chickadees, goldfinches, and sparrows, which relish the seeds.

🐛 **Add plants for a woodland edge.** Traditionally, perennial borders are arranged in a stair-stepped pattern with plants displayed from tallest to shortest. You can use a meadow planting along the edge of a woodland in much the same way—with the tallest plants, such as 6-foot-tall Joe-Pye weed, at the back, and shorter species in front. Plant a few taller plants in the middle front of the bed to break up the pattern and keep the garden exciting. This creates a natural-looking transition between the trees and the lawn and surrounding landscape.

Rosy reds echo through this fall combination in the towering blooms of Joe-Pye weed and in the *Lespedeza thunbergii* 'Gibraltar' at its feet. 'Powis Castle' artemisia adds silvery foliage to complete the picture.

Unforgettable Herbs in Pink and Purple

Billowing mounds of flowers in shades of rose-purple, pink, lavender, and violet make this sophisticated combination one to remember. All the colors share a touch of red, which creates the color echo. The variety of plant shapes and forms add interest. Mounds of catmint are artfully paired with the solid, rounded form of betony, while the spiky flowers of lavender contrast with spherical chives. This planting of herbs is also memorable because the foliage and flowers are fragrant as well. All require rich, well-drained soil and full sun. Nights on the cool side keep the plants in bloom for a month or more.

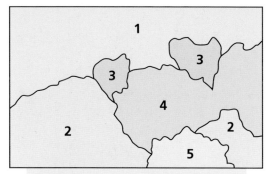

PHOTO KEY
1. **'Six Hills Giant' catmint** (*Nepeta* × *faassenii* **'Six Hills Giant'**); Zones 3 to 8
2. **Big betony** (*Stachys grandiflora*); Zones 2 to 8
3. **Bearded iris** (*Iris* bearded hybrid); Zones 3 to 9
4. **French lavender** (*Lavandula stoechas*); Zones 7 to 9
5. **Common chives** (*Allium schoenoprasum*); Zones 3 to 9

Tips for Terrific Herbs

🌿 **Have your chives and eat them, too.**
It's no secret that chives are a favorite plant of cooks as well as gardeners, but you don't need to relegate them to a kitchen garden. You can harvest leaves from chive plants growing in beds and borders for use in the kitchen. Cutting the plants back encourages fresh, vigorous new leaves to appear. Chive flowers are edible, as well. Gently tear up the rounded clusters, and add them as a color and flavor accent to salads.

🌿 **Consider using a hardier lavender.**
If you garden north of Zone 8, substitute common lavender (*Lavandula angustifolia*) for the less-hardy French lavender in this combination. Common lavender is hardy in Zones 5 to 9, and will survive winters in the milder parts of Zone 4 with winter protection—pile marsh hay or evergreen boughs over the plants after the ground freezes. Both species make fantastic dried flowers. Cut the stems as the buds are showing full color, but before the flowers open. Bind them in small bunches with rubber bands and hang them in a warm, dry, dark place.

🌿 **Keep lavender looking its best.** As lavender plants get old, they tend to get woody and bloom less. To rejuvenate older clumps, prune them in early spring before growth begins: You can cut back the plant to 6 to 8 inches above the soil level. If plants get old and lose vigor, or are likely to be damaged by severe winter weather, take 4-inch cuttings in fall and root them in coarse sand. Set out the new, vigorous plants in spring to replace the old ones.

🌿 **Try shorter plants for a smaller space.** To create a similar color echo combination in a small garden, choose compact versions of the same plants. Substitute 'Blue Wonder' catmint for 'Six Hills Giant' and wood

Color echoes can be subtle, as in this sun-loving, fall-flowering pair of lavender-blue seaside aster (*Aster spectabilis*) and rosy showy sedum (*Sedum spectabile*). Both flowers share blue as a common hue, but the sedum flowers have more red in them than the asters.

betony (*Stachys officinalis*) for big betony. There isn't a smaller form of French lavender, so try 'Munstead', a compact cultivar of common lavender.

An All-White Garden for Partial Shade

Maidenhair Fern

Tulip

Clark's Geranium

Bethlehem Sage

Plant Names	Bloom Color and Season	Height and Spread
'British Sterling' Bethlehem sage	Blue flowers in early spring	8" tall and 2' wide
White old-fashioned bleeding heart	White flowers in spring	3' tall and wide
Maidenhair fern	Lime green foliage	2' tall and wide
'Kashmir White' Clark's geranium	White flowers in early summer	1½' tall and wide
'Dale's Strain' heuchera	Green flowers in late spring	1' to 3' tall and 18" wide

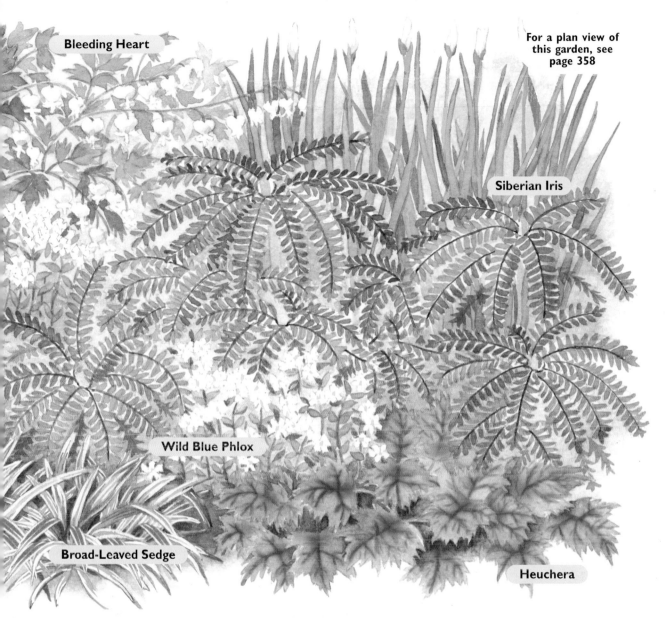

Bleeding Heart

For a plan view of this garden, see page 358

Siberian Iris

Wild Blue Phlox

Broad-Leaved Sedge

Heuchera

Plant Names	Bloom Color and Season	Height and Spread
'Fourfold White' Siberian iris	White flowers in late spring to early summer	2½' tall and wide
'Fuller's White' wild blue phlox	White flowers in spring	1' tall and wide
Creeping variegated broad-leaved sedge	White-striped foliage	6" tall and 12" wide
'Mount Tacoma' tulip	White flowers in spring	1½' tall and 8" wide

A Warm Color Garden

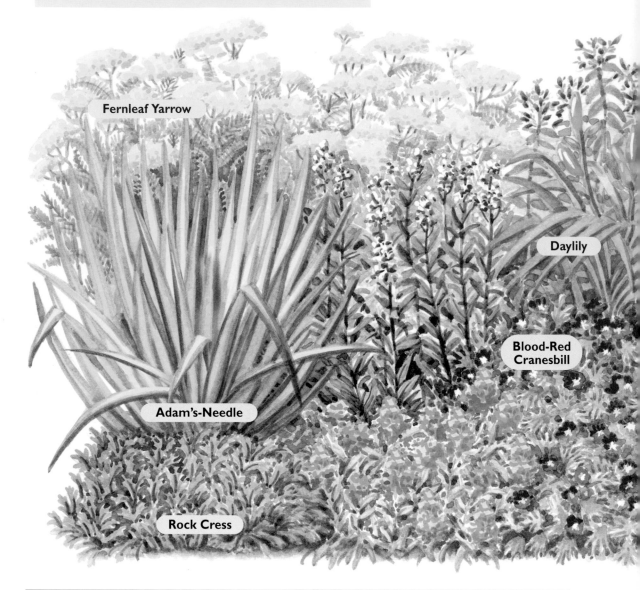

Fernleaf Yarrow

Daylily

Blood-Red Cranesbill

Adam's-Needle

Rock Cress

Plant Names	Bloom Color and Season	Height and Spread
'Bright Edge' Adam's-needle	Yellow-striped leaves/white flowers in summer	4' to 5' tall and 3' wide
Blood-red cranesbill	Magenta flowers in early summer	10" to 12" tall and 2' to 3' wide
Daylily	Orange flowers in summer	3' tall and wide

For a plan view of this garden, see page 355

Garden Phlox

Foxglove Penstemon

Wallflower

Getting the Most from Your Garden

To get the best from this garden of hot-colored perennials, choose a site in full sun with light, well-drained, fertile soil. Throughout the summer, you'll enjoy its bright colors in both flowers and foliage. The rich burgundy foxglove penstemon leaves and the yellow-striped spiky Adam's-needle leaves provide a colorful backdrop for the richly colored flowers that open throughout the season, from the early-spring carpet of purple rock cress to the brilliant late-summer display of red phlox blossoms.

To keep the garden looking its best, cut the daylilies and cranesbills back after hard frost. The garden remains attractive in winter, with ruddy penstemon seedheads, dried lacy flowerheads on the yarrow, and the evergreen bayonetlike Adam's-needle foliage. Cut the dried flower stalks back in early spring to make way for the new growth, and prune any winter-damaged stems of the rock cress and wallflower.

Plant Names	Bloom Color and Season	Height and Spread
'Husker Red' foxglove penstemon	Pink/white flowers in early summer	2' to 4' tall and 2' wide
'Starfire' garden phlox	Cherry red flowers in summer	2' to 2½' tall and wide
'Purple Gem' rock cress	Purple flowers in early spring	4" tall and 1' wide
'Orange Bedder' Siberian wallflower	Orange flowers in spring	4" to 6" tall and 1' wide
Fernleaf yarrow	Yellow flowers in early to midsummer	3' tall and 2½' wide

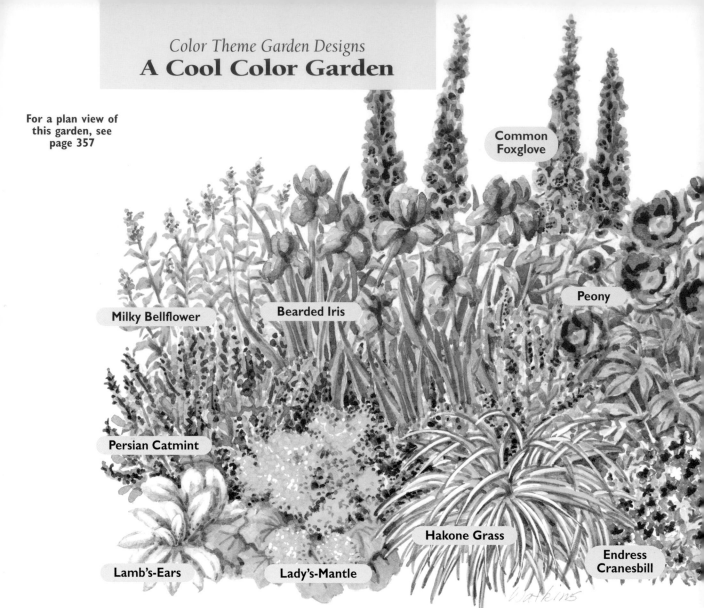

Color Theme Garden Designs
A Cool Color Garden

For a plan view of this garden, see page 357

Common Foxglove

Peony

Milky Bellflower

Bearded Iris

Persian Catmint

Hakone Grass

Lamb's-Ears

Lady's-Mantle

Endress Cranesbill

Plant Names	Bloom Color and Season	Height and Spread
'Pritchard's Variety' milky bellflower	Blue flowers in early to midsummer	3' to 4' tall and 3' wide
'Blue Wonder' Persian catmint	Blue flowers in early summer	1' to 1½' tall and 2' to 3' wide
'A. T. Johnson' Endress cranesbill	Silvery pink flowers in early summer	1' to 1½' tall and 2' wide
Common foxglove	Pink flowers in early summer	3' to 4' tall and 1' to 2' wide
Golden variegated hakone grass	Yellow-striped foliage	1' tall and 2' wide
Bearded iris	Blue flowers in late spring to early summer	2' to 2½' tall and 1' wide

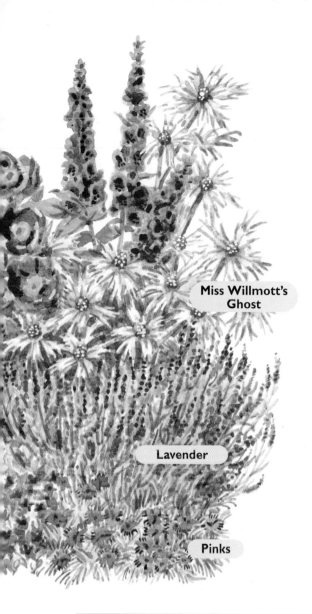

Miss Willmott's Ghost

Lavender

Pinks

Enjoying Your Cool Color Garden

A dreamy garden of soothing colors is the perfect pick-me-up on a hot summer afternoon. This garden would be delightful planted near a backyard patio or garden bench where you can appreciate the details of the planting at close range. This lush garden will produce abundant flowers, so be sure to cut some stems for indoor arrangements. The tall spikes of foxglove, the frothy sprays of lady's-mantle and cat-mint, and a peony blossom or two will grace a vase with color and fragrance.

The peak flowering time for this garden is in the early summer, but lavender and catmint keep the flowers coming through the summer. The lamb's-ears foliage and golden variegated hakone grass will look fresh all through the season. In winter, frost and snow will make enchanting patterns on the tawny grass clumps and the carpet of lamb's-ears.

Plant Names	Bloom Color and Season	Height and Spread
Lady's-mantle	Chartreuse flowers in early summer	1' tall and 2' to 3' wide
Lamb's-ears	Silvery foliage/pink flowers in early summer	4" to 12" tall and 1' to 2' wide
'Hidcote' lavender	Deep blue flowers in summer	1½' tall and 2' wide
Miss Willmott's ghost	Silver bracts/green flowers in summer	3' to 6' tall and 4' wide
'Sea Shell' peony	Pink flowers in early summer	3' tall and wide
Pinks	Pink flowers in early summer	6" to 8" tall and 12" wide

A Contrasting Color Garden

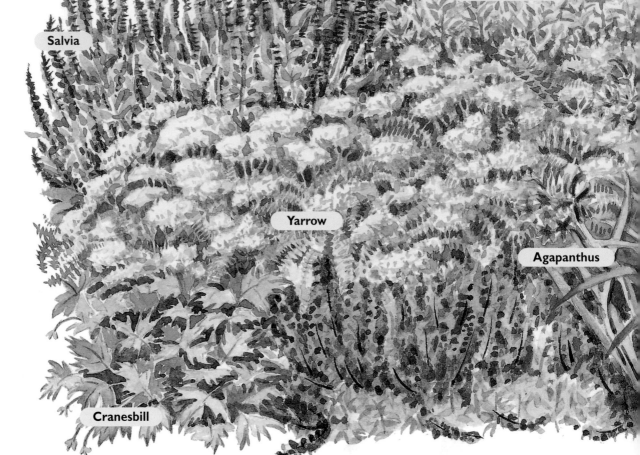

Frikart's Aster

Salvia

Yarrow

Agapanthus

Cranesbill

Plant Names	Bloom Color and Season	Height and Spread
'Bressingham Blue' agapanthus	Deep blue flowers in summer	3' tall and 2' wide
'Monch' Frikart's aster	Lavender-blue flowers in late summer	2½' tall and 3' wide
Black-eyed Susan	Yellow flowers in summer	1' to 2' tall and 1' wide
'Blue Wonder' Persian catmint	Blue flowers in early summer	1' to 1½' tall and 2' to 3' wide
'Mavis Simpson' cranesbill	Pink flowers in early summer	1' tall and 2' wide
Jacob's ladder	Blue flowers in early summer	1' to 3' tall and 1' wide
'May Night' salvia	Purple flowers in early to midsummer	1½' tall and 2' wide
'Moonshine' yarrow	Soft yellow flowers in early summer	1' to 2' tall and wide

For a plan view of this garden, see page 356

Jacob's Ladder

Black-Eyed Susan

Persian Catmint

Getting the Best from Your Garden

To look its best, this group of perennials demands a site with full sun and rich but well-drained sandy soil. If your yard has heavy soil, build up a raised bed with plenty of compost and sand before planting. This garden offers both hot and cool color contrasts. Jacob's ladder and cranebills start the show with blue and pink in late spring, soon followed by blue Persian catmint and purple salvias. To encourage these plants to rebloom in midsummer, cut them back after the first flush of flowers begins to fade.

83

A Color Echo Garden

Phlox

Armenian Cranesbill

Dense Blazing-Star

Chives

Aster

Persian Catmint

Plant Names	Bloom Color and Season	Height and Spread
'September Charm' Chinese anemone (not visible above)	Pink flowers in late summer to fall	2½' to 3' tall and 2' wide
'Patricia Ballard' New York aster	Pink flowers in late summer to fall	2' to 3' tall and 2' to 2½' wide
'Pink Fairy' baby's-breath	Pink flowers in summer	2' tall and 2' to 2½' wide
'Kobold' dense blazing-star	Violet flowers in summer	1' to 2' tall and 1' wide
Prairie blazing-star	Violet flowers in summer	2' to 4' tall and 1' to 2' wide

For a plan view of
this garden, see
page 356

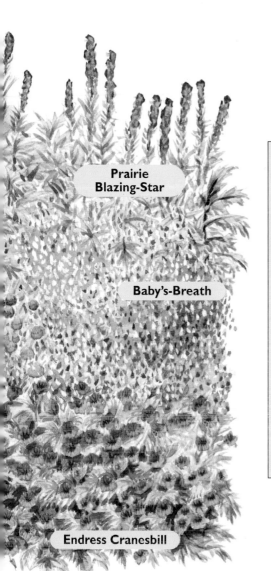

Prairie
Blazing-Star

Baby's-Breath

Endress Cranesbill

Getting the Most from Your Garden

Rich, evenly moist soil that never dries out is the key to success with this pink and purple color echo garden. Catmints, chives, and cranesbills offer early-summer color. Midseason color comes from blazing-stars, long-flowering phlox, and baby's-breath. In the early-summer view here, the Chinese anemones are hidden by a veil of baby's-breath blossoms. The anemone flowers will shoot up in the fall when the asters also come into bloom.

You can add early spring interest to this garden by underplanting some bulbs around the crowns of the perennials. Try the charming, pink daffodil 'Foundling', blue glory-of-the-snow (*Chionodoxa* 'Blue Giant'), and pink and blue Grecian windflowers (*Anemone blanda*).

Plant Names	Bloom Color and Season	Height and Spread
'Dawn to Dusk' Persian catmint	Pink flowers in early summer	1' to 1½' tall and 2' to 3' wide
Common chives	Pink flowers in early summer	1' to 1½' tall and 1' wide
Armenian cranesbill	Magenta flowers in early summer	2' to 4' tall and 3' wide
'Wargrave Pink' Endress cranesbill	Salmon pink flowers in early summer	1' to 1½' tall and 2' wide
'Bright Eyes' garden phlox	Pink flowers with dark centers in summer	3' to 4' tall and 2' wide

Combinations
FOR ALL SEASONS

Perennials are the perfect plants for adding four-season interest in every part of your yard. In this section, you'll find combinations grouped by season, starting with wonderful pairings of spring bulbs and spring-flowering perennials. I've also selected some great combinations for early summer and late summer, and I finished out with terrific perennial groupings for fall color and winter interest. You'll also find garden designs that mix the combinations, resulting in four beds that have different peak bloom seasons, but all offer color and variety from spring through fall.

PHOTO KEY
1. Mixed hybrid daffodils *Narcissus* hybrids); Zones 4 to 8
2. Cowslip primrose (*Primula* hybrid); Zones 4 to 8

Classic Color from Spring Bulbs

Daffodils are a sure sign that winter has run its course and spring is on the way. To proclaim the change of season loud and clear, plant daffodils in generous clumps or large drifts of a single cultivar. And to extend the range of colors and bloom shapes in any daffodil planting, plant old-fashioned hybrid primroses, as shown here, alongside the bulbs. Johnny-jump-ups (*Viola tricolor*) and other cool-weather annuals also make fine planting companions for daffodils, as do other bulbs, such as crocuses, snowdrops (*Galanthus* spp.), glory-of-the snow (*Chionodoxa* spp.), grape hyacinths (*Muscari* spp.), and squill (*Scilla* spp.).

Many daffodils also feature rich fragrance that serves as a reminder that the best of the garden is yet to come. You could substitute almost any of the wide variety of daffodils in this combination. There are 12 categories of daffodils, called divisions. The daffodils are grouped according to the size of the flower's cup (also called the corona) in relation to the petals (the corolla). To enjoy the widest range of shapes, sizes, colors, and bloom times—there are daffodils that bloom in early, mid-, and late spring—plant a few selections from each division.

Secrets for Stunning Spring Color

🐌 **Plan in fall for spring color.** Daffodils are good garden investments because they form long-lived clumps that multiply and produce more flowers every year. And since the bulbs are poisonous, they aren't bothered by rodents, which consume tulip bulbs like caviar. Plant daffodils in fall with 4 to 6 inches above the tops of the bulbs. Space them 3 to 10 inches apart, depending on the size of the bulbs, to give them room to multiply. Instead of aligning them in stiff rows like soldiers, try arranging them in loose, free-form drifts for a more relaxed look.

🐌 **Don't put your daffodils in a bind** Resist the temptation to braid, fold, or otherwise bind up the sprawling foliage of daffodils after the flowers fade—no matter how unattractive it seems. Why? When you bind up the ripening leaves, you reduce or destroy the bulb's ability to produce the food necessary to fuel next year's flowers. So just let the foliage flop a few weeks after bloom, and you'll ensure long life for your bulbs. Once the leaves have turned from green to yellow, cut them off and add them to the compost pile. If you can't stand floppy daffodil foliage, consider choosing miniature daffodils, which are my favorites. While their flowers are not as big as the hybrids', neither is their foliage.

🐌 **Protect your primroses from slugs and snails.** In my garden, primroses are the first plants attacked by slugs. There is something about succulent primrose crowns that makes them simply irresistible to these slimy mollusks. I have to be ever vigilant to keep my plants from being expensive slug bait. My favorite control method is beer traps. I fill small bowls and clay saucers with beer and place them around the garden—I don't bother to bury them. Slugs are born lushes; they climb up the sides of the containers to get to the beer, and then they drown. I empty the traps every other day and refill them. This technique also works for controlling snails.

Ornamental grasses are beautiful garden features throughout the winter. In spring, they serve as a tawny, fine-textured background for masses of golden daffodils.

A Long-Lasting Mix of Groundcovers

For a groundcover bed that's stunning from late winter all the way until fall, try this mix of perennials that sports a variety of shapes and textures. In early spring, creamy white hellebore flowers set against a handsome mix of foliage makes this combination a winner. The design uses a simple trick to make this bed seem deeper than it really is. How does it work? To the human eye, bold textures appear closer and fine textures appear farther away. Thus, the round, bold-textured leaves of wild ginger make the planting seem to stretch toward you, while the fine-textured maidenhair ferns in the background seem to pull away. All the plants in this garden thrive in shade and rich, evenly moist soil.

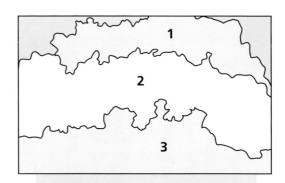

PHOTO KEY
1. **Southern maidenhair fern** (*Adiantum capillus-veneris*); Zones 7 to 10
2. **Garden hybrid hellebore** (*Helleborus* × *hybridus*); Zones 4 to 9
3. **British Columbia wild ginger** (*Asarum caudatum*); Zones 4 to 7

Advice for Great Groundcover Combos

🦂 **Try these early bloomers.** Few flowers are as lovely or as welcome as the nodding saucerlike blooms of garden hybrid hellebores, which begin to open in late winter and last until early summer. The flowers take freezing temperatures and drifting snows in stride. The white flowers gradually fade to green. There also are mauve-pink and maroon forms as well as white ones speckled with dark red. The tough, leathery, dark green leaves are evergreen and add welcome color to the garden all year. Perhaps best of all, Lenten roses are very easy to grow. Give them a spot under deciduous trees so they can enjoy sunshine over winter but be in partial to full shade from late summer onward.

🦂 **Look for these flowers that hide.** The glossy leaves of British Columbia wild ginger hide its curious maroon flowers, which are borne on the ground. Each jug-shaped flower has three lobes with long wiry tails. The flowers are hidden underneath the foliage, so you need to lift up a leaf or two to appreciate them. If you want to see foliage and flowers at the same time, try planting this wild ginger on a slope. That way the flowers will be visible nodding below the leaves at ground level, even when the leaves are fully expanded.

🦂 **Grow a northern fern with southern charm.** Since southern maidenhair fern isn't hardy north of Zone 7, gardeners will need to substitute another plant with a similar soft, airy texture to recreate this combination. The best choice is a close relative, Himalayan maidenhair fern (*Adiantum venustum*). This lovely fern has sea green, horseshoe-shaped fronds that reach 1 to 1½ feet tall and are hardy in Zones 4 to 8.

Evergreen wild gingers like this Virginia wild ginger (*Asarum virginicum*) thrive in shade. It's easy to care for, and its mottled leaves add four-season interest to combinations.

🦂 **Give groundcovers rich soil.** Woodland wildflowers and groundcovers need rich, water-retentive soil to thrive and spread. If your soil is on the lean side or tends to dry out, amend it before you plant wildflowers. Add 3 to 4 inches of organic matter, such as compost or well-rotted manure, over the planting bed, and dig it in to at least 8 inches. Then add a 1- to 2-inch layer of organic matter over the top of the soil. Let the bed settle for three to four weeks before planting, if possible. Don't use peat moss as a soil amendment unless you specifically need acid soil. Peat is low in nutrition and tends to make the soil fluffy without adding fertility.

A Mix of Spring Flowers and Foliage

Combine early-blooming perennials and bulbs with plants that feature handsome foliage, and you have the recipe for a garden that stays attractive for months on end. In this combination, crocuses start off the show in spring, followed shortly by the flowers of the Bethlehem sage. Later in spring, the variegated hosta appears and creates a bright spot of color echoed by the silver-spotted Bethlehem sage leaves. Both of these outstanding foliage plants keep this garden beautiful through summer and into fall. This combination will do best in a partially shady site with moist, rich soil. Try planting it under deciduous trees, so the crocuses can get the full benefit of early spring sun before the trees leaf out.

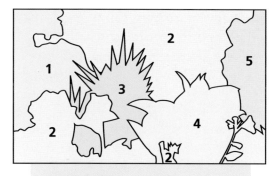

PHOTO KEY
1. Sweet woodruff (*Galium odoratum*); Zones 4 to 8
2. Bethlehem sage (*Pulmonaria saccharata*); Zones 3 to 8
3. Dutch crocus (*Crocus vernus*); Zones 3 to 9
4. 'Univittata' wavy-leaf hosta (*Hosta undulata* 'Univittata'); Zones 3 to 8
5. Garden forget-me-not (*Myosotis sylvatica*); Zones 5 to 9

Expert Tips for a Spring Show

Try growing leopard-spotted pulmonarias. Extra-early spring flowers and long-lasting attractive foliage make pulmonarias invaluable. One of the most popular is *Pulmonaria saccharata* 'Mrs. Moon', which has many shiny silver spots on its leaves and pink buds that open into sky-blue flowers. There are many other garden-worthy pulmonarias you can try, however. Here are a few of my favorites: 'Excaliber', with silver leaves edged in deep green; 'Smoky Blue', with rich blue flowers and large silver spots, 'Little Star', a diminutive plant that has narrow, deep green leaves with sparse spots and deep cobalt blue flowers; 'Milky Way', with large lance-shaped leaves spotted with silver and blue flowers that fade to wine red; and 'Pierre's Pure Pink', with moderately spotted leaves and deep pink flowers.

Depend on handsome hostas. Hostas are perennially popular in shady gardens. They come in a wide range of colors and sizes, and they're virtually care-free, although slugs sometimes damage the leaves. *Hosta undulata* 'Univittata', featured here, is an old-fashioned form with wavy leaves that add extra interest. It's a fast increaser, so if you plant it, you'll end up with plenty of divisions to transplant or give away.

Underplant for extra color. It's easy to tuck spring bulbs among the perennials in combinations like this one. Grassy crocus leaves are the only evidence that spring bulbs added color to this planting before the hosta and Bethlehem sage appeared. Forget-me-nots also poke their flowers up through the other perennials. They're easy to start in place from seeds.

For extra-early spring color, plant combinations of small early-blooming bulbs. White double-flowered snowdrops (*Galanthus nivalis* 'Flore Pleno') and vivid pink hardy cyclamen (*Cyclamen coum* 'Amy') make a delicate pairing for late-winter bloom.

PHOTO KEY
1. **Single late tulip (*Tulipa hybrid*); Zones 3 to 9**
2. **Wild blue phlox (*Phlox divaricata*); Zones 3 to 9**

An Appealing Spring Duo

Snow white tulips rising above a sea of lavender-blue phlox creates a restful, classic garden picture. The fragrance of the wild blue phlox, a native woodland wildflower, fills the warm spring air, making this combination a perfect choice for planting near a terrace or other area where you sit outside. You'll enjoy the fragrance by day and the shine of the luminous white tulips in the evening.

Once the tulips have finished blooming, their bare flower stalks look awkward among the phlox. You can't cut the plants to the ground, because the bulbs need the foliage to make food for next year's flowers. My solution is to cut off the flower stalk flush with the first leaf on the stalk. That way, the foliage can ripen and the gangly stalk is gone. Cut the leaves to the ground once they've turned yellow. The glossy, dark green leaves of the phlox are semievergreen and remain attractive throughout the season and well into winter.

Tips for Tulips and Spring-Blooming Phlox

Encourage your tulips to be perennials. Hybrid tulips have an annoying habit of fading away after a year or two of bloom. By the second or third year, they only produce floppy foliage that looks like a sea green dishrag, and no flowers. To get the best from hybrid tulips, select a spot in full sun with well-drained soil. Plant the bulbs deep, with the tops at least 8 inches down. This also helps to discourage squirrels from digging up the bulbs as soon as you turn your back. Tulips need dry soil in summer for the bulbs to mature, so avoid overwatering the beds where tulips are planted.

Help your phlox to multiply. Wild blue phlox is one of the easiest native wildflowers to grow and propagate. In rich, moist soil, plants increase quickly to form broad clumps smothered with spring blooms. You can divide them in early summer after they bloom, or in fall. Where the plants are happy, they also self-sow freely, and seedlings are easy to move wherever you want them. Tip cuttings are another option. In early summer, take cuttings from the new vegetative shoots when the flower stalks wither. Be sure you get a vegetative shoot, not one that ends in a flower, because flower stalks won't root.

Try a phlox of another color. Wild blue phlox is available in several colors other than lavender-blue, and you could substitute any of them in this combination. 'Fuller's White' bears pure white blooms, while 'Dirigo Ice' is pale lavender. 'Louisiana' has deep blue flowers with purple centers. Fragrant 'Clouds of Perfume' is pale blue, and 'Blue Dreams' is lilac-blue.

A sea of blue Grecian windflowers (*Anemone blanda*) sets off the brilliant flowers of *Tulipa praestans* 'Fusilier'. When these spring flowers fade, interplant annuals that will hide the bulb foliage as it yellows and dies.

Spring Contrast for a Shady Site

Arching sprays of heart-shaped flowers add airy grace to this midspring garden that features contrasting foliage size and texture. The clumps of large-leaved, bold-textured hostas highlight the ferny, delicate foliage of the bleeding hearts. This duo is easy to care for and will thrive in humus-rich, evenly moist soil in light to partial shade. To add early spring interest, underplant the hostas and bleeding hearts with a carpet of early bulbs such as snowdrops (*Galanthus nivalis*) and glory-of-the-snow (*Chionodoxa lucilae*), which will bloom even before the hosta leaves unfurl.

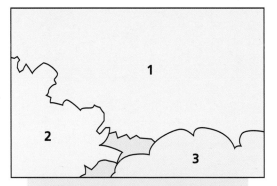

PHOTO KEY
1. Old-fashioned bleeding heart (*Dicentra spectabilis*); Zones 3 to 9
2. 'Krossa Regal' hosta (*Hosta* 'Krossa Regal'); Zones 3 to 8
3. 'Elegans' Siebold's hosta (*Hosta sieboldiana* 'Elegans'); Zones 3 to 8

Secrets for Striking Spring Bloom

❧ Plan for plants to follow bleeding hearts. Bleeding hearts have decorated gardens with their chains of drooping, heart-shaped flowers since this Japanese native was introduced in 1810. The plants bloom for at least a month from spring into early summer. In areas with warm summers, the foliage turns yellow and the plants go dormant shortly after they flower. This leaves an unfortunate gap in the garden, but hostas and ferns are perfect for filling the empty spaces. In cooler zones, bleeding hearts stay attractive for most of the summer if there is ample moisture. Most often in my Zone 4 garden, the plants are looking rough by late summer. I cut them to the ground when the stems start to crimp and fall over. In my garden, the gap they leave is filled with autumn-flowering showy crocuses (*Crocus speciosus*). The crocuses get ample light in spring as the bleeding hearts are emerging, and after the bleeding heart stalks are cleared away in fall, there is plenty of room for the crocus flowers to carpet the ground.

❧ Underplant hostas for an extra-early spring. Since hostas tend to emerge in mid- to late spring, you can plant a wealth of crocuses and other early-blooming bulbs around them to add early spring color to the garden. The bulbs have plenty of time to flower and die back before the hosta foliage has fully emerged.

❧ Double your garden pleasure by layering. The 'Krossa Regal' hosta featured here produces stiff, upright leaves and the plants form a distinctive vase shape. This provides another opportunity for layering, because there's ample room around the clumps for planting smaller perennials. I've added wild gingers (*Asarum* spp.), ferns, violets, and sedges (*Carex* spp.) around the base of my clump, thus growing twice as many plants in the same space.

Wild bleeding heart (*Dicentra eximia*) puts out its first pink flowers in spring and continues to bloom all summer long. Pair it with variegated Solomon's seal (*Polygonatum odoratum* 'Variegatum'), which has dangling white flowers in spring.

A Colorful Woodland Oasis

A simple birdbath surrounded by rich foliage and cool-colored flowers creates an oasis that will attract resident birds like magnets. A mix of shrubs and the arching fronds of ostrich ferns make a sheltering backdrop for wildflowers and ferns that thrive in rich, moist soil. In midspring, the pink buds of Virginia bluebells expand into sky blue flowers that nod over the planting. Woodland primroses add white and rose-pink accents, while the stiff, fuzzy wands of foamflowers poke up through the mass of bluebells. The primroses and bluebells go dormant after they have bloomed, leaving gaps, which are filled by the foamflowers and ferns.

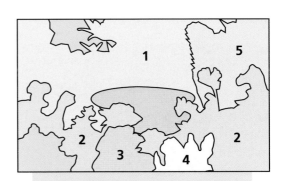

PHOTO KEY
1. Star magnolia (*Magnolia stellata*); Zones 4 to 9
2. Virginia bluebells (*Mertensia virginica*); Zones 3 to 9
3. Japanese woodland primrose (*Primula kisoana*); Zones 3 to 8
4. Wherry's foamflower (*Tiarella cordifolia* var. *collina*); Zones 3 to 8
5. Ostrich fern (*Matteuccia struthiopteris*); Zones 3 to 8

Expert Tips for a Woodland Garden

Grow some bells of blue for spring.
The flower clusters of Virginia bluebells have a
two-toned look because of the pink buds that
open into blue flowers. There's a pure white
form, and if you're lucky, you may find one
growing in your own garden. Bluebells are
prolific seeders, so once you have them in
your garden, you'll always have plants to
share. In addition to the foamflowers and
ferns combined with them here, hostas, wild
blue phlox (*Phlox divaricata*), and pulmonarias
(*Pulmonaria* spp.) will hide the gaps that the
bluebells leave after they go dormant.

Get to know a new primrose. Japanese
woodland primroses are little-known treasures
that begin blooming in midspring and continue for several weeks. The plants form open
clumps from creeping runners, making a
ground-hugging carpet until the plants go dormant in midsummer. They are especially quick
to disappear where the weather is hot and dry.

Keep this giant fern inbounds. While
the ostrich fern featured here easily reaches
3 to 4 feet in height, in rich, moist soil the
fronds can top 5 feet. The fronds form a
graceful, vase-shaped clump that resembles a
giant badminton shuttlecock, a fact that gave
rise to another of this plant's names—shuttlecock fern. It makes an impressive backdrop for
smaller ferns and wildflowers. Left to its own
devices, this fern spreads far and wide by rhizomes (underground stems), eventually
forming huge colonies. In my garden, I keep
it inbounds by removing the new crowns as
soon as they emerge. Cut the rhizome that at-
taches the crowns to the parent plant all the
way back to the parent plant's crown, or the
stub you leave will branch to form two or
more new crowns.

Whorry's foamflower (*Tiarella cordifolia* var. *collina*), with snowy flower
spikes and red-splashed leaves, is a
beautiful choice for spring wildflower
combinations. Try planting it with
trilliums and wild bleeding hearts.

Add water to your combinations. A
simple water feature enhances many perennial
combinations because it adds motion and reflections and will attract birds for you to enjoy
watching. You can use any shallow basin (under
2 inches deep) to make a birdbath. Change the
water every day to keep algae and mosquitoes
at bay. Deeper basins such as cast-iron kettles,
barrels, and decorative containers are good for
miniature water gardens. You can even add a re-
circulating pump to filter and aerate the water.

PHOTO KEY
1. Caucasus geranium
   (*Geranium ibericum*);
   Zones 3 to 8
2. 'Bath's Pink' pinks
   (*Dianthus* 'Bath's Pink');
   Zones 3 to 8

A Combination with Simple Elegance

Let a simple planting of two early-blooming perennials prove that in the garden, sometimes less is more. Caucasus geranium produces clusters of cup-shaped blooms above mounds of fuzzy, rounded leaves with broad, deep lobes. Easy-to-grow 'Bath's Pink' pinks fill the garden with pretty flowers as well as fragrance from late spring into early summer. Its blooms are carried on erect stems above dense mounds of handsome, gray-green, needlelike leaves. Both perennials make excellent additions to the front or middle of beds and borders, where they will weave around the stems of other perennials and carpet the ground. They're especially attractive under peonies and phlox. After a month or more of bloom, the flowers of this long-lasting combination fade, revealing mounds of attractive foliage that make a cool backdrop for perennials like daylilies, balloon flowers (*Platycodon grandiflorus*), and anise hyssop (*Agastache foeniculum*), which bloom in midsummer.

Secrets for Early-Summer Elegance

🌺 **Plant hardy cranesbills for abundant bloom.** Free-blooming, easy-to-grow hardy cranesbills (also called hardy geraniums) are indispensable for the early summer garden. Hardy cranesbills thrive in average to rich soil in full sun or partial shade, although plants bloom more freely in sun. Evenly moist conditions are best, but established plants tolerate drought. Shearing the plants after the first flush of bloom encourages some hardy cranesbills to rebloom and keeps plants looking neat. Some types add fall interest to the garden as well, with foliage that turns lovely shades of wine and red in the fall.

🌺 **Pick a perfect place for pinks.** Plant pinks in full sun or light shade in well-drained soil that has a slightly acid to alkaline pH. If you suspect that your soil is too acidic, check the soil pH, and work lime into the soil as needed before planting to raise the pH. (For advice on soil testing and adding lime, contact your local Cooperative Extension office.) In poorly drained soil or heavy clay, consider planting in raised beds, adding plenty of sand and organic matter such as compost to improve drainage.

🌺 **Rely on tough pinks to take the heat.** Like most pinks, the cultivar 'Bath's pink', featured in this combination, tolerates heat and some humidity, but in the South, plants are subject to rot. A light gravel mulch will help to keep the foliage away from the soil and improve drainage around the crown of the plant, thus reducing problems with fungal diseases.

For an early-summer–blooming color echo, combine bushy, pink-flowered *Centaurea hypoleuca* with bearded iris, pinks, and white-flowered mother-of-thyme.

PHOTO KEY

1. **'General Sikorski' clematis (Clematis 'General Sikorski');** Zones 4 to 9
2. **Delphinium (Delphinium hybrid); Zones 3 to 7**
3. **'Ruby Regis' herb tree mallow (Lavatera trimestris 'Ruby Regis');** annual

A Mixed Planting for Beautiful Bloom

Mixed plantings of perennials, annuals, and vines, like this grouping of delphinium, herb tree mallow, and clematis, have decided advantages for small gardens. While most perennials have limited bloom seasons, an-nuals like the mallow commonly flower all season, giving the garden long-lasting color. Vines add height and color to a combination without taking up much space. Here, the clematis climbs a pillar, creating a column of color that towers over the stately spires of delphiniums. The clematis will flower for a month or more, and some varieties reflower throughout the season.

Secrets for Beautiful Summer Bloom

🔊 **Get the most from clematis.** Clematis prefer rich, well-drained soil and a shady, well-mulched area to spread their roots. For best growth, be sure the soil pH is neutral to slightly acidic. The vines bloom best in sunlight, so train them up a trellis or pillar. Or, make shrubs do double duty as vine supports. Plant the clematis a foot or so from the shrub's crown. Then train its stems up through the shrub's branches, tying them loosely until the plants are large enough to ramble at will.

🔊 **Stake delphiniums for dramatic results.** Delphiniums need staking or they'll topple over or break off in wind and rain. Provide each stem with a tall, thin, sturdy stake. Tie stems to the stakes with soft string or yarn.

🔊 **Use a delphinium substitute in the South.** Delphiniums grow best in areas with low humidity and cool nights. In warm areas, like the humid South, substitute mulleins (*Verbascum* spp.), which have tall flowering spires in shades of yellow and pink.

🔊 **Start mallow from transplants.** The saucer-shaped flowers of herb tree mallow look like miniature hibiscus flowers. The pink flowers of 'Ruby Regis' look perfect in this combination of pinks and purples, but there's also a lovely white cultivar called 'Mont Blanc' that would combine well with white clematis and delphiniums. If you live in a region with cool summers, you may find that these free-blooming annuals will self sow in light soil. For best results in other regions, set out established transplants each spring after danger of frost is past. If you're designing combinations of your own and want to include herb tree mallow, keep in mind that it can grow as tall as 6 feet by season's end!

Larkspur (*Consolida ambigua*) is a self-sowing annual that makes a great substitute for perennial delphiniums, which can be tricky to grow, especially in warm climates. Here, pink larkspur makes a great companion for perennial pinks (*Dianthus*).

A Summer-Long Perennial Parade

Hardy, durable, and long-lived, peonies are the backbone of the early summer garden. Their showy flowers come in shades of pink, red, and white that look lovely combined with a wide range of early summer-blooming perennials. Once the flowers fade, their handsome, dark green foliage provides a backdrop for summer's blooms. In this combination for a moist-soil site in full sun to partial shade, single peonies contrast nicely with rounded, lacy-textured star of Persia. The airy, cream-colored plumes of goat's beard and the spiky, rich blue flowers of blue false indigo add the finishing touch in this early summer view. The foliage of Siberian iris, which is soon to bloom, adds a spikey accent and contrasts nicely with the bold, ribbed leaves of hostas, which bloom later in summer.

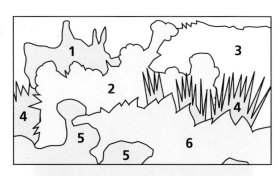

PHOTO KEY

1. **Blue false indigo (***Baptisia australis***); Zones 3 to 9**
2. **'Sea Shell' peony (***Paeonia lactiflora* **'Sea Shell'); Zones 3 to 8**
3. **Goat's beard (***Aruncus dioicus***); Zones 3 to 7**
4. **Siberian iris (***Iris sibirica***); Zones 2 to 9**
5. **Star of Persia (***Allium cristophii***); Zones 4 to 8**
6. **'Honeybells' fragrant hosta (***Hosta plantaginea* **'Honeybells'); Zones 3 to 8**

Expert Advice for a Summer-Long Perennial Parade

❧ Add extra enjoyment with fragrant flowers. Most peonies feature fragrant flowers, which makes them as enjoyable in the garden as they are indoors in bouquets. The 'Honeybells' fragrant hosta in this combination has fragrant flowers too, as does the double-flowered cultivar 'Aphrodite'.

❧ Enjoy less work with single peonies. I prefer single-flowered peonies over doubles because their blooms look more graceful in the garden. There's a practical reason to grow single peonies, too: They don't need staking. While heavy-flowered double peonies topple without support, the lighter single blooms stand tall on their own.

❧ Plan ahead for the rising stars. Star of Persia, an ornamental onion, grows from a hardy bulb that must be planted in fall for bloom the following spring and early summer. Plant the bulbs with their tops at a depth of three times the height of the bulb. Star of Persia is not commonly available at garden centers but is available from mail-order bulb suppliers.

❧ Fill the gap when foliage falls. Keep in mind that after star of Persia flowers, the foliage dies back. When you plant star of Persia bulbs in fall, set the bulbs around the crowns of spreading perennials that will fill the gaps they leave. In this combination, hosta foliage will cover up the space, but plants such as hardy cranesbills (*Geranium* spp.) and catmints (*Nepeta* spp.) also will take care of their inevitable departure. Don't tidy up the star of Persia seedheads that are left standing when the foliage fades, however. They remain attractive in the garden for several months. Or, you can cut them as soon as the seed capsules begin to split, and hang them upside down until they're fully dry to use for dried flower arrangements.

In early summer, this perennial border stars our featured combination, as well as the frothy spikes of *Nepeta* X *faassenii* 'Blue Wonder', white peonies, pink hardy cranesbills, and silvery lamb's-ears.

PHOTO KEY

1. Knautia (*Knautia mace-donica*); Zones 4 to 9
2. Bearded iris (*Iris* bearded hybrid); Zones 3 to 9
3. Big betony (*Stachys grandi-flora*); Zones 2 to 8
4. Edging boxwood (*Buxus sempervirens* 'Suffruticosa'); Zones 6 to 10
5. 'Vera Jameson' sedum (*Sedum* 'Vera Jameson'); Zones 4 to 9
6. Blood-red cranesbill (*Geranium sanguineum*); Zones 3 to 8

Summer Scene in Red and Pink

In rich, well-drained soil and full sun, this gorgeous combination will stay in bloom much of the summer. It features red and pink flowers, which aren't always easy to combine. This grouping works because the deep red knautia blossoms have a hint of purple that complements the rose-pink big betony and the magenta-pink cranesbill. The strappy iris foliage adds a vertical accent and serves as a reminder that this garden began blooming in late spring. The mound of 'Vera Jameson' sedum leaves have a hint of pink to them, echoing the pink-flowered perennials. The sedum will come into its own in late summer to early fall, when dusty rose-pink flowers cover the foliage. Edging boxwood is an evergreen shrub, added here to provide structure and color in winter when the perennials go dormant.

Plants for Beautiful Summer Scenes

❧ Long bloom in maroon. Knautia is a nonstop bloomer that produces clumps of attractive, deeply lobed foliage topped with loads of maroon flowerheads from early summer until frost. Plants stand 2 feet tall, and mature clumps measure several feet across. If red's not your color, try blue buttons (*Knautia arvensis*), which bears pink pincushionlike flowers blushed with a hint of pale blue. It grows to 3 or more feet tall, producing fewer flowers at a time on more open plants. Like its cousin, it blooms nearly all summer. Both are hardy in Zones 4 to 9.

❧ The best blooming cranesbill. Blood-red cranesbill is one of the longest blooming cranesbills. It produces mounded clumps of deeply cut leaves that are covered with flowers for a month in early summer. After the main flush of bloom, additional flowers appear sporadically through the season. Cultivars with paler flowers are available, including 'Album', a white-flowered form, and 'John Elsley', with rose-pink blooms.

❧ Foliage and flower feast. Big betony is worth growing for both its beautiful flowers and its foliage. The plants form low, spreading clumps of broadly oval, scalloped leaves that are lovely as a groundcover when plants are out of bloom. The spikes of tubular flowers appear for a month or so in summer. The variety *robusta* is a particularly hearty form with deep rose-pink flowers.

❧ Bearded iris at its best. Planting bearded iris with drought-tolerant companions gives you the best this perennial has to offer of both flowers and foliage. When planted with perennials that need supplemental watering, iris foliage fades fast. But in dry sites, the spiky gray-green foliage stays healthy and attractive, adding interest to a combination long after the flowers are finished.

❧ Extra color from annuals. If you're looking for a fast way to add even more color to a perennial border, try adding long-blooming annuals such as dwarf forms of flowering tobacco (*Nicotiana alata*) and cosmos, along with weather-tolerant garden petunias.

Soft pink Lancaster cranesbill (*Geranium sanguineum* var. *striatum*) is an ideal edging plant because of its creeping habit and long bloom. Combine it with other pastel perennials to add color in early summer and beyond.

PHOTO KEY

1. Heartleaf crambe (*Crambe cordifolia*); Zones 6 to 9
2. Sweet scabious (*Scabiosa atropurpurea*); annual
3. 'Bowl of Beauty' peony (*Paeonia* 'Bowl of Beauty'); Zones 3 to 8
4. 'Ann Folkard' cranesbill (*Geranium* 'Ann Folkard'); Zones 5 to 9
5. Purple toadflax (*Linaria purpurea* 'Canon J. Went'); Zones 5 to 9
6. Bearded iris (*Iris* bearded hybrid); Zones 3 to 9

Powerful Perennials for Big Effects

If you have enough garden space to spare, take advantage of shrub-size perennials like heartleaf crambe, which looks like a baby's-breath on steroids when in bloom. Despite its size, crambe provides a delicate, airy backdrop for the focal point of this combination, exquisite 'Bowl of Beauty' peony. I like the balance between fine and bold textures and rounded and spiky forms. The toadflax stems that weave through the clumps of iris add a soft base for their spiky leaves. Colors are nicely balanced, too, with the creamy white crambe flowers picking up the white at the center of the peonies.

This combination likes full sun and rich, well-drained soil. The crambe and peony will spend most of their energy making roots for the first few years in the garden. After that, they'll bloom for years. Both resent being disturbed once they're established. Iris, on the other hand, needs to be divided in summer or early fall every two to five years.

Expert Advice for Big Effects

❧ Enjoy lovely flowers, hide homely leaves. Heartleaf crambe produces its flowers high above a rosette of large, succulent kale-like leaves. The leaves are attractive as they emerge, but are best hidden by a plant with long-lasting foliage because insects, slugs, and weather will damage the crambe leaves fairly quickly. (In this garden, the peony serves to screen the crambe foliage.)

❧ Give 'em room to spread. Don't crowd large perennials at planting time, so they can attain their full size without smothering their neighbors. Heartleaf crambe measures 4 feet across at maturity, so space plants 2 feet apart on all sides at planting. Peony clumps spread to 3 feet across, so give them 1½ feet on all sides.

❧ Choose full-flowered peonies. Peonies come in single-, semidouble-, and double-flowered forms. 'Bowl of Beauty', featured here, is an anemone or Japanese-type peony that has semi-double flowers with a tuft of showy, petal-like stamens at the center, making the flowers look very full.

Create the illusion of an early-summer snowfall by planting snow-in-summer (*Cerastium tomentosum*). Its frothy white flowers pair beautifully with blue catmint, and pink peonies form a shrub-like background.

109

Swimming in Early-Summer Color

In early summer, a sprinkling of color graces this garden, which will come into full bloom a bit later in the season. Nevertheless, a school of bronze fish seem to be enjoying the sea of yellow Jerusalem sage, yarrow, and lily leek flowers. 'East Friesland' salvia adds a splash of contrasting purple and also gives the combination a vertical accent. The tiered clusters of Jerusalem sage flowers echo the vertical line of the sage. The crimson flag and sedum will provide late-summer and fall color.

As you can see in the photo on the facing page, this combination is part of a sweeping perennial border. The yellow theme of the combination continues in the lady's-mantle flowers, while the frog sculpture perched in the birdbath extends the pondlife theme of the garden art.

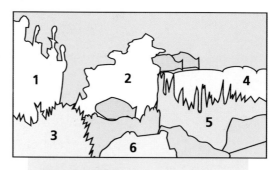

PHOTO KEY
1. Jerusalem sage (*Phlomis russeliana*); Zones 4 to 9
2. Yarrow (*Achillea taygetea*); Zones 3 to 8
3. Crimson flag (*Schizostylis coccinea*); Zones 7 to 9
4. 'Autumn Joy' sedum (*Sedum 'Autumn Joy'*); Zones 3 to 10
5. 'East Friesland' salvia (*Salvia × sylvestris* 'East Friesland'); Zones 4 to 7
6. Lily leek (*Allium moly*); Zones 3 to 9

Secrets for Long-Lasting Color

🌸 **Try tiers of color.** Jerusalem sage bears curious tiered clusters of hooded, pale yellow flowers on 3-foot stems that always attract attention. The erect stalks are carried high above felted, heart-shaped leaves that form a ground-hugging carpet. Give plants a position with light, well-drained soil in full sun. Where space is available, they spread into broad clumps.

🌸 **Use ornamental onions for beds and borders.** While most ornamental onions bear flowers in shades of pink, rose, lilac, violet-purple, or white, the lily leek in this garden features lemon yellow blooms. Its dense, showy heads of star-shaped flowers are borne above gray-green foliage that turns rich yellow as plants go dormant after flowering. Lily leeks increase rapidly in rich, well-drained soil in full sun or light shade. Combine them with bushy perennials or spreading herbs to hide the gaps they leave.

🌸 **Add a hardy, long-blooming sage.** *Salvia* × *sylvestris* is a striking perennial that's hardy as far north as Zone 3 with protective winter mulch of snow, evergreen boughs, or straw (wait until the ground freezes in late fall to lay the mulch). Plants produce abundant flower spikes covered with small, purple-blue blooms in early summer. Cut them back after the first flowers appear, and plants will rebloom later in summer. *Salvia* × *sylvestris* cultivars like 'East Friesland', 'Blue Hill', 'Rose Queen', and 'Snow Hill' may also be listed as *S. nemorosa* or *S.* × *superba* in catalogs and plant lists. Whatever their names, they're great choices for long-lasting color.

Pink- and blue-flowered cranesbills, spiky Siberian iris, and chartreuse-flowered lady's-mantle are neighbors in an early summer border that features the combination shown on the facing page.

A Glowing Late-Summer Duo

Glowing clusters of goldenrod dominate this informal planting, but splashes of lilac-blue, courtesy of the bellflowers, add dazzling contrast. Flower forms—from frothy to saucer-shaped—also add contrast. There's a bit of a trick involved in this dynamic combination. While goldenrods bloom late in the summer, bellflowers are early-summer bloomers. The bellflowers here have been coaxed into reblooming by careful deadheading of the early blooms. For more intense blue, you could also add balloon flowers (*Platycodon grandiflorus*) to this combination.

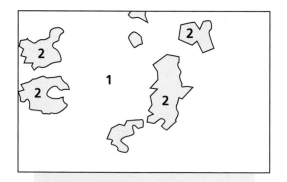

PHOTO KEY
1. **Goldenrod (*Solidago*); Zones 3 to 8**
2. **Peach-leaved bellflower (*Campanula persicifolia*); Zones 3 to 7**

112

Tips for a Glowing Garden

Get to know the goldenrods. Many goldenrods make great garden plants, but it pays to know whether you're planting running or clumping types. The runners—including European goldenrod (*Solidago virgaurea*) and Canada goldenrod (*S. canadensis*)—quickly spread by creeping underground runners to form large clumps. They're best suited to large gardens and meadow plantings where their roving habit is an asset. Clump-forming goldenrods are the best choice for small gardens. These spread very slowly to form fountainlike mounds that add color to the garden without taking it over. Some of the best clumpers include showy goldenrod (*S. speciosa*), stiff goldenrod (*S. rigida*), early goldenrod (*S. juncea*), and dwarf goldenrod (*S. sphacelata*).

Goldenrods are more than a just a pretty face. The fluffy flowers of goldenrods along highways and in meadows across the country are a sure sign that the season is drawing to a close. But goldenrods do more than just decorate gardens or mark the passing of the seasons. They're terrific for attracting beneficial insects because they're rich in pollen and nectar. Several species also yield yellow or greenish dyes, including gray goldenrod (*Solidago nemoralis*), which also makes a lovely garden plant. Goldenrods also have been used in various herbal remedies for centuries.

Don't kill these bellflowers with kindness. For years I failed with peach-leaved bellflowers because I pampered them too much. I gave them rich soil and ample moisture, but they rewarded my efforts by dying. Finally, I learned not to pamper them and to just satisfy their simple needs. Plant them in average, well-

For a late-summer combination with a rich variety of textures, pair the feathery flower spikes of white mugwort (*Artemisia lactiflora*) with bold black-eyed Susans. Be sure to keep the soil evenly moist, or the mugwort will tend to wilt.

drained soil and don't overwater. They will reward you with a month or more of exquisite lilac-blue flowers. There are also cultivars with white and violet-blue flowers.

Fabulous Flowers for Late-Summer Fireworks

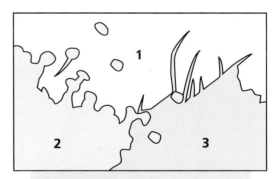

PHOTO KEY
1. 'Fireworks' rough-stemmed goldenrod (*Solidago rugosa* 'Fireworks'); Zones 3 to 8
2. 'Pamina' Japanese anemone (*Anemone × hybrida* 'Pamina'); Zone 4 (with winter protection) or Zones 5 to 8
3. Russian sage (*Perovskia atriplicifolia*); Zones 4 to 9

Arching streamers of yellow goldenrod and hot pink anemone bombs create a planting that rivals any summer fireworks display. This long-blooming combination starts in high summer, when the graceful spikes of Russian sage first appear. In late summer, the goldenrod and anemones join the show. All three plants continue flowering into early fall. In this combination, plant placement plays an important role. Putting the goldenrod at the back keeps its explosive fountains of flowers from overpowering the airy Russian sage and creates a contrasting backdrop for the dense, round anemone blooms.

Techniques for Fabulous Flowers

❧ Try a goldenrod with three seasons of glory. 'Fireworks' goldenrod offers more than just showy late-season flowers. The emerging buds add a lovely, pale green texture to the garden through most of the summer, and the flowers begin opening in August and continue for a month or more. The show continues after the flowers fade, because the sprays of shiny, silvery seedheads catch the low, arching rays of the late-autumn sun. The plants add texture and color to the winter landscape, and a topping of snow turns the arching rows of starry brown flowerstalks into delicate lace.

❧ Seek sage advice for winter interest. The silvery gray stems and dried flower clusters of Russian sage are lovely in the fall and winter landscape. They also look beautiful in dried flower arrangements. Cut the stems after a hard frost, when the leaves begin to curl, and hang them to dry thoroughly before using them. Or, cut them when the flowers are opening and enjoy the added bonus of the blue color.

❧ Plan for a progression of anemones. The common name Japanese anemone is used for more than one species, a fact that's helpful to know since they bloom at slightly different times. First to bloom in August is *Anemone tomentosa*, followed shortly in late summer to early fall by *A. hupehensis* (also called Chinese anemone) and *A. hupehensis* var. *japonica*. Hybrid Japanese anemones (*A. × hybrida*) tend to bloom toward the end of the anemone season. To enjoy anemones from August through October, plant a selection of species and hybrids. Give them full sun or partial shade and rich, moist, well drained soil.

❧ Breathe easily around goldenrods. Goldenrods, which are pollinated by insects, don't deserve their reputation for causing hay fever, because their heavy pollen isn't released into the air. Their bad rap stems from the fact that they bloom at the same time as ragweed, a notorious nemesis of hay fever sufferers.

Bright yellow 'Fireworks' goldenrod sets fire to this late-summer combination. The hot-colored theme continues in the fiery blooms of *Salvia greggii*, the red-brown switchgrass flowers, and rich purple canna foliage. Blue yucca leaves add contrast in both form and color.

A Modern Grassy Planting

Bold masses of ornamental grasses and perennial flowers with long-lasting color and interesting texture carry this meadow-inspired garden through the entire season. A broad drift of fine-textured feather reed grass, which blooms in midsummer but is shown in seed, stands out against a backdrop of huge, bold-textured Joe-Pye weed. A mass of Russian sage echoes the texture and spiky form of the grass and adds a touch of lilac-blue flowers for two months in summer. The dried stems of the sage and grasses will decorate the fall and winter landscape until growth resumes in spring. This combination features versatile plants that require little more than a spot in full sun and average to rich, well-drained soil to thrive. In spring, cut all the plants to the ground to make way for fresh new growth.

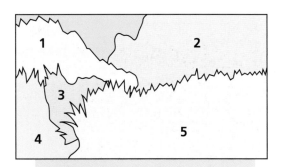

PHOTO KEY

1. Tall moor grass (*Molinia caerulea* subsp. *arundinacea*); Zones 5 to 9
2. 'Atropurpureum' Joe-Pye weed (*Eupatorium maculatum* 'Atropurpureum'); Zones 2 to 8
3. Russian sage (*Perovskia atriplicifolia*); Zones 4 to 9
4. Frost grass (*Spodiopogon sibericus*); Zones 3 to 8
5. Feather reed grass (*Calamagrostis* × *acutiflora* 'Stricta'); Zones 4 to 9

Secrets for a Bold Grass Garden

🍂 **Save this dramatic plant for big gardens.** Joe-Pye weed is a fantastic plant for gardens large enough to accommodate its huge size. Mature clumps can reach 6 or more feet in height, with an equal spread. A site with moist, rich soil and full sun yields the largest plants. The vanilla-scented flowers open in late July and persist for a month or more. They're a magnet for butterflies and bees, and the giant flowerheads are always abuzz with activity. Dozens of monarchs, along with tiger swallowtail and fritillary butterflies, may dance around a single plant. The fuzzy seedheads are attractive through fall and winter, long after the flowers fade.

🍂 **Plant a handsome four-season grass.** Feather reed grass is a cool-season grass, which means it starts growing in early spring when the soil is still cool. It blooms in June (earlier than most grasses), and by mid-summer, decorative seedheads form. Unlike some cool-season grasses, which don't hold up well and add little to the late-summer garden, feather reed grass remains attractive even after the seeds drop. The bare, straw-colored stalks persist through winter, making it a valuable addition to the garden all year round.

🍂 **Choose some warm-season grasses.** Two of the grasses in this planting—tall moor grass and frost grass—are warm-season plants. They start growing late in the season, after the soil has warmed, and bloom in late summer and fall. Their dried seedheads grace the garden all winter long. Fountain grass (*Pennisetum alopecuroides*) is another beautiful and versatile warm-season grass. Its bright green leaves form an arching fountain of foliage and turn sandy-colored in the fall and winter. Fountain grass also has stiff flowers that emerge in midsummer, and birds will flock to eat the seeds in fall.

Prairie dropseed (*Sporobolus heterolepis*) adds a beautiful, light texture to the front of a border in late summer, and its pumpkin orange stalks and airy seedheads create a lovely display in fall even after the surrounding perennials start to fade.

A Towering Late-Summer Border

Brilliant color, bold contrast, and large drifts of big and tall perennials may be just the ticket for brightening up a drab spot. In this garden, a long drift of 5-foot-tall, double-flowered ragged coneflowers tower over an equally bold clump of garden phlox. Trees behind the planting put it in partial shade and add a deep green backdrop. A combination like this one, with contrasting colors and bold flowers, is ideal if you're planting a garden that you commonly enjoy from a distance— looking out a window and across the lawn, for example.

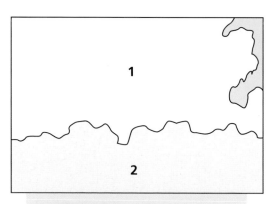

PHOTO KEY
1. 'Golden Glow' ragged coneflower (*Rudbeckia laciniata* 'Golden Glow'); Zones 3 to 9
2. Garden phlox (*Phlox paniculata*); Zones 3 to 8

118

Secrets for Late-Summer Borders

❧ **Choose seeds for extra show.** Ragged coneflower comes in both single and double forms—the one in this combination has double flowers. I prefer the single-flowered form, and it's a good choice for a more natural-looking meadow-style garden. Attractive buttonlike seedheads appear after the flowers fade, and in fall the seeds are magnets for goldfinches—I've counted 30 in a single flock feeding on the seeds. One problem with the single-flowered form is seedlings. Any seeds that the birds miss will probably sprout, and you'll need to weed out the volunteers. If you'd rather avoid this chore, you'll probably prefer the double form, because the buttonlike centers of the flowers are filled with showy petals that don't produce seeds.

❧ **Plan on adding early-summer interest.** To keep a planting like this one looking its best all season, add early-blooming perennials, such as bold clumps of peonies accented by a drift of rich blue Siberian iris (*Iris sibirica*). Clumps of yellow daylilies and purple coneflowers would carry the garden until the phlox begins to bloom. An edging of lady's-mantle (*Alchemilla mollis*) and blood-red cranesbill (*Geranium sanguineum*) will round out the planting.

❧ **Extend flowers into fall.** There are several wonderful perennials that would add more color to this combination in late summer and continue blooming into the fall. Pink turtlehead (*Chelone lyonii*) has pretty spikes of tubular pink flowers, while 'Firetail' mountain fleece (*Persicaria amplexicaulis* 'Firetail') produces red flower spikes on bushy plants that reach 3 feet tall. Bottle gentian (*Gentiana andrewsii*) has sprawling stems with bright blue, bottlelike flowers in clusters. All of these plants grow well in rich, moist soil in light to partial shade.

'Goldsturm' black-eyed Susans and the frothy heads of Rhone asters (*Aster sedifolious*) create a striking gold and lavender combination in late summer that's perfect for a small garden.

A Perennial Pair for Every Garden

Asters and black-eyed Susans are a tried-and-true duo that's as familiar as the sunny meadows where these plants grow wild. Blue and yellow flowers combine to make a complementary color pair that leaps from the garden. Placing the blue flowers in front of a backdrop of yellow makes the colors seem more intense. Black-eyed Susans brighten up the summer garden like no other flower can, and they're virtually care-free. This late-summer pair would work equally well in a border or an informal garden and will thrive as long as it has full sun and well-drained soil.

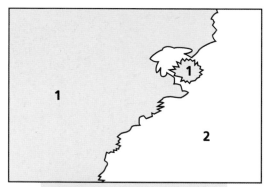

PHOTO KEY
1. 'Monch' Frickart's aster (*Aster* × *frikartii* 'Monch'); Zones 5 to 8
2. Orange coneflower (*Rudbeckia fulgida* var. *sullivantii*); Zones 3 to 9

More Practically Perfect Perennials

Beautiful black-eyed Susans. Black-eyed Susans (*Rudbeckia* spp.), or coneflowers, thrive in full sun or light shade in almost any soil. The common species *R. hirta* is an annual or short-lived perennial. On the taller side, thin-leaved coneflower (*R. triloba*) has dense, branched crowns of small orange-yellow flowers. Sweet coneflower (*R. subtomentosa*) has lemon yellow flowers on 2- to 3-foot stems, while great coneflower (*R. maxima*) towers above the competition with 5- to 8-foot stems sporting showy, blue-gray leaves crowned with huge 4-inch flowers. When the rich yellow petals fall, the huge conelike centers accent the late-summer garden.

Low-growing asters for the front of the border. The shortest of the asters are alpine asters (*Aster alpinus*), which have rich blue-purple flowers with a yellow center. 'Dark Beauty' is similar, but the flowers are richer purple. 'Goliath' has large blue flowers, while compact 'Happy End' is rose-pink. For dry sandy soils, try seaside aster (*A. spectabilis*) with rich blue flowers and stiff, 1- to 2-foot stems.

Asters for the middle of the border. If blue is your color, you're sure to love smooth aster (*Aster laevis*) with its purple-stained, blue-green leaves and airy, branched spikes of sky blue flowers. 'Bluebird' has strong, upright stems and dense flower spikes. Sky-blue aster (*A. oolentangiensis*) is similar, but the flowers are smaller and the sprays branch closer to the ground. In semishade, try heart-leaf aster (*A. cordifolius*), with sky blue flowers on 2- to 3-foot stems. Flat-topped aster (*A. umbellatus*) has flattened heads of starry white flowers in late summer.

A simple color echo for late summer pairs dusty blue Russian sage (*Perovskia atriplicifolia*) with free-flowering Frikart's aster (*Aster × frikartii*). Place this combination in a spot with full sun or light shade in well-drained soil.

PHOTO KEY
1. **'Herbstsonne' shining coneflower** (*Rudbeckia nitida* **'Herbstsonne'**); Zones 4 to 9
2. **Brazilian vervain** (*Verbena bonariensis*); Zones 7 to 9
3. **Giant hyssop** (*Agastache barberi* **'Tutti Frutti'**); Zones 6 to 10
4. **Hybrid rose mallow** (*Hibiscus moscheutos* hybrid); Zones 5 to 10
5. **Balloon flower** (*Platycodon grandiflorus*); Zones 3 to 8
6. **Blue oat grass** (*Helictotrichon sempervirens*); Zones 4 to 9

A Riot of Colors for Late Summer

Large clumps of oversize perennials create a memorable picture in this border filled with shocking color contrasts. A massive clump of 'Herbstsonne' shining coneflower, which can range from 5 to 7 feet tall and can easily spread to 3 or 4 feet, towers over the garden and forms a backdrop of bright yellow daisies. The vibrant yellow coneflowers, pink saucers of rose mallow, and raspberry spikes of giant hyssop create the most jolting combination.

You either love it or you don't. Fine-textured clumps of blue-green oat grass form a cool-colored edging at the front of the garden. This ornamental grass echoes some of the cooler shades of purple in this otherwise hot-colored mix.

Overall, this garden features masses of fine textures, but the huge rose mallow blooms add a vital note of contrast. The large blocks of color unify the design and keep it from looking jumbled. This mix of long-blooming hardy and tender perennials fills this garden with color from late summer through frost.

Secrets for Nonstop Color

Take a fresh look at annuals. Giant hyssop and Brazilian vervain are tender perennials, but they're commonly grown as annuals. They're easy to raise from seeds sown in early spring. These and many other new annuals have exciting potential for combining with perennials. Unlike the stiff ball-like flowers of marigolds, giant hyssop and Brazilian vervain have a more open form and graceful flower clusters that complement the form and flowers of perennials.

Try bold, easy-to-grow rose mallows. Rose mallows lend a tropical air to any garden. Established plants can rival even the biggest perennials for sheer size and the amount of color they add to the garden. They can range from 4 to 8 feet tall and easily spread into broad clumps. The huge flowers are showstoppers and come in white, pale to rose-pink, and brilliant red. Although each flower lasts only a day, mature plants produce dozens all through the dog days of summer. Hardiness varies from cultivar to cultivar, and some thrive even in Zone 4. In general, red-flowered cultivars are less hardy than white and pink selections. Grow rose mallow in full sun or light shade in rich, evenly moist soil.

Grow a grass with cool-colored leaves. Most ornamental grasses have plain green leaves and are grown primarily for their showy plumed flowers and seedheads. Blue oat grass is an exception. Its steely blue leaves form spiky, rounded evergreen clumps that are topped in early summer by tall wispy flower plumes. The seedheads break apart by midsummer and are best removed, allowing the foliage to take center stage. For a blue-leaved accent in a smaller garden, consider planting blue fescue (*Festuca cinerea*). 'Elijah Blue' has steely gray-blue leaves.

For rosy purple color from midsummer to frost, match up purple coneflowers with Brazilian vervain (*Verbena bonariensis*). Although the verbena isn't hardy north of Zone 7, it will reseed as far north as Zone 4.

PHOTO KEY
1. **Gooseneck loosestrife (*Lysimachia clethroides*); Zones 3 to 8**
2. **Variegated obedient plant (*Physostegia virginiana* 'Variegata'); Zones 3 to 9**
3. **Hardy mum (*Chrysan-themum × morifolium*); Zones 4 to 9**

A Combination with Frosty Foliage

Long before the chilly nights of early winter spread frost over the garden, the foliage of variegated obedient plant appears heavily lined with frost. Its creamy edged leaves make a bright contrast with its clear rosy pink flowers. From a distance, they add a bright spot of color to the deep green loosestrife foliage in the background. Adding plants like variegated obedient plant that have colored foliage to your perennial beds will add lots of interest in the fall, when only a few of your plants may be left in bloom. In this combination, the spiky obedient plant stems contrast nicely with the more rounded form of the mums, which are just coming into bloom. As fall progresses, the plant will be smothered in flowers, creating a mound of color. Planting fall-blooming crocuses will also help extend the display.

Expert Tips for Mums and More

❧ Try mums of all shapes and sizes. Chrysanthemums are one of the most popular fall-flowering perennials. Flower size ranges from gargantuan mop headed pompons to miniature button mums. Exotic spider shaped and curious spoon shaped petals are common. Flower color ranges from white through all shades of pink, red, and yellow, so chances are there's a mum that will work well in nearly any fall combination you can imagine. Hardy mums like the ones in this combination are easy to grow.

❧ Choose "Minn" mums for the far North. Gardeners in very cold climates need to be selective about the cultivar of mum they buy. Researchers at the University of Minnesota have developed mums with iron-clad hardiness. These special cultivars have names starting with "Minn," like 'Minnglow'. Early-blooming selections are sure to bloom before hard frost.

❧ Keep not-so-obedient plant under control. If you've ever grown the rambunctious obedient plant, which romps through the garden like a playful child, you may wonder how it ever got its name. The reasoning behind the name has to do with its flowers, which are attached to the stem on flexible stalks that can be bent into any position. Once moved, the flowers obligingly stay in the new position—hence its name. To keep your obedient plant from overtaking your bed, try planting it in a large plastic pot with the bottom removed. The container will confine the roots, but you'll have to divide the plants every year or two to keep them vigorous.

To give perennial favorites like 'Alma Potshcke' New England aster and 'Autumn Joy' sedum a new look, contrast them with the fine texture of ornamental grasses like *Miscanthus sinensis* 'Morning Light' and *Lespedeza thunbergii* 'Gibraltar'.

A Fall Flower Fiesta

Masses of flowers in fiesta-bright hues create a vibrant fall combination. Bright pink and lavender-purple hues create a color echo, while garden mums in burnt orange add striking contrast to the mix (you can substitute any burnt orange mum if you can't find 'Moira' at your local garden center or nursery). Color contrast is especially important here, because all the textures and flower forms are so similar. Without color contrast, the combination would have much less impact. As an added benefit, all the plants in this combination bloom over a long season, thus ensuring that the garden stays at full glory for nearly a month.

Keep in mind that if you plant this combination, you'll have little early-season interest except for the stonecrop flowers, which will form in summer, but be light green. You may want to interplant some flowering annuals to add summer interest.

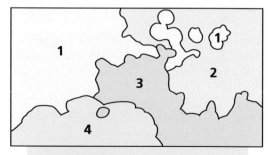

PHOTO KEY
1. **'Prince Henry' Japanese anemone (*Anemone × hybrida* 'Prince Henry', also known as *A. × hybrida* 'Prinz Heinrich'); Zone 4 (with winter protection) or Zones 5 to 8**
2. **'King George' Italian aster (*Aster amellus* 'King George'); Zones 5 to 8**
3. **'Moira' garden mum (*Chrysanthemum* 'Moira'); Zones 4 to 9**
4. **Showy stonecrop (*Sedum spectabile* 'September Glow'); Zones 4 to 9**

Secrets for Showy Fall Flowers

❧ Add an Italian aster for American gardens. Our native New England and New York asters are well-known plants for fall, but for something different, try Italian aster. It bears starry, 1-inch flowers in shades of lilac-blue, purple, and violet with bright yellow centers. Unlike native asters, which thrive in rich, evenly moist soil, the Italian aster featured here requires excellent drainage to succeed and will rot in moist or wet conditions. Give it full sun and soil that is average to rich but very well drained.

❧ Use vigorous anemones for fall. Fall-blooming anemones are the result of crosses between several species, and they bloom at slightly different times. 'Prinz Heinrich', featured here, is an especially vigorous cultivar that starts in September and blooms for nearly a month. 'Honorine Jobert' bears white flowers and 'September Charm' bears pale pink ones.

❧ Pinch your mums for compact growth. Garden mums start growing early in spring, but they do not bloom until late summer and fall. As a result, the stems can get quite tall during the growing season, and when the flowers open, their weight causes the stems to flop. To avoid this problem and to encourage plants to form dense, well-branched mounds, pinch the stems at least once early in the growing season. When stems are 6 to 8 inches tall, pinch them back to about 4 inches. When sideshoots have about eight leaves, pinch them back again, leaving from two to four leaves. Don't pinch mums after July 1, or you may remove the flower buds that have formed.

❧ Expand your sedum horizons. 'Autumn Joy' sedum, which bears deep pink blooms that turn bronzy maroon in fall, is one of the most popular sedums. Pink-flowered 'September Glow', featured here, is more delicate looking and can be easier to work into some combinations. 'Vera Jameson' is another spectacular pink-flowered fall-blooming sedum, which also features purple-pink leaves.

For a fresh view of garden mums, try combining them with ornamental grasses. Here, crimson-flowered 'Raquel' garden mum brings out the red highlights in the fall foliage of prairie dropseed (*Sporobolus heterolepis*).

A Colorful Autumn Meadow Garden

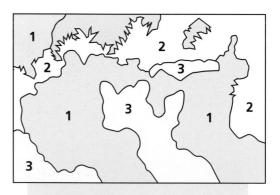

Richly hued asters and goldenrods mingle with the white blooms of snakeroots in this autumn combination of wild meadow perennials. The color contrasts add power to this combination of fine textured plants. The spiky goldenrod plumes add height to the planting and stand out against the rounded shapes of the asters and snakeroot. An added attraction of this combination is the butterflies that will dance between the colorful blooms to sip nectar.

This combination needs full sun, well-drained soil, and plenty of room to spread. If you'd like summer flowers as well, try adding purple coneflowers and Joe-Pye weed.

PHOTO KEY
1. **New England aster (*Aster novae-angliae*); Zones 3 to 8**
2. **Tall goldenrod (*Solidago altissima*); Zones 3 to 9**
3. **White snakeroot (*Eupatorium rugosum*); Zones 3 to 7**

Secrets for Meadow Plants and Gardens

🐝 **Grow a golden smorgasbord for beneficials.** Goldenrods are more than a colorful face in the garden. They earn their keep by feeding wildlife. Their nectar and pollen feeds a huge array of butterflies, bees, beetles, and other insects, including many beneficial ones. And many of the insects that visit goldenrods are a food source for birds and other animals. For this reason, planting goldenrods not only beautifies your garden but also helps the environment.

🐝 **Move meadow plants to borders.** In a meadow garden, the unruly forms of plants are celebrated rather than censured, but if you're growing New England asters in a border, you don't want them flopping all over other plants. To keep them looking their best, in June, when the new shoots are 1 to 1½ feet tall, cut them back by half and prune out any weak or floppy stems. The plants will branch from side buds and form more compact, flop-resistant clumps. You may still need to stake taller asters to keep them standing erect.

🐝 **Try tough, versatile white snakeroot.** Sun or shade, moist soil or dry, white snakeroot takes them all with aplomb. This late-season wildflower is one of the last plants to bloom before frost. It is especially useful in dry shade, where the white flowers brighten the darkest recesses. An attractive purple-brown leaved cultivar called 'Chocolate' is winning admirers for its unusual foliage and dramatic contrast with the flowers.

🐝 **Manage mildew.** Powdery mildew can be a problem on the leaves of New England asters and tall goldenrod. The best way to keep the leaves disease-free is to keep the plants from wilting. If you grow them in rich, continually moist soil, mildew generally will not be a major problem. The plants will perform better as well, because they are native to wet meadows and prairies.

Compact *Solidago sphacelata* 'Golden Fleece' is crowned with fountainlike sprays of lemon yellow flowers in late summer and fall. It's a beautiful companion for rounded asters like 'Purple Dome' New England aster.

Rich Textures for Late Fall

Silvery foliage of wormwood and lamb's-ears provides bright spots of color that set off the ripening fall foliage around them in this garden. As the season draws to a close, the structure that plants add to a garden—branches, overwintering foliage, seedheads—becomes especially important. The seed capsules of Siberian iris in this combination turn chocolate brown and stand out against the yellow leaves. They'll add a touch of elegance through the winter months. Perennial seedheads and foliage can also provide food and shelter during the winter months for birds and beneficial insects.

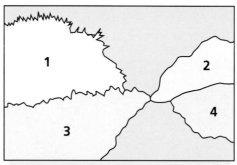

PHOTO KEY
1. **Siberian iris (*Iris sibirica*); Zones 2 to 9**
2. **Wormwood (*Artemisia arborescens*); Zones 4 to 8**
3. **Lamb's-ears (*Stachys byzantina*, also offered as *S. lanata*); Zones 4 to 8**
4. **'Blue Hill' salvia (*Salvia × sylvestris* 'Blue Hill'); Zones 5 to 9**

Expert Tips for Fall to Winter Interest

Enjoy the glories of the fall garden.
If your inclination is to begin cleaning up the garden as soon as the last flowers fade, don't be such a neatnik. Wait at least a week or two after hard frost, and take time to enjoy the splendor of the season before beginning your fall cleanup. Remove iris foliage after it has fully ripened and been flattened by frost, but leave its seed pods standing for winter interest. In fact, as a general rule, I cut down all plants that have weak leaves or stems that flop once they are frosted—lilies, peonies, and hostas are a few examples. I leave any plants with stiff stems standing until spring, along with those that feature decorative seedheads. They'll add winter interest to the landscape and also provide food for winter songbirds. Most ornamental grasses, including Japanese silver grass, are prime contributors to the winter landscape because of their massive clumps of tawny leaves. Other plants that deserve to remain standing through the winter include coneflowers, baptisias, sedums, and Joe-Pye weed.

Give wormwood special care. Wormwood is a shrub rather than a herbaceous perennial, and its woody stems will persist through the winter. In cold climates, protect the stems with a tent of straw over winter. From Zone 6 south the plants don't require protection. In spring, remove the straw and prune the stems hard to remove winter-damaged wood and encourage new growth.

Spruce up lamb's-ears for spring.
Lamb's-ears have persistent leaves that stay attractive even after hard frost. By spring, however, they're bedraggled and browned. Neaten up the plants for spring before growth starts by cutting the creeping stems back to where they're firmly rooted in the soil and removing the old foliage. The clumps will quickly resprout and make a pleasing backdrop for early-flowering bulbs.

For a late-season splash at the front of the border, try white autumn crocuses (*Colchicum speciosum* 'Album'). Here the crocuses echo the silvery leaves of licorice plant (*Helichrysum petiolare* 'Variegatum'), a tender perennial, and feathery artemisia foliage.

Color Echoes for a Shaded Fall Border

Bright yellow foliage in this woodland border echoes the colors of the changing leaves in the trees overhead. This combination makes excellent use of foliage texture and color to keep things interesting late in the season. Glowing clumps of yellow-foliaged variegated hakone grass repeat along the border's curving edge, tying the design together. A clump of Solomon's seal, a native woodland wildflower, echoes the yellow color of the fine-textured grass and provides a plumelike accent. Clumps of glossy black-green wood spurge accentuate the yellow hues of the surrounding foliage. A glossy, bold clump of heuchera catches the light and shimmers among the chartreuse fountains of hakone grass.

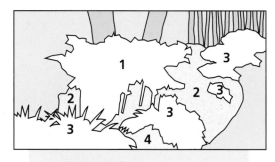

PHOTO KEY
1. Solomon's seal (*Polygonatum biflorum*); Zones 3 to 7
2. Wood spurge (*Euphorbia amygdaloides* var. *robbiae*); Zone 6 (with winter protection) or Zones 7 to 8
3. Golden variegated hakone grass (*Hakonechloa macra* 'Aureola'); Zones 5 to 9
4. 'Dale's Strain' heuchera (*Heuchera americana* 'Dale's Strain'); Zones 4 to 9

132

Plants for a Shaded Fall Border

❧ **A giant Solomon's seal.** Gardeners familiar with diminutive 1- to 2-foot Solomon's seal (*Polygonatum biflorum*) found in deciduous woodlands are shocked to see the towering stems this plant produces in cultivation. In rich garden soil, free of root competition, the plants can attain their full size; in my garden, that means 5 feet or more. Clusters of three to ten green bell-like flowers hang below the stems, followed in autumn by blue berries relished by robins and thrushes. If you want a small Solomon's seal, try fragrant Solomon's seal (*P. odoratum*) from Japan. To brighten up a shaded spot, use 'Variegatum', which has leaves edged in creamy white.

❧ **A solid green grass.** Although yellow variegated hakone grass is far more popular, the plain green wild form, *Hakonechloa macra*, has charms of its own. Where subtle color is called for, use a clump as an accent or to add fine texture to a group of bold leaves. It also makes a nice contrast next to plants with variegated leaves. In northern gardens, where the variegated selection is not reliably hardy, use the species, which is hardy to Zone 4, to add simple elegance to a design. You can also use it in place of bamboo, which is invasive in the South and not hardy in the far North.

❧ **Where the grass meets the garden.** A smooth carpet of emerald turf sets off a long border like this one to great advantage. A clean edge keeps the lawn looking neat and the garden looking its best. Use an edging tool or sharp spade to edge the beds in spring. An edging strip will keep a crisp edge for years without the need for annual edging.

Let strong foliage combinations keep your fall garden lively. Combine the chartreuse foliage of variegated hakone grass with a red-leaved wood spurge (*Euphorbia amygdaloides* 'Purpurea'), and deep green hostas.

A Frost Hardy Combination for Early-Winter Beauty

Even after killing frosts have destroyed the last of the late-blooming perennials, subtle color and texture keep this garden interesting. Ornamental grasses are the stars of the winter landscape, with their feathery seedheads and graceful clumps of dried leaves, which will stand until spring. While grasses are lovely alone, they're even more dramatic when contrasted with the ghostly stems of Russian sage. The evergreen leaves of the arum and lilyturf add welcome greenery to this planting through winter.

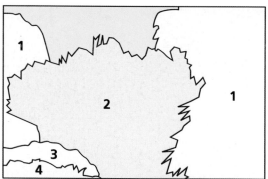

PHOTO KEY
1. Japanese silver grass (*Miscanthus sinensis*); Zones 4 to 9
2. Russian sage (*Perovskia atriplicifolia*); Zones 4 to 9
3. Italian arum (*Arum italicum*); Zones 6 to 9
4. Big blue lilyturf (*Liriope muscari*); Zones 6 to 9

Secrets for Winter Beauty

🌿 **Try a plant that grows in winter.** Italian arum has a life cycle that's the reverse of most perennials. The plants are dormant in summer and produce new foliage in fall that lasts through winter. Greenish white flowers appear in spring and then the foliage disappears for the season. Erect spikes of showy red berries are left behind to adorn the late summer and fall landscape.

🌿 **Rely on evergreen plants for winter interest.** In areas with mild winters where the ground is not consistently covered by snow, perennials with evergreen leaves add color to the garden from late fall through winter. Lily turf is a fine-textured evergreen groundcover perfect for planting under shrubs or among tall perennials that have decorative winter stems. Other evergreen perennials include hellebores, thymes, European wild ginger (*Asarum europaeum*), and sedges (including *Carex hachioensis* 'Evergold' and *C. morrowii*).

🌿 **Be sure the time is right for winter mulch.** Freezing and thawing cycles and bitter winds can wreak havoc with plants, especially evergreen ones, over winter. In northern gardens, winter mulch is essential, but even in warmer zones, plants that have succulent leaves, like bergenia, are easily damaged by drying winds and fluctuating temperatures. While it's tempting to mulch when you tidy up the garden for winter, wait until the ground freezes. If you spread mulch too early, plants won't fully harden off and go dormant, making them vulnerable to plummeting temperatures.

Hellebores are some of the best-loved winter-flowering perennials. In areas with mild winters, stinking hellebore (*Helleborus foetidus*) blooms in February and March, and an occasional coating of frost highlights the foliage.

A Spring Garden

Variegated Solomon's Seal

Old-Fashioned Bleeding Heart

Virginia Bluebells

Wild Blue Phlox

Wild Ginger

Bethlehem Sage

Plant Names	Bloom Color and Season	Height and Spread
'Mrs. Moon' Bethlehem sage	Pink buds, blue flowers in spring	6" to 12" tall and 1' to 2' wide
Old-fashioned bleeding heart	Pink flowers in spring	3' tall and wide
Wild bleeding heart	Pink flowers in spring to summer	1' to 2' tall and wide
Virginia bluebells	Sky blue flowers in spring	1' to 2' tall and 1' wide
'Peeping Tom' daffodil	Yellow flowers in spring	1' tall and 6" wide
Ostrich fern	Bright green fronds	2' to 5' tall and 3' wide

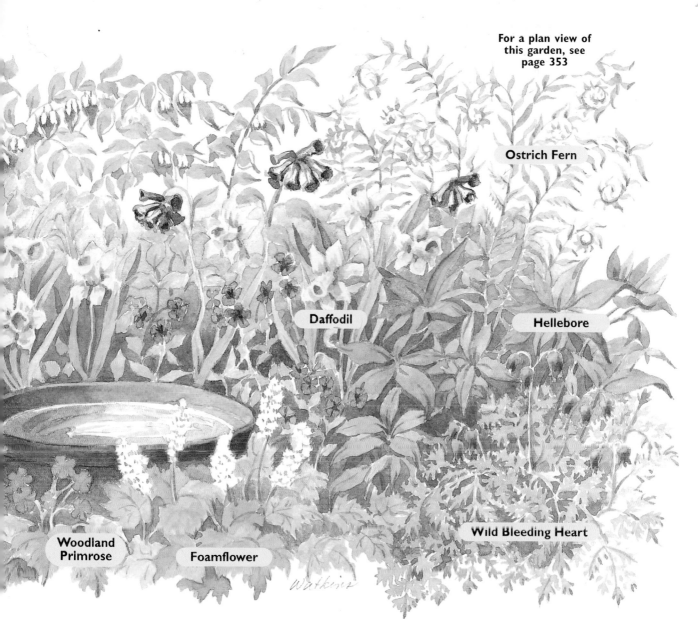

For a plan view of
this garden, see
page 353

Ostrich Fern

Daffodil

Hellebore

Wild Bleeding Heart

Woodland
Primrose

Foamflower

Watkins

Plant Names	Bloom Color and Season	Height and Spread
Allegheny foamflower	White flowers in spring	6" to 12" tall and 1' wide
Canada wild ginger	Maroon flowers in spring	6" to 12" tall and 1' to 2' wide
Garden hybrid hellebore	Pink or white flowers in spring	1' to 2' tall and wide
Wild blue phlox	Blue flowers in spring	1' tall and wide
Woodland primrose	White or magenta flowers in spring	6" tall and 6" to 12" wide
Variegated Solomon's seal	White-edged leaves	1' to 2' tall and 2' wide

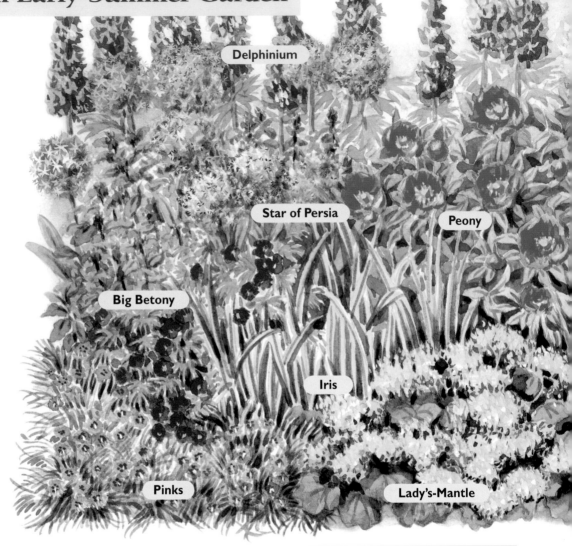

Garden Designs for All Seasons

An Early-Summer Garden

Delphinium

Star of Persia

Peony

Big Betony

Iris

Pinks

Lady's-Mantle

Plant Names	Bloom Color and Season	Height and Spread
Big betony	Rose-pink flowers in summer	1½' to 2' tall and wide
'Souvenir d'Andre Chaudron' catmint	Blue flowers in early to midsummer	2' to 3' tall and wide
Heartleaf crambe	White flowers in early to midsummer	4' to 6' tall and wide
Delphinium	Blue flowers in early summer	3' to 5' tall and 2' to 3' wide
Blue false indigo	Rich blue flowers in early summer	2' to 3' tall and 3' wide
Caucasus geranium	Deep blue flowers in early summer	1' to 1½' tall and 2' wide
Variegated sweet iris	Blue flowers in early summer	2' to 2½' tall and 1' wide

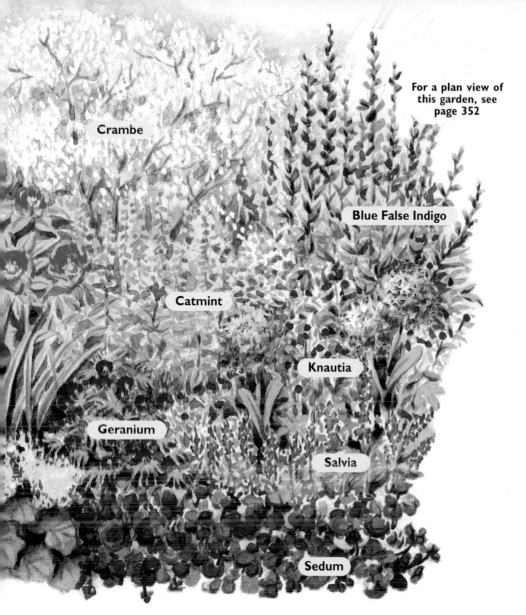

Crambe

For a plan view of
this garden, see
page 352

Blue False Indigo

Catmint

Knautia

Geranium

Salvia

Sedum

Plant Names	Bloom Color and Season	Height and Spread
Knautia	Deep red flowers in summer	1' to 2' tall and 1' wide
Lady's-mantle	Chartreuse flowers in early summer	1' tall and 2' to 3' wide
'Sea Shell' peony	Shell pink flowers in early summer	3' tall and wide
'Bath's Pink' pinks	Pink flowers in early summer	6" to 12" tall and 1' wide
'May Night' salvia	Purple flowers in early to midsummer	1½' tall and 2' wide
'Vera Jameson' sedum	Rose purple flowers in late summer to fall	1' tall and 2' wide
Star of Persia	Silvery lilac flowers in early summer	1' to 2' tall and 1' wide

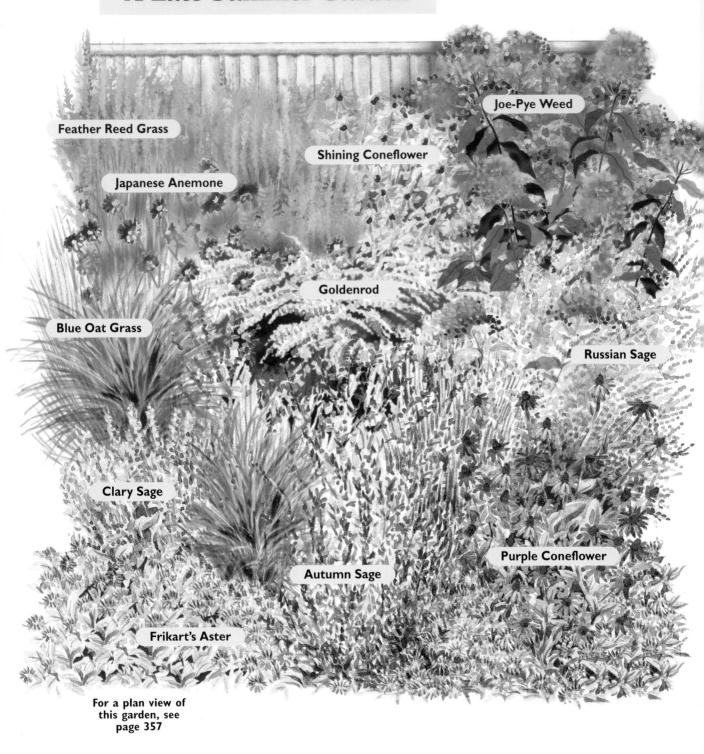

Feather Reed Grass

Japanese Anemone

Shining Coneflower

Joe-Pye Weed

Blue Oat Grass

Goldenrod

Russian Sage

Clary Sage

Autumn Sage

Purple Coneflower

Frikart's Aster

For a plan view of
this garden, see
page 357

140

Plant Names	Bloom Color and Season	Height and Spread
'Pamina' Japanese anemone	Deep pink flowers in late summer to fall	2' to 3' tall and 2' wide
'Monch' Frikart's aster	Lavender-blue flowers in late summer	2 to 2½' tall and 3' wide
Blue oat grass	Blue-gray leaves/straw flowers in summer	2' to 3' tall and 2' wide
Purple coneflower	Rose-purple flowers in summer	2' to 4' tall and 1' to 2' wide
'Herbstsonne' shining coneflower	Yellow flowers in late summer	3' to 4' tall and 2' to 3' wide
'Fireworks' rough-stemmed goldenrod	Yellow flowers in late summer to fall	3' to 4' tall and 3' wide
'Atropurpureum' Joe-Pye weed	Rose-pink flowers in late summer	4' to 6' tall and wide
Feather reed grass	Greenish flowers with pink tones in early summer	2' to 3' tall and 2' wide
Russian sage	Blue flowers in late summer to fall	3' to 5' tall and wide
Autumn sage	Scarlet flowers in summer and fall	2' to 3' tall and 3' wide
Clary sage	Pink or blue flowers in summer	2' to 3½' tall and 3' wide

Enjoying Your Late-Summer Garden

Late summer and early autumn are a celebration in this sumptuous cottage-style garden. It's a garden for full sun and rich, loamy, well-drained soil. Butterflies will be frequent visitors throughout the summer and early fall, attracted by the feast of nectar from the coneflowers, asters, goldenrod, sages, and Joe-Pye weed. To get even more enjoyment from your garden, try cutting a few bouquets for indoor arrangements. The abundant sprays of flowers offer more than enough bounty, so the ones you cut won't be missed. Ornamental grasses and the dried seedheads of purple coneflower, Joe-Pye weed, Russian sage, and goldenrod continue to look attractive right through the winter, particularly when laced with snow. Goldfinches will mob the plants, vying for a choice place to feed on the seeds.

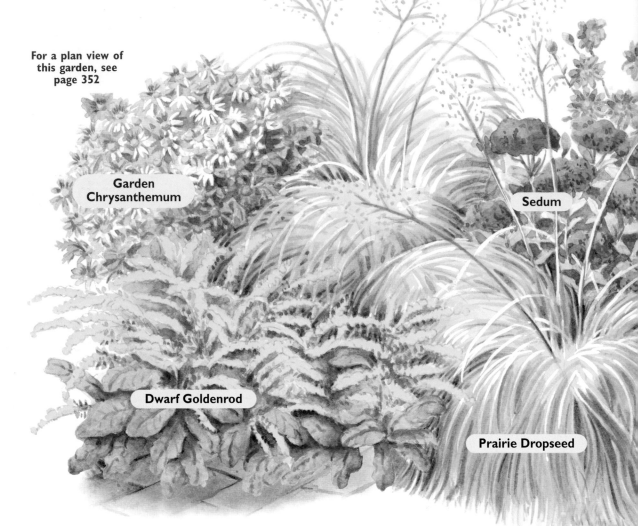

For a plan view of this garden, see page 352

Garden Chrysanthemum

Sedum

Dwarf Goldenrod

Prairie Dropseed

Plant Names	Bloom Color and Season	Height and Spread
'Prince Henry' Japanese anemone	Pink flowers in late summer to fall	2' to 3' tall and 2' wide
'Blue King' Italian aster	Blue flowers in late summer to fall	2' tall and 2' to 2½' wide
'Clara Curtis' hardy garden chrysanthemum	Rose-pink flowers in fall	1' to 2½' tall and wide
Prairie dropseed	Green leaves in spring and summer, gold leaves in fall	1' to 3' tall and 3' wide
'Golden Fleece' dwarf goldenrod	Yellow flowers in fall	1' to 2' tall and wide
'Autumn Joy' sedum	Rose-pink flowers in late summer	2' tall and wide

Japanese Anemone

Italian Aster

Getting the Most from Your Garden

Fall gardens are a great alternative for gardeners who travel a lot during the summer and don't want to put time and money into plants they won't be at home to enjoy. With autumn comes cooler temperatures and clear days. It's a great time to be outdoors enjoying the flowers and the butterflies they attract. Plus, working in the garden is more enjoyable when it's cool. This pocket-size garden of fall delights is perfect for a narrow bed along a driveway or even for a large planter. Place this garden in a spot with full sun or light shade and rich, well-drained soil.

If you have a long bed to fill, you can repeat this pattern in two directions, with the 'Clara Curtis' chrysanthemum and 'Golden Fleece' goldenrod doubled up at the center. For a deep bed, add a backdrop of airy Russian sage (*Perovskia atriplicifolia*) and brilliant yellow sneezeweeds (*Helenium autumnale*) to complete the picture. Try adding bright spring bulbs, such as daffodils and tulips, for spring interest. Cut down the dried stalks of sedum, goldenrod, and dropseed in early spring to make way for the bulbs and new growth of the other plants.

Combinations
FOR SPECIAL SITES

The amounts of light, soil, and moisture that create your yard's unique growing conditions affect your plant choices and garden style. In this section, you'll find inspirational combinations that will turn "problem" garden conditions like shady sites and wet soil into great garden opportunities. I've even chosen several terrific combinations that will thrive in discouragingly heavy clay soil. I've also combined the best plants from each combination into colorful designs that offer season-long interest from both flowers and foliage.

A Sunny Trio for Spring

Decorate a dry, sunny bank with this stunning mix of tough, easy-to-grow perennials in magenta, lilac-blue, and lime green. Lime green, or chartreuse, is a versatile color that blends well with nearly any other color. The startling magenta flowers of the phlox make a handsome background for the chartreuse euphorbia flowers, while the lilac-blue phlox helps to tone down this otherwise hot-colored combination. Although there's little contrast in texture or flower size and shape, the striking colors add more than enough interest to this planting, which will thrive in tough conditions where few other perennials would be happy.

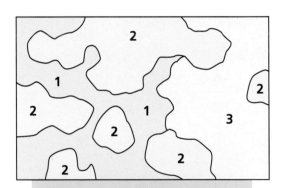

PHOTO KEY
1. 'Emerald Cushion Blue' moss phlox (*Phlox subulata* 'Emerald Cushion Blue'); Zones 2 to 9
2. Cypress spurge (*Euphorbia cyparissias*); Zones 4 to 9
3. Moss phlox (*Phlox subulata*); Zones 2 to 9

Techniques for Sunny Spring Spreaders

🌿 Try a dainty but tough groundcover.
Moss phlox is a popular perennial that comes in a rainbow of shades, including lilac-blue, pink, red, and pure white—there are even striped cultivars. A few of my favorites include 'Blue Hills', with medium blue flowers; 'Candy Stripe', with pink-and-white flowers (like a peppermint stick!); 'Coral Eye', which has pale pink flowers with dark centers; soft lavender 'Dirgo Arbutus'; crimson red 'Red Wing'; and 'Snow White', with pure white flowers on compact plants. Once established, a single plant of moss phlox will cover several square feet of ground. Set young plants 2 feet apart in a groundcover planting, and in time they will interweave to form a dense mat. Mulch between the plants to control weeds until they grow together. Established plants are heat- and drought-tolerant, so they seldom need watering, and the mats are so thick that most weeds can't get a toe hold.

🌿 Plant moss phlox in rock walls. Moss phlox is a great choice for a rock wall planting.
Just tuck the plants into spaces between rocks as you build the wall. To plant an existing wall, buy small plants and use a chopstick to tuck the roots into the crevices between rocks. The plants will spread slowly at first, but once the roots get established, they will take off and produce mats of flowers that spill down the wall.

🌿 Enjoy this blessing and avoid its curse. Although cypress spurge adds delicate foliage and unique flowers to the garden, it's a vigorous spreader that's best used in tough spots where few other plants will thrive. In more congenial surroundings such as beds and borders, you'll need to control its spread by regularly removing the running stems that spread in every direction. If you do include cushion spurge in a spot where it's likely to spread, try planting it in a plastic pot sunk in the ground. Every year or so, you'll need to lift the pot, divide the plants, and replant them in fresh soil. They make long-lasting cut flowers, too. Let the ends of the stems dry before placing them in a vase.

Cheery yellow sundrops (*Oenothera pilosella*) and deep pink smooth phlox (*Phlox glaberrima*) make a bright combination of contrasting summer colors for a tough, sun-baked spot.

Rich Color for a Sunny Summer Spot

Cool-colored Hungarian speedwell tumbles over a mass of brilliant cherry red pinks to form a flamboyant combination at the front of this border. The tiny pink flowers of rock soapwort trail through the planting, helping blend the other colors together. All three of these perennials need well-drained soil. Although they grow in most regions of the country, they perform best in areas with cool summer nights and moderate humidity. Here, a gravel mulch helps assure sharp drainage and keeps the soil cool. This combination would also look great in a decorative container on a deck or patio.

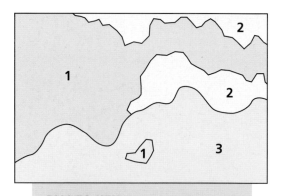

PHOTO KEY
1. 'Crater Lake Blue' Hungarian speedwell (*Veronica teucrium* 'Crater Lake Blue'); Zones 3 to 8
2. Rock soapwort (*Saponaria ocymoides*); Zones 3 to 7
3. Pinks (*Dianthus*); Zones 3 to 9

Sun-Loving Plants
for Rich Summer Color

❧ Keep your veronicas blooming.
Veronicas, also called speedwells, bloom for weeks in early summer, but they don't have to stop there. When flowering begins to wane, take up your clippers and shear the plants back by one-half to two-thirds. They will soon start to bloom all over again. Where summers are cool and sun is plentiful, you can keep them blooming all season with careful deadheading after each flush of bloom.

❧ Get the most out of pinks. Pinks grow best in regions where summer humidity is moderate and the soil is slightly alkaline. Plant them in light, well-drained, near-neutral soil, and give them plenty of sun and fresh air. The profuse, fragrant flowers appear in early summer, with scattered rebloom throughout the season. Use pruning shears to remove the spent flowers—cut the stems back to the height of the foliage so you don't leave a forest of unattractive stalks standing. Even after the plants have stopped blooming, the neat clumps of spiky gray or green foliage remain attractive,

so they're a good choice for planting along the edges of walks and at the front of borders with later-flowering plants such as poppy mallow (*Callirhoe involucrata*) and asters tumbling over them. Most pinks have evergreen foliage that adds color to the winter landscape.

❧ Try this useful soapwort. Rock soapwort is a terrific little groundcover that blooms nonstop for a month or more in summer. Plants form broad, flat clumps in record time and make an attractive groundcover for well-drained sunny sites, such as rock gardens. If allowed to scramble through taller perennials, rock soapwort will visually "knit" together the tall plants, as it has in this combination. Or, plant it in crevices in rock walls. For a more dramatic display, try larger-flowered *Saponaria* × *lempergii* 'Max Frei'. This soapwort bears rich pink, 1-inch flowers that cover the mounds of foliage in mid- to late summer. They look great with bright blue bellflowers, plumbago (*Ceratostigma plumbaginoides*), and 'Golden Fleece' goldenrod.

A mass of mixed pinks (*Dianthus* spp.) perfumes the air around a perky clump of Johnny-jump-ups (*Viola tricolor*) in this sun-loving late-spring combination.

PHOTO KEY
1. Blue oat grass (*Helictotrichon sempervirens*); Zones 4 to 9
2. Purple coneflower (*Echinacea purpurea*); Zones 3 to 8
3. Sea lavender (*Limonium latifolium*); Zones 3 to 9
5. Poppy mallow (*Callirhoe involucrata*); Zones 4 to 6
6. Lamb's-ears (*Stachys byzantina*); Zones 4 to 8

A Colorful Water-Wise Combination

Sizzling sun and dry summer weather won't stop these delicate-looking yet rugged perennials. Flowers begin to appear in early summer, when the poppy mallow opens its first flowers, but this planting really hits its stride in mid- to late summer. By then, the coneflowers and sea lavender, punctuated by the sprawling poppy mallow stems, are in full bloom. Flowering continues into fall.

Color echoes and contrasting textures add interest to this mix of long-blooming perennials. The woolly, silver-gray leaves of lamb's-ears backed by an airy cloud of sea lavender blossoms make a soothing combination. The poppy mallow ambling over the lamb's-ears add splashes of bright color that echo the rosy purple of the coneflowers. The fine-textured, airy mound of sea lavender looks especially soft compared to the bold coneflowers. In the background, a thin veil of oat grass flowers catches the afternoon light, yet doesn't block the view of the drifts of flowers behind it.

Tips for a Water-Wise Garden

🐚 **Grow poppy mallow for long bloom and easy care.** The poppy mallow that weaves through this combination flowers profusely throughout the summer without pinching or deadheading. Although the plants may trail for several feet, the stems are never dense enough to smother the plants they grow over. In the fall, the leaves will turn clear yellow, a nice complement to the silver and gray fall foliage around them.

🐚 **Try tough-as-nails sea lavender.** Sea lavender may look as delicate as lace, but this native of salt marshes and tempest-tossed dunes is up to any challenge. It tolerates salt, sandy soil, hot sun, dry soil, and punishing wind, yet never looks anything but perfect. Plants form thick taproots that help them endure dry spells. When the plants are in full bloom, you hardly see the lush, glossy oblong leaves, but even after the blooms fade, the leaves look great all year. The flowers last for months and are perfect for cutting and drying.

🐚 **Put lamb's-ears along the edge.** To give a new planting of perennials a nicely finished look, plant lamb's-ears along the edge of the bed. Despite its soft-looking leaves, lamb's-ears is a tough plant that spreads quickly to cover the hard edge between soil and pavement.

🐚 **Add more tough plants for dry spots in sun.** Other perennials to try in a dry sunny spot include torch lilies (*Kniphofia* spp.), lesser calamint (*Calamintha nepeta*), butterfly weed (*Asclepias tuberosa*), salvias, globe thistle (*Echinops ritro*), penstemons, and sea hollies (*Eryngium* spp.). For foliage interest, try yuccas and prickly-pear cactus (*Opuntia* spp.). Another unexpected choice for both flower and foliage interest on a dry site is bearded iris. Bearded iris is actually quite drought-tolerant, and when planted in a dry garden, the foliage stays healthy and attractive all season, adding interesting texture contrast and a vertical accent to many combinations.

For a delightful combination, plant 'Anne Folkard' hardy cranesbill with 'Silver Brocade' artemisia. The silver, ferny artemisia contrasts nicely with the deeply cut cranesbill leaves, and the magenta cranesbill flowers add a definite punch.

Dynamic Color for Summer's Dog Days

Flowers can be hard to come by during the dog days of summer, but heat and humidity are no match for durable perennials like Russian sage, sunflower heliopsis, and coneflowers. Large drifts of color keep this combination from looking fussy and maximize the impact from each plant. White coneflowers, a form of our native purple coneflower, play an important role in making this combination work. They add contrast in both color and shape when grown with Russian sage, while their orange centers echo the bright orange double heliopsis flowers. This trio is drought-tolerant and rarely suffers from any insect or disease problems.

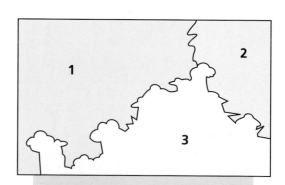

PHOTO KEY
1. Russian sage (*Perovskia atriplicifolia*); Zones 4 to 9
2. 'Golden Plume' sunflower heliopsis (*Heliopsis helianthoides* 'Golden Plume'); Zones 3 to 9
3. White purple coneflower (*Echinacea purpurea* 'Alba'); Zones 3 to 8

Plants for Summer's Dog Days

❧ A late starter that's worth the wait.
Russian sage flowers for weeks in summer and
looks fantastic even when it's not in bloom.
The deeply cut leaves are late to emerge in
spring. It won't leaf out until after the tulips
bloom. 'Blue Mist' flowers early, 'Filagran' has
deeply cut leaves and pale flowers, and
'Longin' is a 4-foot-tall cultivar with erect stems
and coarsely lobed leaves.

❧ Coneflowers of a different color.
While purple-pink coneflowers are best known,
white-flowered selections also are great garden
plants. 'White Swan' has white flowers that
have a green tint, while 'White Lustre' has large
pure white flowers. Some of the best of the
pink-flowered types include: 'Bright Star', a
seed-grown strain with large, rose-pink flowers;
'Magnus', which has 7-inch-wide, purple-pink
flowers; and 'Springbrook Crimson Star', which
has deep rosy purple flowers and gracefully
drooping petals.

❧ More than just a pretty face. Purple
coneflowers are popular among gardeners because they provide a wealth of flowers in return
for little care, but herbalists also appreciate these
sturdy plants. Native Americans have used coneflowers medicinally, and today *Echinacea* roots
are made into extracts or teas to boost the im-
mune system and help the body recover from
colds and flu. The plant is also used to make a
cream that helps heal cuts and skin abrasions.

❧ A deep-rooted combo. Purple coneflowers, heliopsis, grasses, and Russian sage
have thick, fleshy roots or taproots that store
water. These roots help the plants survive
drought without extra watering. However, the
taproots of plants like Russian sage make them
difficult to divide. These roots may reach
down several feet, so it's hard to dig them up
without harming the plants. To propagate
them, take cuttings of new growth in early
summer instead.

Rosy-flowered swamp
milkweed (*Asclepias incarnata*) and ornamental
grasses are part of the
background in this sunny
border that features
the combination shown
on the opposite page.

A Mix of Herbs and Flowers

Parsley and many other herbs make perfect companions for sun-loving perennials that thrive in well-drained soil. This low-growing, drought-tolerant combination, perfect for the front of a sandy soil border, contrasts rich green, ruffled leaves of parsley with woolly, gray-green lamb's-ears. A clump of purple-leaved sedum with rosy flowers adds both color and contrasting shape to the planting. To round out this beautiful and mostly edible combination, you could also plant a bright yellow thyme, such as *Thymus* × *citriodorus* 'Aureus', or golden oregano (*Origanum vulgare* 'Aureum') and deep purple opal basil (*Ocimum basilicum* 'Purpurascens').

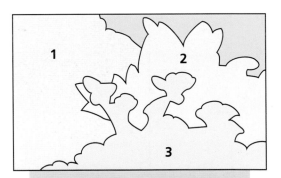

PHOTO KEY
1. 'Vera Jameson' sedum (*Sedum* **'Vera Jameson'**)**; Zones 4 to 9**
2. Lamb's-ears (*Stachys byzantina*, **also offered as** *S. lanata*)**; Zones 4 to 8**
3. Curly parsley (*Petroselinum* **crispum var. crispum**)**; Zones 5 to 8**

154

Secrets for Mixing Herbs and Flowers

 Let the sun bring out this sedum's best. Sedum 'Vera Jameson', featured in this combination, needs rich, well-drained soil in full sun to light shade. The more sun the plant receives, the darker purple the foliage will be. Plants also maintain a more mounded form in sun—they tend to flop in the shade.

 Try two types of parsley. Parsley is a wonderful herb for use in salads, soups, and other dishes. It's also a great source of vitamins A and C, as well as a number of minerals. Curly parsley, pictured here, is one of two forms that are available. Flat-leaved, or Italian, parsley has divided leaves with flattened, deeply cut lobes. It's ideal for use in sauces and soups. Curly parsley is more tender and is great when used fresh in salads. Both forms are biennials, not perennials, meaning that they produce foliage the first year, then flower and die the second. Replant parsley annually to ensure a continuous supply of this super herb.

 Add more herbs to the mix. Several other culinary herbs, both perennial and annual, make fine additions to ornamental gardens. Consider including thyme, chives, and sage to full-sun plantings in well-drained soil. Mint is generally too invasive to use among other perennials, but it can be included in wild areas. Oregano, another vigorous spreader, makes a fine groundcover for a sunny spot with soil that's on the dry side. Basil, especially purple-leaved types and Thai basil, is an annual suitable for sunny gardens with rich, evenly moist soil. Dill is a reseeding annual that adds ferny foliage and flat clusters of yellow flowers. It thrives in sun and well-drained soil.

Starry lavender 'Peter Harrison' New York asters and rosy *Sedum sieboldii* 'Nana' are guaranteed to provide a late-summer and autumn show for the front of a sunny, well-drained perennial bed.

PHOTO KEY
1. **Red valerian (*Centranthus ruber*); Zones 4 to 8**
2. **Lance-leaved coreopsis (*Coreopsis lanceolata*); Zones 3 to 8**
3. **Gray rabbitbrush (*Ericameria [Chrysothamnus] nauseosus*); Zones 5 to 8**
4. **'May Night' salvia (*Salvia × sylvestris* 'May Night'); Zones 5 to 9**
5. **Catmint (*Nepeta × faassenii*); Zones 3 to 8**

Summer Blooms for a Tough Site

A rich display of fiery reds and yellows tempered by cool blues and silver makes a lively summer-blooming mix for a dry, sunny site. Most of the plants in this combination have fine textures and spiky forms. The rounded mass of the rabbitbrush and the bold, round coreopsis flowers offer a pleasing contrast. The rabbitbrush will bloom in late summer and will be covered with fuzzy yellow flowers that will last into winter. This group of drought-tolerant plants doesn't like pampering and will grow best in alkaline soil.

156

Expert Tips for a Tough, Dry Site

🌰 **Include plants tailor-made for tough spots.** The adaptable plants in this garden are perfectly happy in lean, dry soils and a spot with plenty of bright sunshine. That makes this combination a perfect choice for a seaside garden or a planting in the High Plains, in the Southwest, or on a hot, dry slope.

🌰 **Add some early-season color.** While most of the perennials in this combination bloom in summer, you can encourage an early season start by underplanting with tulips, which thrive in areas where they get a hot, dry period for their summer dormancy. Species tulips, such as *Tulipa tarda*, are especially attractive and will rebloom reliably for many years.

🌰 **Extend the life of coreopsis.** Lance-leaved coreopsis is a short-lived perennial, persisting only a few years in most gardens. Competition hastens the plant's demise, because in a garden jam-packed with exuberant perennials, coreopsis is easily elbowed out. To keep plants thriving, give them plenty of room

to breathe, and keep surrounding plants from flopping over and smothering them. If you give plants rich, well-drained soil and remove spent flowers, they will bloom all summer and last for a few extra years before you need to replace them. Self-sown seedlings will appear if you let some flowers set seeds.

🌰 **Try versatile red valerian.** Also called Jupiter's beard, this rugged, beautiful perennial is surprisingly easy to please. It thrives in dry, alkaline soil, but also is happy in the average, well-drained soil found in most garden beds and borders. The plants even grow in narrow crevices in rock walls where there is seemingly no soil at all. They will self-sow under good conditions.

🌰 **Shear to promote continuous bloom.** After the first wave of early summer bloom in this garden, cut back the stems of catmint, sage, and rabbit brush by half. The plants will resprout from side shoots and give you another month of bloom. Shear the red valerian if the plants become too floppy.

Mounds of lavender form a fragrant, showy edging for clumps of pink mallows and spiky red and white penstemons in this midsummer planting that thrives in sunny, well-drained conditions.

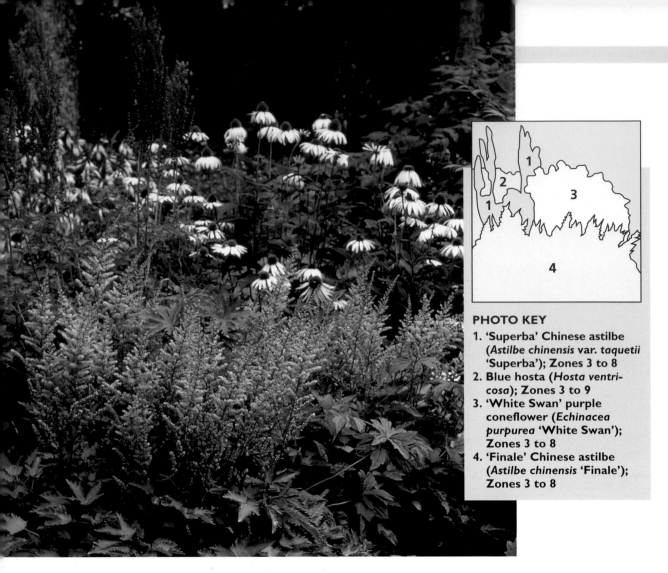

PHOTO KEY

1. 'Superba' Chinese astilbe (*Astilbe chinensis* var. *taquetii* 'Superba'); Zones 3 to 8
2. Blue hosta (*Hosta ventricosa*); Zones 3 to 9
3. 'White Swan' purple coneflower (*Echinacea purpurea* 'White Swan'); Zones 3 to 8
4. 'Finale' Chinese astilbe (*Astilbe chinensis* 'Finale'); Zones 3 to 8

Astilbes for a Woodland Edge

Drifts of perennials in pastel colors make a showy yet restful planting for the edge of a woodland. The setting for this midsummer-blooming combination adds a special beauty because the drifts of sunlit flowers are highlighted against a backdrop of tall trees and rich foliage. Spikes of 'Superba' astilbe flowers echo the vertical trunks of the trees, making a transition between the garden and the woods. The round, bold-textured coneflowers offer the perfect contrast to the spikes of fine-textured 'Finale' astilbes.

This combination is part of a border that faces southeast. The site is shaded in the morning and again in midafternoon, so the plants receive about six hours of direct sun daily. Sun-loving coneflowers grow alongside shade-tolerant astilbes in this New England garden. Although coneflowers are prairie plants native to full sun, as long as they receive six hours of direct sun daily, they bloom just fine. In areas with cool summers, shade-loving astilbes will take a great deal of sun. In warmer southern gardens, they are best grown in full shade.

Secrets for Sensational Astilbes

🍂 **Divide astilbes when the time is right.** Mature astilbes form dense, woody crowns with dozens of stems and a thick tangle of foliage. If plants outgrow their site or become so crowded they begin to bloom less, it's time to divide them. Either lift the crowns in early spring, just as the leaves are emerging, or dig the plants after they've finished flowering. Use a sharp knife or shears to cut the crown into smaller sections. Replant the divisions into soil enriched with compost or manure. Astilbes are heavy feeders and benefit from an annual topdressing with composted manure.

🍂 **Keep astilbes moist in southern sites.** Hybrid astilbes suffer where summer nights are hot. In the South, give them full but open shade and rich, continually moist soil. Chinese astilbe (*Astilbe chinensis*) and star astilbe (*A. simplicifolia*) are the most heat-tolerant of the astilbes.

🍂 **Try heat-loving astilbe substitutes.** Phygelius (*Phygelius* spp.), which have spiky flower clusters with nodding, tubular flowers in a wide range of colors, are good heat-tolerant astilbe substitutes. Another possibility is bear's-breeches (*Acanthus* spp.), which have lush foliage and erect spikes of white-and-violet flowers. Or consider some of the long-blooming salvias, which bloom from early summer to frost, such as autumn sage (*Salvia greggii*) and its hybrids, in a range of reds, pinks, and white.

Diminutive mid-summer-blooming *Astilbe chinensis* var. *pumila* is the perfect vertical accent for a small, partly shaded garden where large astilbes won't fit. Plants spread to form low, broad clumps and make a lovely groundcover, too.

PHOTO KEY

1. Himalayan fleeceflower
   (*Persicaria affinis*); Zones
   3 to 7
2. Japanese painted fern
   (*Athyrium niponicum*
   'Pictum'); Zones 4 to 8

A Simply Elegant Groundcover Duo

If you have a rock wall or steps in a partly shaded area, try dressing it up with this elegant pairing of a fern and a perennial groundcover. The mat-forming stems of fleeceflower make a neat, tight carpet under a single clump of Japanese painted fern. The plain green fleeceflower leaves highlight the showy silver-and-maroon fronds of the fern, adding a dash of interest that keeps the planting from becoming monotonous.

The trailing stems of the fleeceflower spill gracefully over the edge of the wall, and in time, they'll fill the crevices between boulders and cover the entire face of the wall. When the fleeceflowers begin blooming in summer, their dense wands of pink flowers complement the silvery fern fronds and add a vertical accent. The flower spikes dry to a rich reddish brown in autumn. The leaves turn golden yellow and dry to chocolate brown as winter arrives.

Plants for a Groundcover Duo

🐚 **Give this fern some sun.** Japanese painted ferns are lovely additions to any garden picture. Unlike native ferns, such as wood ferns (*Dryopteris* spp.) and shield ferns (*Polystichum* spp.), which are woodland plants that prefer full shade, Japanese painted ferns need bright light or some direct sun to bring out the best color in the fronds. The first time I grew this plant, I made the mistake of putting it in deep shade, where it languished. When I saw it growing to perfection in a friend's partially shaded garden, I knew my mistake.

🐚 **Enjoy your fern volunteers.** Where Japanese painted ferns are happy, they are among the most generous garden ferns. The plants spread by rhizomes (underground stems) to form broad clumps and also by spores. Some of the offspring have green fronds, while others are beautifully colored in shades of sea green, silver-gray, and pink. In fact, many of the offspring that grow from spores are superior to the parents. If you don't like the plain ones, weed them out.

🐚 **Grow a noninvasive knotweed.** Fleeceflowers, also called knotweeds, are relatives of some feisty weeds, including serious spreaders with alarming names like mile-a-minute-vine. Fortunately, not all knotweeds are weeds. The Himalayan fleeceflower in this combination is a well-behaved groundcover. A few of the best cultivars include: 'Border Jewel', which has light pink flowers; 'Darjeeling Red', with rich rose-red flowers; 'Donald Lowndes', which has double, salmon-pink flowers; and 'Dimity', with thick spikes of pale flowers that blush to crimson as they age.

Himalayan fleeceflower (*Persicaria affinis*) is a slow-spreading groundcover that forms mats of glossy leaves. It flowers for weeks in summer, and it's a good companion for verbenas and veronicas on a lightly shaded site.

161

A Planting to Welcome Summer

Texture, soothing colors, and handsome foliage create a combination that welcomes summer, yet remains good-looking long after the flowers have faded. Frothy white astilbe flowers create a fine-textured focal point, but phlox and iris hold their own because of their bright colors and more solid forms. The contrast between white and blue gives this planting a peaceful glow, while the brilliant pink phlox adds a dash of excitement. Ferny astilbe leaves and strap-shaped iris foliage keeps this combination attractive long after the flowers have faded. To keep this combination looking its best, plant it in humus-rich, moist soil.

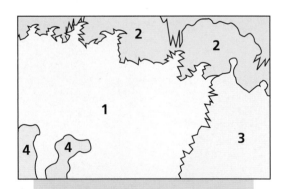

PHOTO KEY
1. **Astilbe (*Astilbe × arendsii*);** **Zones 3 to 9**
2. **Siberian iris (*Iris sibirica*);** **Zones 2 to 9**
3. **'Spring Delight' mountain phlox (*Phlox ovata* 'Spring Delight');** **Zones 4 to 8**
4. **Serbian bellflower (*Campanula poscharskyana*); Zones 3 to 7**

Tips for Long-Lasting Summer Color

❧ **Lighten dark spots by planting white flowers.** I use lots of white flowers, along with plants that feature white variegation on their leaves, to brighten up spots in partial to full shade. White reflects light and enlivens the garden during the day and in the evening. To add more white to this combination after the astilbe fades, try white border phlox (*Phlox paniculata* 'David'), along with variegated Solomon's seal (*Polygonatum odoratum* 'Variegatum') and creeping variegated broad-leaved sedge (*Carex siderostica* 'Variegata'). For a tropical touch, plant a white-leaved caladium.

❧ **Add some late-blooming perennials.** This combination goes out of bloom by early summer, and by July, it needs a new source of color to complement the lush foliage textures. Masterwort (*Astrantia major*) is a long-blooming perennial for summer with open clusters of starry white or pink flowers. 'Firetail' mountain fleece (*Persicaria amplexicaulis* 'Firetail') blooms all summer with cherry red spikes over graceful, rich green leaves. For fall interest, try turtleheads (*Chelone* spp.), with their white or pink hooded flowers. Add spotted toad lilies (*Tricyrtis* spp.) and woodland asters to keep the garden blooming until frost.

❧ **Don't touch those clippers!** Don't be too hasty to make things look neat as flowers fade. The green seed capsules that follow astilbe and iris flowers add interesting texture for the rest of the summer. In fall, they turn brown. I leave them standing in my garden through the winter, when the dried pods and seedheads jut out of the snow drifts.

If you want to fill lots of space in a partly shaded garden, try goatsbeard (*Aruncus dioicus*), which forms clumps up to 4 feet tall and wide. Its white flower plumes combine well with lupines, peonies, blue stars (*Amsonia* spp.), and bellflowers (*Campanula* spp.).

Cool Silvers and Blues for Summer

A rich mix of foliage in shades of blue-green and silver-gray creates a cool-colored planting that would add a restful touch to any lightly shaded spot. A dramatic fountain of silvery blue oat grass occupies center stage. The silver- and maroon-splashed foliage of the heuchera picks up the silver theme, while its rounded leaves add an attractive contrast. A downy silver-gray carpet of lamb's-ears knits the planting together by blending the blues and silvers. In early summer, columbine flowers add a dash of color, but the richly textured foliage in this garden remains attractive until the end of the season, long after columbine flowers fade.

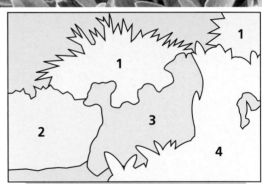

PHOTO KEY
1. Blue oat grass (*Helictotrichon sempervirens*); Zones 4 to 9
2. 'Dale's Strain' heuchera (*Heuchera americana* 'Dale's Strain'); Zones 4 to 9
3. Dwarf fan columbine (*Aquilegia flabellata* 'Nana'); Zones 3 to 9
4. Lamb's-ears (*Stachys byzantina*, also offered as *S. lanata*); Zones 4 to 8

Secrets for a Healthy Blue-and-Silver Mix

Replant heucheras to keep them happy. Heucheras are perennials for full sun or partial shade that thrive in rich, evenly moist soil that has good drainage. They have sturdy crowns that become woody as the plants age, and after a few years in the garden, the crowns tend to rise above the soil surface. In colder zones, low winter temperatures may damage crowns that are above ground. To keep plants healthy and prolong their life, lift the clumps in late summer or early fall, and replant with the crowns at soil level.

Extend the life of short-lived columbines. Columbines can be short-lived perennials, but they're well worth the effort it takes to keep them healthy and vigorous. Give them rich, well-drained soil and full sun to partial shade. They will self-sow readily, and young seedlings will gradually replace the older plants, which decline and disappear. Borers, which tunnel into the crown and hollow out the taproots as they feed, are one pest that shortens the life of columbines. Healthy plants that collapse dramatically are probably infested. To prevent borers, remove dead stalks and foliage at the end of the growing season. If you spot borers in a plant's stems, cut off and discard infected stems before the borers tunnel into the taproot.

Trim lamb's-ears when they flower. In early summer, lamb's-ears send up furry 1- to 1½ -foot-tall stalks with small magenta flowers that may be too tall for the edge of a bed. When your lamb's-ears get out of proportion, cut off the flower stalks to the ground. This keeps plants at the right height and makes the carpet of foliage thicker.

For a sharp color contrast to lighten a shady spot, try a pure white fan columbine (*Aquilegia flabellata* 'Nana Alba') with a brilliant scarlet azalea. Both will grow well in rich, well-drained soil and light to partial shade.

Give blue oat grass good drainage. Blue oat grass is an evergreen, cool-season ornamental grass that prefers full sun to light shade. It doesn't grow well in areas with hot, humid summers. In heavy clay or poorly drained conditions, root rot may be a problem.

165

A Shade-Loving Groundcover Mix

Wood ferns and long-blooming hardy cranesbills create a groundcover planting that transforms a lightly shaded spot from boring to beautiful. This combination is perfect for a spot with moist soil, and the plants will survive even in heavy clay. Blood-red cranesbill is one of the few cranesbills that will bloom all season—a spot that receives several hours of direct sun daily will ensure continuous bloom. Because of its contrasting foliage shapes and textures, this combination would work well under showy, spring-blooming shrubs or small trees, such as magnolias or serviceberries. Underplanting with spring bulbs will add early spring color.

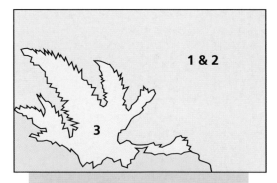

PHOTO KEY
1. **Blood-red cranesbill (***Geranium sanguineum***); Zones 3 to 8**
2. **Lancaster cranesbill (***Geranium sanguineum* **var.** *striatum***); Zones 3 to 8**
3. **Soft shield fern (***Polystichum setiferum***); Zones 6 to 8**

Secrets for Shade-Loving Groundcovers

&. **Try blood-red cranesbills in different colors.** Popular, free-blooming blood-red cranesbills thrive in rich, moist soil in sun or partial shade. Since established plants have extensive, fleshy roots, they can withstand some drought. Blood-red cranesbills come in a variety of colors and sizes suitable for a range of gardens. 'Album' has pure white, cup-shaped flowers on 8-inch-tall plants. 'Alpenglow' is a vigorous, 1- to 1½-foot tall, mat-forming selection with vibrant rosy flowers. 'Cedric Morris' has unusually large magenta flowers. 'Max Frei' forms 8-inch mounds studded with vivid red flowers. 'Shepherd's Warning' has vibrant rose-pink flowers on rounded, 6-inch-tall plants.

&. **Grow this adaptable, easy-care fern.** Soft shield fern, featured here, is a terrific garden plant that grows in full to partial shade but also tolerates sites that receive some sun each day. The arching fronds normally reach 2 feet in length but can be considerably longer in rich, moist soil. Plants spread gradually to form broad clumps, which you can divide for propagation or to keep the ferns from taking up too much room in the garden.

&. **Plant some shield ferns in dry soil.** Unlike many ferns, which require rich, moist soil to thrive, some evergreen shield ferns (*Polystichum* spp.) tolerate short periods of drought. Soft shield fern is one of the best for dry sites. Others that handle adversity include Christmas fern (*P. acrostichoides*), brittle fern (*P. polyblepharum*), Makino's holly fern (*P. makinoi*), and *P. rigens*.

&. **Try this combo for shade.** In a moist, shady spot, recreate the feel of this combination using male fern (*Drypoteris filix-mas*) with shade-loving, pink-flowered wild cranesbill (*Geranium maculatum*).

The brilliant yellow variegated leaves of hostas like 'Lakeside Symphony' or 'Gold Standard' are perfect for brightening up a dull, shady spot. To heighten their color, pair them with black-green *Helleborus foetidus*.

A Sumptuous Woodland Border

Bold drifts of perennials create an eye-catching combination, which is especially important in a garden like this that's viewed from afar. A planting composed of small clumps of many different plants will look jumbled and confusing from a distance. Planting large drifts is more successful because you can enjoy the overall effect of the combination, rather than be overwhelmed by a complex and visually confusing planting. This garden is planned with the tallest perennials in back and the shortest in front to create a transition between the trees and the lawn. The garden is at its peak of bloom in this early-summer view, but the bergenia and lady's-mantle foliage will add interest all season.

PHOTO KEY

1. **Black snakeroot (*Actaea [Cimicifuga] racemosa*); Zones 3 to 8**
2. **'Fujiyama' garden phlox (*Phlox paniculata* 'Fujiyama'); Zones 3 to 8**
3. **'Chatterbox' hybrid coral bells (*Heuchera* × *brizoides* 'Chatterbox'); Zones 3 to 8**
4. **Leather bergenia (*Bergenia crassifolia*); Zones 3 to 8**
5. **Lady's-mantle (*Alchemilla mollis*); Zones 3 to 8**
6. **'Loddon Anna' milky bellflower (*Campanula lactiflora* 'Loddon Anna'); Zones 3 to 7**
7. **'Palace Purple' heuchera (*Heuchera* 'Palace Purple'); Zones 4 to 8**

Plants for a Woodland Border

🌿 **Try dwarf bellflowers for small gardens.** Full-size milky bellflowers like 'Loddon Anna', pictured here, can reach 3 to 4 feet. If you have a small garden, you may want to try white-flowered 'Pouffe', a dwarf plant that grows just 2 feet tall.

🌿 **Consider what to plant where it's hot.** Milky bellflower thrives where summer days are moderate and summer nights are cool. In areas with hot days and humid, steamy nights, try substituting early phlox (*Phlox maculata*), which blooms at the same time. 'Omega' has light pink flowers similar to 'Loddon Anna'. 'Rosalind' is a deep pink selection of *Phlox carolina*. Black snakeroot is heat sensitive, too, so in hot climates, substitute Culver's root (*Veronicastrum virginicum*), which has similar spikes of white flowers.

🌿 **Plan for autumn beauty with snakeroot.** While black snakeroot (*Actaea* [*Cimicifuga*] *racemosa*) blooms in late spring and early summer, its relative Kamchatka bugbane (*A. simplex*), produces dramatic, 3- to 6-foot-tall wands of fragrant white flowers in September and early October. 'White Pearl' is compact and reaches only 3 feet, while 'Atropurpurea' is a purple-leaved selection.

🌿 **Prepare for a heuchera revolution.** 'Palace Purple', the first heuchera grown primarily for its leaves, produces clumps of bronzy red leaves that have a metallic luster and loose clusters of tiny whitish flowers in early summer. When plant breeders crossed it with silver-leaved selections of our native *Heuchera americana*, they started a revolution. Now, there are dozens of cultivars with showy silver and purple leaves, each more beautiful than the last. 'Pewter Veil' has silvery leaves,

Black snakeroot (*Actaea* [*Cimicifuga*] *racemosa*) produces spiky flowering candelabras in early summer. The tall spikes are perfect when contrasted with the mounding forms of meadow rue (*Thalictrum* spp.), phlox, and ferns.

while 'Montrose Ruby', 'Ruby Veil', and 'Plum Pudding' have maroon and silver mottled ones.

🌿 **Anticipate the trials of tree roots.** A woodland provides a dramatic backdrop, but also puts perennials in competition with greedy tree roots for water and nutrients. The simplest solution is to pull the bed forward, as far outside the drip line of the trees as possible. Place a path across the back to provide access for maintenance.

169

Early-Season Flowers for Shade

Snowdrops and garden hybrid hellebores bloom from late winter to early spring, taking advantage of the sunshine streaming through the still-bare branches of overhanging trees. By the time the trees leaf out the snow-drops will have flowered, and their foliage will have died back for the summer. The hellebores will finish flowering and their new umbrella-like leaves will expand to cover the spaces left by the snowdrops. The Italian arum leaves, which were green over winter, die back in summer, leaving behind pretty red berries that add interest in the shady months.

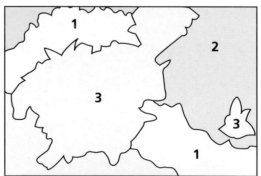

PHOTO KEY
1. **Common snowdrop (*Galanthus nivalis*); Zones 3 to 9**
2. **Italian arum (*Arum italicum*); Zones 6 to 9**
3. **Garden hybrid hellebore (*Helleborus* × *hybridus*); Zones 4 to 9**

Secrets for Decorating the Shade in Spring

🌿 **Clear away winter-worn foliage.** Even where winters are mild, the evergreen foliage of hellebores looks quite bedraggled by spring. As soon as the snow melts and before the flowers start to emerge, I cut off the old leaves. The flowers show off better when they aren't hidden by winter-browned foliage.

🌿 **Enjoy self-sown hellebores.** Hellebores are prolific self-seeders. Once you have a plant or two, you'll find seedlings coming up all over the garden, especially in gravel paths where the seeds settle in the crevices among the gravel. If you have the room, let your seedlings grow to blooming size to see which ones have the best flower form and color—you may find seedlings with creamy white, maroon, purple-pink, and white with maroon spots. Look them over carefully, and save the best. Dig up the plants that don't meet your standards. Unless you're ruthless, Lenten roses will fill up your garden in short order. Give your extras away, or pack them off to the compost pile.

🌿 **Grow undemanding snowdrops for early flowers.** Easy-to-grow snowdrops are undaunted by freezing temperatures—they can withstand being covered by snow even when in full bloom. They thrive for years without division, and they reseed prolifically. In time, they can form vast carpets, even in the dry shade of huge lawn trees. The most common species available is 4-inch-tall *Galanthus nivalis*, which blooms in late winter and early spring. 'Flore Pleno' is a double-flowered form. Giant snowdrop (*Galanthus elwesii*) blooms a little later and has larger

For the earliest bloom in shady gardens, plant hellebores (*H. orientalis*), which flower in late winter. Hellebores thrive in partial to full shade, provided they have sun in winter. They do best in rich, well-drained soil.

flowers with green spots at the base and tip of the inner petals. The 5- to 9-inch plants have broad, gray-green leaves. Or try fall-blooming *G. reginae-olgae*, which has dark green leaves that emerge after the flowers. It grows best in dry soil.

A No-Fail Pair for a Shady Site

Ajuga and spotted lamium are a shade gardener's dream. They feature beautiful flowers and foliage, yet both are so easy to grow they're almost indestructible. The silvery, green-edged foliage and snow white flowers of 'White Nancy' spotted lamium brighten up shady spots on even a dark day, and in this simple groundcover planting, they provide a bright contrast to the rich blue spikes of ajuga. Versatility is another advantage of this dynamic duo: Both plants grow in either moist or dry soil as well as partial or full shade.

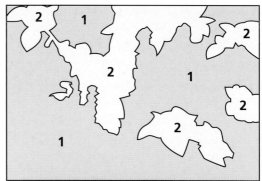

PHOTO KEY
1. Ajuga (*Ajuga reptans*, also offered as *A. repens*); Zones 3 to 9
2. 'White Nancy' dead nettle (*Lamium maculatum* 'White Nancy'); Zones 3 to 8

Tips for Easy-Care Shade Gardens

❧ **Mow old ajuga.** Carpets of ajuga are beautiful in bloom, but after the flowers fade, the old stalks look messy. Cutting down each stalk by hand is time-consuming, but your lawnmower makes it easy to keep your ajuga carpet looking great. Set the lawnmower blade at a height of 2 to 3 inches, and simply run it over the clumps after the flowers fade. The new leaves will grow in and fill out the carpet of foliage that lasts for the rest of the summer.

❧ **Color the shade with fabulous ajuga foliage.** Two of my favorites are 'Burgundy Glow' (sometimes sold as 'Tricolor'), which has leaves splashed with pink, white, and green, and 'Gray Lady', with gray-green leaves. 'Aboretum Giant' has large, leathery, 6-inch-long leaves edged in purple, and 'Bronze Beauty' has metallic, bronze-purple leaves and bright blue flowers. If you want a slow spreader, try 'Purple Brocade', which has deep purple, crinkled leaves.

❧ **Plant a combo for dry shade.** A planting of ajuga and spotted lamium is especially valuable for dry shade, one of the most difficult challenges shade gardeners face. Both plants will quickly carpet the ground under mature trees, along a shrub border, or on a shady slope.

❧ **Experiment with lamiums.** There are several choices of lamiums that you can combine with the ajugas mentioned above. 'Album' has white flowers and silver-striped leaves, and 'White Nancy' has silver leaves. If you prefer flowers with soft color, try 'Pink Pewter', which has silvery pink flowers. 'Aureum' has chartreuse leaves and pink flowers; 'Beedham's White' is similar, but has white flowers.

For a stunning but tough combination to plant under trees or shrubs, mix *Lamium maculatum*, which has rose-purple flowers, with the yellow-edged leaves and white flowers of *Lamium album* 'Friday'. This duo will even survive in dry areas under the eaves of your house.

A Tried-and-True Foliage Combination

Hostas and ferns, the mainstays of shade gardens across the country, thrive with a minimum of care, adapt to a wide range of sites, and look great. Contrasting textures make this combination a beauty: The bold foliage of 'Francee' hosta stands out against the finely cut feathery fronds of the maidenhair fern. Both plants remain attractive all season. Plant this combination in partial to full shade. Average to rich, moist, well-drained soil is ideal. Both plants will spread to form broad clumps in time.

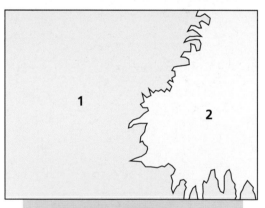

PHOTO KEY
1. 'Francee' hosta (*Hosta* 'Francee'); Zones 3 to 8
2. Maidenhair fern (*Adiantum pedatum*); Zones 3 to 8

Secrets for Successful Foliage Plantings

☙ **Lighten up the shade with variegated foliage.** Leaves splashed or edged with white or yellow are invaluable for adding long-lasting color to shady spots. White reflects light, making hostas and other plants with white-marked leaves especially useful for brightening up all-green foliage combinations.

☙ **Plan a layered garden.** Hostas need plenty of room to spread out their foliage, but they're slow to emerge and can leave gaps in the spring garden. To fill the gaps and enjoy two rounds of bloom in the same space, plant snowdrops, crocuses, and other early bulbs around the hosta clumps. The bulbs will bloom early, before the hostas emerge, and as they're going dormant, the unfurling hosta leaves will cover the yellowing bulb foliage.

☙ **Divide hostas on your schedule.** Hostas will grow for years without a lot of fuss, and eventually form huge, dramatic clumps. When they grow too big for their space, dig and divide them in either early spring or fall. Established clumps have such thick roots and dense crowns that you'll need a sharp knife or shears to cut the plant into sections. Another option is simply to slice them into sections with the blade of a sharp spade. Once replanted, the plants will recover so quickly you'll never even know they were disturbed.

☙ **Be patient with ferns.** Ferns have a reputation for being temperamental, but that's because most kinds take a year or two to settle in before they begin growing in earnest. Maidenhair ferns are especially slow the first year they're in the garden, but once established they'll form long-lived, luxuriant clumps.

Sweet woodruff (*Galium odoratum*) adds its lacy white flowers to this trio of shade-loving foliage plants, including silvery Japanese painted fern (*Athyrium niponicum* 'Pictum'), variegated *Hosta undulata* 'Univittata', and the rounded, lobed leaves of bloodroot (*Sanguinaria canadensis*).

A Spring Fling for the Shade

Mounds of wild blue phlox and comfrey fill a shady spot with soothing color in late spring. Wild blue phlox, a sweetly fragrant native woodland wildflower, blooms for several weeks in mid- to late spring. Once the creamy white comfrey flowers have faded, its broad, lance-shaped leaves will create a thick, textured groundcover that contrasts beautifully with the fine-textured phlox foliage. A clump of stiff Christmas fern fronds adds a vertical accent. Try this versatile combination in moist or dry soil in partial to full shade.

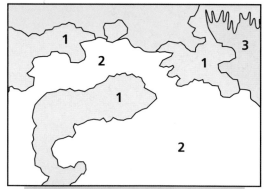

PHOTO KEY

1. Wild blue phlox (*Phlox divari-cata*); Zones 3 to 9
2. Comfrey (*Symphytum grandi-florum*); Zones 5 to 9
3. Christmas fern (*Polystichum acrostichoides*); Zones 3 to 8

Plants for a Spring Fling

🌿 **A fragrant woodland wildflower.** The fragrant flowers of wild blue phlox have endeared it to generations of gardeners. The plants produce loose clusters of ¾-inch flowers on erect, 10- to 15-inch-tall clumps above lance-shaped, evergreen leaves. They spread steadily to form broad clumps. As an added bonus, wild blue phlox also will self-sow where it's happy. While the species has powder blue flowers, several cultivars have been selected for color and fragrance. 'Clouds of Perfume' is an extremely fragrant selection with medium lavender-blue flowers. 'Fuller's White' is a compact, 8-inch-tall cultivar with pure white flowers. 'Blue Dreams' bears rich lilac-blue flowers on 10-inch plants.

🌿 **Tough, tolerant comfrey.** White comfrey is the perfect choice for a dry, shaded spot. The plants will form a dense, weed-free groundcover even in tough spots, such as around the roots of mature trees. Watch it carefully in richer soil, however. The plants can spread vigorously by rhizomes (underground stems) and become quite invasive. Small pieces of rhizome left in the soil grow into full-size plants. White comfrey is related to common comfrey (*Symphytum officinale*), an herb used to make dye and medicinally to soothe and soften the skin, to heal broken bones, and to cleanse wounds.

🌿 **A handsome, easy fern.** Christmas fern is an adaptable, easy-to-grow fern that makes a great plant for nearly any shade garden. The ferns thrive in moist, rich soils and grow in light to full shade. They'll tolerate tougher conditions as well, because this is one of the most drought-tolerant ferns. They will grow on dry banks and even in heavy clay soil. The evergreen fronds have been gathered for hol-

Drifts of wild blue phlox highlight a planting of spring-blooming perennials. As you can see, wild blue phlox isn't always blue.

iday decorations since colonial times. That's why it's called Christmas fern.

🌿 **Spores spell new ferns.** Take a look at the tips of mature Christmas fern fronds, and you'll see that the individual leaflets, called pinnae, are narrow and crinkled. Turn them over and you'll see brown undersides. This is not a disease, it's the fern's equivalent of flowers—the part of the frond where the spores are produced. Once the dust-size spores are released into the air, the ones that settle onto moist soil and germinate eventually will form new ferns.

A Soothing Mix for a Woodland Path

Bold clumps of strap-shaped hosta leaves make a stunning partner for the delicate-looking flowers of creeping phlox. The hosta is by far the boldest plant in this low-growing, shade-loving combination, which borders a woodland path. Its leaves stand out against the contrasting fine-textured phlox flowers and the grasslike variegated black sedge. Heart-shaped epimedium leaves add a rounded shape to the mix and create a backdrop for the hostas. In early spring, the pale yellow epimedium flowers complement the emerging yellow-edged hostas. If you can't find a nursery that sells rohdea-leaf hosta, try substituting *Hosta helonioides* 'Albopicta'.

PHOTO KEY
1. **Variegated black sedge (*Carex nigra* 'Variegata'); Zones 3 to 9**
2. **'Sulphureum' Persian epimedium (*Epimedium* × *versicolor* 'Sulphureum'); Zones 4 to 8**
3. **Rohdea-leaf hosta (*Hosta rohdeifolia*); Zones 3 to 8**
4. **'Porter's Purple' creeping phlox (*Phlox stolonifera* 'Porter's Purple'); Zones 3 to 8**

Plants for a Woodland Mix

Subtle sedges. Sedges are grasslike plants that often are overlooked in the garden, but their beauty lies in their subtlety. I use their fine texture to contrast with bolder leaves. Many have very short stems, so the leaves often radiate directly from the crown to form handsome, low mounds. When stems are present, you'll be able to see the characteristic that distinguishes these plants from grasses: The stems don't have joints, as true grasses do, and they're triangular in cross section, so they have three distinct edges. The variegated black sedge in this combination produces low clumps of evergreen leaves. Grow it in evenly moist soil.

A charming woodland creeper. Creeping phlox is a versatile, easy-to-grow woodland wildflower that spreads steadily to form a dense evergreen groundcover of shiny leaves. Its trailing stems root as they grow. Best of all, you'll find a color to fit every design. This combination features 'Porter's Purple', but you may also want to grow 'Bruce's White', which has white flowers with a yellow center. 'Iridescens' has lavender flowers flushed with blue and 'Melrose' has rich pink flowers. Once the flowers fade, cut the stalks to the ground to keep the clumps tidy and to encourage thick, healthy mats of foliage.

Groundcovers with early spring flowers. Epimediums are among the earliest perennials to bloom in spring. The flowers emerge before the foliage in shades of yellow, rose, purple-pink, orange, and white. Once the leaves appear, they quickly form dense, 6- to 12-inch-tall mats that weeds rarely penetrate. Epimediums thrive in partial to full shade and rich, well-drained, evenly moist soil, but established plants will grow well in dry shade as well. The leaves of many epimediums are

Variegated grasses, such as variegated hakone grass (*Hakonechloa macra* 'Aureola'), light up shady gardens. The frothy white flowers and dark leaves of *Rodgersia sambucifolia* and the pink plumes of *Filipendula purpurea* add a richly colored backdrop.

evergreen in warmer zones, and some leaves may overwinter in the north. Either way, cut down the old foliage in late winter, before the flower stalks begin to show; otherwise, the foliage will detract from the spring flowers.

A Fanciful Foliage Combination

Most shade-loving perennials bloom in spring, so by the time summer rolls around, foliage is the focus of shade plantings like this one. Bold hosta leaves form the focal point, while a drift of silver-mottled heuchera creates a striking contrast in both color and shape. Silver-leaved pulmonarias add a bright white accent that echoes the dainty white flowers of corydalis. This group of shade-loving perennials will do best in rich, moist soil; in dry conditions, the plants will suffer or go dormant. By filling shady spots with perennials like these in a rich mix of foliage textures and colors, it's possible to keep your garden looking great right up to fall.

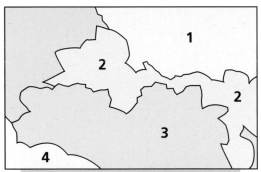

PHOTO KEY
1. Pale corydalis (*Corydalis ochroleuca*); Zones 5 to 8
2. 'Albo-picta' Fortune's hosta (*Hosta fortunei* 'Albo-picta'); Zones 3 to 8
3. 'Pewter Veil' heuchera (*Heuchera* 'Pewter Veil'); Zones 4 to 8
4. 'Excalibur' pulmonaria (*Pulmonaria* 'Excalibur'); Zones 4 to 8

Secrets for Stunning Foliage

🌺 **Try easy-care corydalis.** Corydalis may be new to you, but it's well worth trying. Flowering begins in spring and continues all summer, even in the shade. It self-sows freely but is seldom invasive—if you have too many plants, just pull them up. In addition to creamy-flowered *Corydalis ochroleuca*, pictured here, try yellow-flowered *C. lutea* or *C. flexuosa*, which bears beautiful, true-blue flowers. *C. flexuosa* is hardy to about Zone 5, but the plants don't tolerate high heat in summer. Some gardeners grow *C. flexuosa* with ease; others find it temperamental. In my cool Minnesota garden, I find it needs more light than other species. I give it four to six hours of direct sun. I also mulch it with marsh hay in the winter.

🌺 **Grow striking foliage plants for shade.** For foliage color and texture in shade, don't just stick to well-known choices like hostas. Variegated Solomon's seal (*Polygonatum odoratum* 'Variegatum') has featherlike stalks of oval leaves with a creamy edge. Variegated Siberian bugloss (*Brunnera macrophylla* 'Variegata') has heart-shaped leaves with wide, creamy margins accented by sky-blue flowers in spring. Epimediums, hellebores, and ferns also have striking, deeply cut leaves that add textural interest long after the flowers are gone.

🌺 **Add a tropical touch with tender perennials.** Many tender perennials have foliage that adds pizzazz to any shady spot in summer. Coleus thrives in shade and comes in an astounding array of patterns. Elephant's ear (*Colocasia esculenta*) gives shady spots a lush tropical look, as do the caladiums, which come in a rainbow of colors. I grow sun-loving cannas in partial to full shade. They don't bloom as heavily, but the foliage is lush and tropical.

The strappy leaves of Japanese roof iris (*Iris tectorum*) add punch to a shade garden. The striped leaves of variegated broad-leaved sedge (*Carex siderostica* 'Variegata') echo the shape of the iris leaves, while purple-green 'Palace Purple' heuchera makes a restful foreground.

A Long-Blooming Mix for Clay

Long-flowering perennials that create soothing color echoes and bright contrasts create a winning combination for any sunny site with clay soil. The yellow daisies of Coreopsis 'Moonbeam' cover the plants nonstop from early summer to fall. The royal purple petals of early-blooming asters contrast with the coreopsis, while the buttonlike centers of the aster flowers echo the soft yellow of the coreopsis. Behind the fine-textured coreopsis and asters, the green broccoli-like heads of 'Autumn Joy' sedum form a bold, solid mass. The sedum will become the focal point once its rosy flowers begin to open. By fall, they will age to rusty red, still accompanied by the coreopsis.

Secrets for Long-Blooming Perennials

 A beautiful 'Moonbeam'. 'Moonbeam' coreopsis is so tough, versatile, and easy-to-grow that it was voted Perennial Plant of the Year in 1993. All coreopsis thrive in full sun and average to rich soil, and plants will grow in clay as long as it's well drained. Once established, coreopsis are quite drought-tolerant. 'Moonbeam' forms 1- to 2-foot mounds that literally bloom for months. Shearing or deadheading the plants regularly helps keep the flowers coming.

 More great coreopsis. If you love brilliant, rich yellow, try other cultivars of *Coreopsis verticillata*. You'll get the same fine-textured foliage and a wealth of blooms. 'Golden Showers' forms 1½- to 2-foot-tall mounds with golden yellow flowers. 'Zagreb', also with golden yellow flowers, is a dwarf se-

lection that tops out at about 1 foot and is perfect for the front of a bed or border.

 Dwarf asters for the front of the border. Dwarf asters stay under 15 inches tall, and a few are even shorter, making them excellent plants for adding color to the front or the middle of beds and borders. Most dwarf asters are either hybrids or cultivars of New York aster (*Aster novi-belgii*). 'Audrey' is 1 foot tall with lilac flowers. 'Royal Opal' has white flowers flushed with blue. 'Snow Cushion' has white flowers on 8-inch plants. 'Violet Carpet', also 8 inches tall, has rich violet flowers. To keep even dwarf asters extra small and compact, pinch or shear the stems back to 6 inches in June. They will resprout from side shoots and bloom, forming a colorful carpet of flowers.

Sedum 'Autumn Joy' thrives in some of the toughest garden conditions. It tolerates heavy clay and poor, dry soil, and it blooms right through summer heat and drought. Plus, it looks great with many other perennials, including bear's-breeches (*Acanthus* spp.), artemisias, and lavender.

A Cottage-Style Mix for Clay

Awealth of summer-blooming perennials mixed together in a cottage-style design create an appealing garden that anyone would admire. The bright mix of colors is typical of plantings of free-spirited cottage gardeners. All the plants in this garden are tough, deep rooted perennials that thrive in clay soil as well as in many other soil types. Fleshy tap-roots allow coneflowers to probe deeply for water, and the thick tuberous roots of daylilies are expert clay-busters. Long after flowers fade, the black-eyed Susan seedheads will carry the garden through the winter season, crowned by caps of snow.

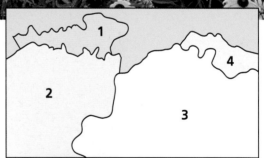

PHOTO KEY
1. **'Little Fellow' daylily** (*Hemerocallis* 'Little Fellow'); Zones 3 to 9
2. **'Stella de Oro' daylily** (*Hemerocallis* 'Stella de Oro'); Zones 3 to 9
3. **Black-eyed Susan** (*Rudbeckia fulgida* var. *speciosa*); Zones 4 to 8
4. **White purple coneflower** (*Echinacea purpurea* 'Alba'); Zones 3 to 8

Expert Tips for Cottage-Garden Style

Try a different black-eyed Susan.
Gardeners everywhere are familiar with the orange-yellow daises of 'Goldsturm' black-eyed Susans. I find them a bit stiff looking and prefer some of their more informal relations. For the relaxed look of a cottage garden, *Rudbeckia fulgida* var. *speciosa,* pictured here, is a good substitute. Like 'Goldsturm', it blooms nonstop, but the stems are more delicate, the plant is more open, and the slightly smaller flowers have drooping petals that aren't as stiff. Plants are easy to grow, and they thrive in full sun or partial shade in almost any soil.

Rely on daylilies. Daylilies are one of the toughest garden perennials you can grow. (Proof: The garden of a friend who lives near the ocean was flooded with salt water for 2 months after a hurricane. Every plant in the garden died except the daylilies.) Their thick, fleshy roots store vast amounts of food and water, providing reserves designed to help them through cold winters and dry summers. That's why daylilies are so easy to grow in clay soils: They love the moisture when it's available in winter and spring, and they have ample reserves to thrive in summer as clay soil dries out. Although they bloom best in the sun, they also thrive in a wide range of light conditions, from full sun to partial shade.

Take a taste of daylilies. Daylilies aren't just tough and beautiful, they're edible, too. The flowers are delicious eaten raw in salads or fried in a light tempura batter. The buds are great when steamed like asparagus or stir-fried with vegetables or tofu. Next time you're in the garden, pick off a fresh petal or two and give them a try. Different cultivars actually have different flavors. You can spend a day discovering your best-tasting daylily.

If you have tough clay soil, rely on combinations featuring easy-care daylilies like 'Cherry Cheeks', a stunning hybrid that produces a profusion of huge, 6-inch flowers.

Let seeds fall where they may. In this "anything goes" style of garden, plants are free to seed where they will, and volunteers are welcome additions. In this combination, the black-eyed Susans and coneflowers all self-sow if you leave their seedheads in place. They look great in winter, and birds appreciate the seeds. Self-sowing annuals like cleome (*Cleome hassierana*) also work well in cottage-style gardens.

Showy Summer Flowers for Clay

Few plants beat these showy summer bloomers for dressing up a site with heavy clay soil. That's because they're all descended from plants that grow wild in heavy clay soils along streams and in wetlands. They'll grow in well-drained conditions, too, and will provide a month or more of color in a spot with full sun or light shade. A large, dense mound of rosy pink bee balm takes center stage. The salmon-flushed pink daylilies echo the color of the bee balm and add a mass of bolder texture. Obedient plant weaves through the garden, popping up wherever space allows.

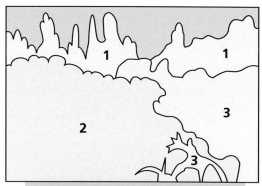

PHOTO KEY
1. 'Summer Snow' obedient plant (*Physostegia virginiana* 'Summer Snow'); Zones 3 to 9
2. 'Marshall's Delight' bee balm (*Monarda* 'Marshall's Delight'); Zones 4 to 8
3. Daylily (*Hemerocallis* hybrid); Zones 3 to 9

More Plants for Showy Blooms

❧ Species daylilies change the pace.
Species daylilies may not be as showy as some hybrid daylilies, but they're beautiful and graceful in the garden, and many are fragrant, as well. Some of the best include early daylily (*Hemerocallis dumortieri*), which has brown buds that open to yellow flowers in spring; lemon daylily (*H. lilioasphodelus*), with lemon yellow flowers unsurpassed for their heady fragrance; and Middendorff daylily (*H. middendorfii*), which has fragrant, yellow to orange flowers.

❧ Hybrid bee balms have lots to offer.
Many hybrid bee balms are crosses between bee balm (*Monarda didyma*), a long-flowering species with scarlet or violet flowers, and wild bergamot (*M. fistulosa*), which has pink to soft lavender flowers. While wild bergamot is native to dry fields, prairies, and high plains, bee balm grows in wet ditches and meadows. Bee balm contributes its rich color to these hybrids, while wild bergamot offers resistance to powdery mildew. One of the best hybrids is 'Marshall's Delight', which features rich pink color, disease resistance, and nonstop flowering. 'Gardenview Scarlet' and 'Jacob Kline' are brilliant red and mildew-resistant. 'Blue Stocking' has violet flowers, while 'Beauty of Cobham' is pink.

❧ Obedient plants add plenty of color.
A variety of hybrid obedient plants have lots to offer gardeners as well. While the regular species is a soft rosy pink, gardeners can opt for a brighter hue by planting 'Vivid', a cultivar that bears brilliant rose-colored flowers. 'Variegata', with rose-pink flowers, features leaves with creamy white margins. 'Summer Snow', shown in this grouping, is quite a departure, because its pure white flowers open a month before the other selections. It's also slower spreading—another desirable trait, because obedient plant can actually be quite disobedient, taking over the garden.

Two great clay-busters— dense blazing-star (*Liatris spicata* 'Kobold') and an old-fashioned yellow-flowered daylily—make a fantastic pair for heavy soil. They'll tolerate winter wet and summer drought and still bloom to perfection in mid-summer.

PHOTO KEY

1. Swamp sunflower (*Helianthus simulans*); Zones 6 to 9
2. Porcupine grass (*Miscanthus sinensis* var. *strictus*); Zones 4 to 9
3. Giant sunflower (*Helianthus giganteus*); Zones 3 to 9
4. 'Gold Sword' Adam's needle (*Yucca filamentosa* 'Gold Sword'); Zones 5 to 10 (4 with protection)

A Cheerful Combo for Dry Clay Soil

Instead of breaking your back trying to improve dry clay soil, let tough, adaptable perennials with deep, probing roots do the work for you. Giant sunflower, with its exuberant masses of yellow daisies, simply defies the difficult conditions of this dry clay garden. The golden-striped yucca foliage echoes the yellow flowers and creates a spiky-textured carpet under them. The yellow-striped foliage of the porcupine grass, just visible behind the sunflowers, also echoes the yellow theme.

Plants for Gardens with Dry Clay Soil

☙ Meet the perennial sunflowers. The best-known sunflowers are annuals, but they have some beautiful perennial cousins that make excellent garden plants. All are suitable for clay soil and offer a month or more of nonstop bloom in late summer and fall. After the flowers fade, their seeds provide food for birds. In addition to giant sunflower (*Helianthus giganteus*) and swamp sunflower (*H. simulans*), which are featured in this combination, consider trying thin-leaved sunflower (*H. decapetalus*), a 4- to 6-foot-tall plant topped by masses of pale yellow 2- to 3-inch flowers in late summer. Willow leaf sunflower (*H. salicifolius*) produces fountains of handsome, threadlike, gray-green leaves and narrow clusters of flowers in fall. Huge maximilian sunflower (*H. maximiliani*) produces 8-foot stalks with spiky clusters of rich yellow flowers in fall.

☙ Love your yucca. Yuccas are invaluable garden plants, especially in tough sites. They'll grow in dry clay or sandy soil, and they thrive in full sun or light shade despite heat and drought. Their stiff, spiky leaves add height and drama to the garden and are the perfect contrasting companions for fine textures and rounded or creeping plants. They also produce huge branched flowerheads of waxy, nodding white blossoms in summer.

☙ Choose the best variegated grass. There are several types of Japanese silver grass (*Miscanthus* spp.) with yellow banded leaves. Porcupine grass, pictured here, and zebra grass (*M. sinensis* 'Zebrinus') are 5 to 6 feet tall and have striking horizontal yellow bands across their green leaves. Porcupine grass is more upright and stronger than zebra grass, which tends to flop over in midsummer. The best of all may be *Miscanthus sinensis* 'Tiger Cub', which is very compact and sturdy. Dwarf 'Little Dot', barely 3 feet tall, is ideal for small gardens. All Japanese silver grass cultivars produce feathery flower plumes in late summer, which will look attractive through the winter. Here's a hint: If your grass tends to flop, try tying it at the base to keep it standing longer.

Clumps of 'Gold Sword' Adam's needle surrounded by the lacy flowers of hardy ageratum (*Eupatorium coelestinum*) make a showy late-summer combination that thrives in clay soil.

A Native Perennial Border for Clay

For a wealth of late-spring bloom on a site with clay soil, try planting combinations of wildflowers native to the eastern United States. In this garden, a carpet of pink smooth phlox forms the focal point, while a large, shrublike mound of willow blue star adds a vertical accent. All of these tough wildflowers thrive in a garden where the soil is moist in spring but may get dry in summer. Plant them in full sun or light shade. For best results, work organic matter, such as compost, into the soil at planting time—you'll reap the benefit of more vigorous and free-flowering plants.

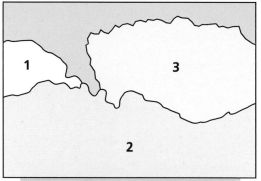

PHOTO KEY
1. Foxglove penstemon (*Penstemon digitalis*); Zones 4 to 8
2. Smooth phlox (*Phlox glaberrima* ssp. *triflora*); Zones 4 to 8
3. Willow blue star (*Amsonia tabernaemontana*); Zones 4 to 9

Wildflowers for a Border in Clay Soil

&. Beautiful blue stars. Blue stars are native wildflowers that gardeners love because of their starry, steel blue spring flowers, their attractive, pest-free foliage, and their bright orange and russet fall color. Willow blue star, pictured here, has shiny, lance-shaped leaves and round clusters of steel blue flowers on 2- to 3-foot stems. Arkansas blue star (*A. hubrectii*) has needlelike leaves that turn brilliant orange and gold in fall. All blue stars thrive in average to rich soil in light to partial shade. They tolerate full sun in the North.

&. Penstemons for clay soil. Penstemons have a reputation for being difficult to grow. That's because they need full sun, cool nights, and good drainage, and for gardeners in the East and Midwest, these conditions aren't easy to achieve. Luckily, there are native eastern penstemons that grow in both heavy soil and sultry summers. The foxglove penstemon used in this combination is one of the easiest to grow, in sun or shade, and it even tolerates wet soil. For a drier spot in heavy clay, try gray penstemon (*Penstemon canescens*), with pale pink flowers; hairy penstemon (*P. hirsutus*), with purple flowers; or Small's penstemon (*P. smallii*), with rose-pink blooms.

&. More groundcover phlox. Gardeners familiar with the tall border phloxes may be surprised to discover the early-blooming groundcover species. These natives of open woods and roadsides thrive in rich, well-drained soil and partial shade. Creeping phlox (*Phlox stolonifera*) produces prostrate mats of foliage and 4-inch-tall stalks crowned with pink, white, or lilac-blue flowers in midspring. Wild blue phlox (*P. divaricata*) has fragrant blue flowers, and many beautiful cultivars are available. The hybrid 'Chattahoochee' is

Make a bold statement in a clay-soil garden with meadow perennials in contrasting colors. Plant bright yellow 'Zagreb' coreopsis; towering 'Herbstsonne' coneflower; and airy, purple-flowered butterfly bush (*Buddleja davidii* 'Petite Indigo') against a backdrop of tall evergreens.

slightly later-flowering and has lavender-blue flowers with red centers.

&. More wildflowers for light shade. There are several other native wildflowers that you could add to this combination, including purple coneflower (*Echinacea purpurea*), Bowman's root (*Gillenia trifoliata*), blue false indigo (*Baptisia australis*), Culver's root (*Veronicastrum virginicum*), and woodland sunflower (*Helianthus divaricatus*).

PHOTO KEY
1. Variegated Japanese silver grass (*Miscanthus sinensis* 'Variegatus'); Zones 4 to 9
2. 'Ogon' dwarf sweet flag (*Acorus gramineus* 'Ogon'); Zones 5 to 8
3. Perennial nemesia (*Nemesia fruticans* 'Alba'); Zones 9 to 11

Fountains of Grass from Heavy Soil

A huge, vase-shaped clump of variegated Japanese silver grass takes center stage in this combination, with golden variegated dwarf sweet flag accenting it at the base. Low-growing perennial nemesia weaves among the grasses. If you garden north of Zone 9, substitute sweet woodruff (*Galium odoratum*) for the nemesia. Many ornamental grasses are a great choice for making a bold display in gardens with clay soil. The beauty of ornamental grasses lies in their fountainlike form, coupled with their airy flower plumes and seedheads. The seedheads are beautiful in the garden through fall and even into the winter, plus you can cut them and bring them indoors for dried flower arrangements.

Secrets for Fountains of Grass

🍃 **Select just the right silver grass.** This combination features variegated Japanese silver grass, which is beautiful but tends to flop open as the flower plumes emerge. To avoid that problem, you can substitute the cultivar 'Morning Light', which has narrow leaves edged in creamy white. 'Sarabande' is similar. If you want a grass with broad leaves, try 'Cabaret', which has a wide white stripe down the broad leaves. 'Cosmopolitan' also has wide, striped leaves and an upright habit.

🍃 **Divide silver grass one clump at a time.** Japanese silver grass can produce huge clumps over time. Eventually, the clump be gins to die out in the middle and loses its lovely fountainlike appearance. To rejuvenate the plant, you need to divide it. I sometimes wish for a backhoe and a chain saw when I have to divide large ornamental grasses, because the root systems are deep, and the crown is several feet across. The easiest way is to lift sections of the clump one at a time. You may need to use an ax, a pick, or a mattock to cut off divisions from the plant. Keep as much root attached to the divisions as possible. Discard the dead central portion, amend the soil with rich compost, and replant a healthy clump.

🍃 **Plant a pot of gold.** The cream and green fountains of variegated dwarf sweet flag look like pots of gold set into the garden. This attractive, easy-care groundcover is often called an ornamental grass, but it's actually a type of plant called an arum, related to the jack-in-the-pulpit. The tight clumps form overlapping fans of leaves that create a full, fountainlike appearance. In the wild, sweet flags are native to wetlands, but they're very adaptable in the garden. They thrive in sun or shade, in wet or average

A fountain of Japanese silver grass is the focal point in this clay soil garden that features the combination shown on the opposite page. Clumps of lamb's-ears continue the silvery color theme along the path.

soil. They may need watering during droughty conditions. Crush some of the foliage or break the roots and you'll notice the scent of citrus. 'Licorice' sweet flag has bright green leaves and smells of anise.

A Combination for Sand and Sun

While perfect, humus-rich loam is ideal for many popular perennials, here's a simple but stunning duo that thrives in poor to average sandy soil. The fine-textured, silver-gray stems of artemisia make a lovely backdrop for the bright, rosy purple flowers of wallflower. Both plants need full sun, and they'll form rounded clumps that are smothered in flowers in early summer. To add contrasting textures and shapes in this planting, try adding a clump of spiky-leaved yucca or a bearded iris, which also features stiff swordlike leaves and is quite drought tolerant.

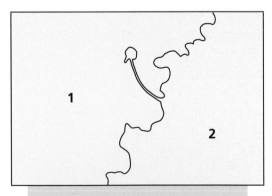

PHOTO KEY
1. **'Silver King' artemisia** (*Artemisia ludoviciana* **'Silver King'**); Zones 3 to 9
2. **Persian wallflower** (*Erysimum linifolium*); Zones 7 to 9

Secrets for Successful Sandy Gardens

❧ **Feed sandy soil with organic matter.**
Sandy soil is challenging for gardeners because
it's low in nutrients and prone to drought. The
good news is that many perennials require the
quick drainage that only sand provides. The
key to success with sandy soil is to add plenty
of organic matter such as compost at planting
time, and replenish it annually. (Organic
matter helps hold water and nutrients in the
soil.) Keep the soil mulched—shredded leaves
or pine needles are attractive choices for
perennial gardens—and water during periods
of drought.

❧ **Grow wonderful wallflowers.** Few
plants are as lovely and easy-to-please as wallflowers (*Erysimum* spp.). Give them full sun
and well-drained neutral to alkaline soil, and
they're completely satisfied. Their blooms
begin opening as soon as the weather warms in
spring. If deadheaded, plants will bloom off
and on all season, especially in areas where
nights are cool. Wallflowers are tender, short-
lived perennials that last only two to three

years in areas where they're hardy. Plant new
plants each spring, or take cuttings after flowering or in fall and overwinter them indoors in
a cool, sunny window.

❧ **Experiment with artemisias.** To add
coarser texture to this combination, substitute
'Silver Brocade' artemisia (*Artemisia stelleriana*
'Silver Brocade'). Its deeply cut leaves resemble
small oak leaves, and the plants tolerate tough
conditions, including salt spray. Common
wormwood (*A. absinthium*) is taller, with gray-
green leaves on mounded, 2-foot-tall plants;
'Lambrook Silver' has rich silver-gray leaves.
For more height, try shrubby, 3-foot-tall
'Powis Castle' artemisia, which has finely dis-
sected, silvery leaves.

❧ **Prune artemisia to keep it bushy.** After
flowering, artemisias frequently flop open and
look downright ratty, especially in areas with
hot, humid summer weather. When the plants
flop open, cut the stems back to the ground,
and fresh, attractive growth will soon appear.

'Silver Mound' artemisia
creates a river of silver
between black-eyed Su-
sans in this simple, easy-
care combination for a
sunny, sandy site. Unlike
other artemisias, 'Silver
Mound' forms neat
mounds of foliage that
are about a foot tall.

A Combination for Color and Fragrance

Showy flowers, handsome foliage, and rich fragrance make this easy-care combination a winner. The flat-topped clusters of yarrow, borne above mounds of fernlike gray-green leaves, provide color for over a month in early summer. Cut back the flowers as they fade and enjoy repeat bloom into early fall. The bright green, grassy leaves and round, rosy purple blooms of the chives accent the yarrow in form, foliage, and color, while low-growing thyme and Mexican daisy form a carpet of color that weaves the planting together.

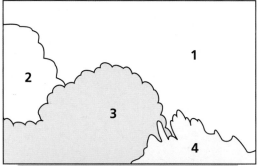

PHOTO KEY
1. 'Moonshine' yarrow (*Achillea* 'Moonshine'); Zones 3 to 8
2. Mexican daisy (*Erigeron karvin-skianus*); Zones 5 to 7
3. Common chives (*Allium schoenoprasum*); Zones 3 to 9
4. Thyme (*Thymus vulgaris*); Zones 4 to 8

Expert Tips for Rich Color and Pungent Fragrance

❧ **Please touch these plants.** We all use our sight to appreciate gardens, but we often forget to use the senses of touch and smell. To enjoy this combination to the fullest, you need to use all your senses. Feel the velvety texture of the gray-green yarrow leaves and enjoy their pungent aroma. Then run your fingers through the clumps of smooth, hollow, grassy chive leaves, and brush the soft mats of thyme foliage. Pinch off a leaf or two to get a whiff of their distinctive scents, and carry them around the garden with you.

❧ **Meet a little daisy that never stops.** Blooming, that is. All season long, the Mexican daisies in this combination produce clouds of rosy pink buds that open into white flowers, creating a two-toned effect that adds to the plants' charm. In areas where the plants aren't hardy, they still come back year after year because they're prolific self-seeders. Try Mexican daisies in one of your gardens, and plants soon appear everywhere, even in cracks in the pavement and in gravel walkways.

❧ **Give herbs poor soil to get pungent aromas.** Rich, moist soil doesn't bring out the best in most herbs. Instead, poor, sandy soil that's well drained and contains a good complement of organic matter yields plants with the best fragrance and flavor.

❧ **Dry some yarrow for indoor color.** Yarrow is a delightful cut flower, and its blooms hold their color when dried, as well. Cut them just as the flowers begin to open, leaving as long a stalk as possible. Strip off the leaves, bind them into loose bundles, and hang them upside down in a warm, dark place to dry.

For a contrasting color combination on a sandy, sunny site, plant snow-in-summer (*Cerastium tomentosum*) beside tall purple spikes of Rocky Mountain penstemon (*Penstemon strictus*) and yellow 'Moonshine' yarrow flowers.

Long-Blooming Prairie Perennials

F iery sage, luscious purple poppy mallow, and true blue Texas bluebonnets glow in this long-blooming combination that's perfect for a sandy site. All three of these plants are native to the high plains of states like Kansas, Missouri, and Texas, so they're adapted to well-drained sandy soil and can withstand heat and drought. Poppy mallow blooms all season long, as does the autumn sage, keeping this combination lively even in the dog days of summer. Cut back the spent flower spikes of the sage in mid-summer to encourage new growth and blossoms. Texas bluebonnets add a splash of spring color, then fade away after blooming.

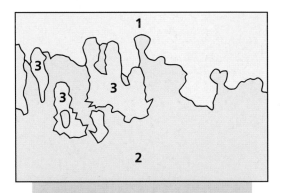

PHOTO KEY
1. Autumn sage (*Salvia greggii*); Zones 7 to 9
2. Poppy mallow (*Callirhoe involucrata*); Zones 4 to 9
3. Texas bluebonnet (*Lupinus texensis*); Zones 6 to 9

Techniques for Prairie Perennials

❧ Reseed Texas bluebonnets for yearly bloom. Several wild species of lupines (*Lupinus* spp.) are known as bluebonnets. Most are perennials, but the Texas bluebonnet featured in this combination is a true annual. To succeed with this popular wildflower, you need well-drained, neutral or alkaline soil and full sun. Sow the seeds on a well-prepared seedbed. Plants will self-sow where conditions are to their liking, but if you want to grow Texas bluebonnets outside their native range, you'll need to sow fresh seed each year.

❧ Pick a lupine to suit your soil. If bluebonnets aren't native to your area, try another lupine instead. If you live in the Plains states and have alkaline soil, try silky lupine (*L. sericeus*). If you live in the Midwest or the East and have acid soil, plant wild lupine (*L. perennis*). Both are perennial and are available from wildflower nurseries.

❧ Give poppy mallows plenty of sun. Poppy mallows (*Callirhoe involucrata*) are powerhouse perennials that bloom nonstop from spring through frost. Though they're native to warm southern regions, they're hardy to Zone 4. The beautiful flowers open from delicately twisted buds and close each evening. The variety *tenuissima* has soft lavender flowers. Winecups (*C. digitata*) grows upright, with rich red-purple flowers and 1- to 3-foot wiry stems. Full sun and good drainage are the keys to success with poppy mallow and winecups.

❧ Shear autumn sage for best results. Autumn sage is a long bloomer that's perfect for continuous color in Zone 7 and warmer. The plants get shrubby with age, but you can reduce their size and stimulate fresh new growth by shearing them in spring. Give plants full sun and well-drained soil with a little extra humus added, and the plants will flower until frost.

Texas sage (*Salvia texana*) produces spikes of rich blue flowers on compact plants. Watch for this new perennial in wildflower catalogs. Pair it with yellow sundrops (*Calylophus serrulatus*) in sandy soil for a flowering show in spring and early summer.

A Summer-Long Mix for Sandy Soil

Pale pink and bright yellow make a pleasing color contrast in this late-spring combination. A cheerful clump of golden yellow lily leeks with strappy, gray-green leaves stands out against the soft colors and finer textures of the surrounding plants. By midsummer, the lily leeks will have gone dormant, leaving behind their starry, dried seedheads. By then, foliage colors, shapes, and textures become the focus of this planting. Mounds of maplelike bigroot geranium foliage will draw attention, and the fernlike, gray-green prairie smoke leaves will add a delicate note of contrasting texture.

PHOTO KEY
1. **Prairie smoke (*Geum triflorum*);** Zones 2 to 8
2. **Lily leek (*Allium moly*); Zones** 3 to 9
3. **Bigroot cranesbill (*Geranium macrorrhizum*); Zones 3 to 8**

Secrets for Dry-Soil Flowers and Foliage

🌰 **Grow bigroot cranesbill for foliage and flowers.** Bigroot cranesbill produces broad, felted leaves that have a rich, musky odor. This adaptable plant also features pink flowers in early summer. The cultivar 'Album' has white flowers, while 'Bevan's Variety' is a low, spreading plant with magenta flowers. 'Ingwerson's Variety' has pale pink flowers and glossy leaves. 'Spessart' has dark rose-pink flowers.

🌰 **Plant a prairie native named for its seeds.** A wildflower native to dry prairies, prairie smoke is an easy-to-grow plant that forms a bright green groundcover of ferny leaves accented in summer by rose-pink flowers. The name prairie smoke refers to the plumed seedheads, which are composed of long, fuzzy strands with the seed attached at the bottom. They emerge pink and fade to smoky white as they age, suggesting a smoldering prairie fire.

🌰 **Rely on bulbs in dry, sandy soil.** Lily leeks are ornamental onions that grow from bulbs, and they can withstand hot, dry summers because the bulbs store water and nutrients. After the plants bloom, the foliage fades back for the rest of the season, and the plants draw on their underground reserves to survive the long dormant period.

🌰 **Learn more ways that plants survive drought.** Bigroot cranesbill is named for its thick, fleshy stems, called rhizomes, and its deep taproots. These water-storing organs help the plant endure dry conditions in much the same way bulbs do. Unlike a bulb, however, the rhizomes trap enough water to enable the plant to keep growing throughout the season. While bigroot cranesbill rhizomes trail along the surface of the soil, the rhizomes of prairie smoke run just under the soil surface.

The nodding, rose-pink spring flowers of prairie smoke will change to white smoky plumes in early summer. It's a perfect choice for sandy soil or a rock garden, along with sedums and moss phlox (*Phlox subulata*).

A Dramatic
Dryland Mix

Drought-tolerant perennials, such as Spanish bayonet, lavender, and santolina, can transform a parched, dry spot into a lush, colorful garden. Desert heat and dry, poor soil are not a problem for this showy mix of easy-to-grow plants. Mounds of lavender and santolina spill gracefully over the face of a low wall, while spiky-leaved clumps of Spanish bayonet add a dramatic vertical accent. On hot, sunny days, both lavender and santolina perfume the air with their heady fragrances.

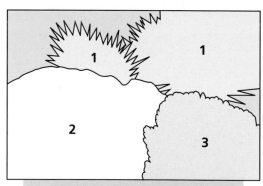

PHOTO KEY
1. Spanish bayonet (*Yucca baccata*); Zones 5 to 9
2. Lavender cotton (*Santolina chamaecyparissus*); Zones 6 to 8
3. Lavender (*Lavandula angustifolia*); Zones 5 to 9

Secrets for Successful Dryland Gardens

🍂 **Learn to manage reflected heat.** Paved surfaces and rocks reflect intense heat, especially in hot, sunny climates. They also store heat and radiate it back long after the sun is down. (Think of walking barefoot across the hot sand at the beach, and you'll understand the brutal conditions plants have to cope with in a hot, sunny site.) The first line of defense in a hot, dry garden is to grow heat-tolerant, drought-adapted plants. Use mounding plants, such as lavender and santolina, anywhere reflected heat may be a problem—along the edges of beds and to cover the soil and large rocks. Let the plants billow out over paved areas so their dense stems will shield the pavement from the sun's rays and help keep it from heating up. If possible, place a tree or large shrub to block the hottest afternoon sun.

🍂 **Meet the perfect edging plant.** Santolinas are attractive when planted along the top of a wall or near rocks that echo their rounded form. You can also shear them to form a low hedge. They actually are small shrubs, and their stems get quite woody in time. Cut plants back after flowering to encourage fresh, succulent foliage.

🍂 **Count on lavender to be tough.** Lavender looks delicate and smells heavenly, but it thrives on adversity. It likes well-drained to dry soil in full sun and grows best when days are hot and dry and nights are cool.

For the look of a bright cottage garden on a sandy site, try pink musk mallow (*Malva moschata*), golden marguerite (*Anthemis tinctoria*), and yellow 'Early Sunrise' coreopsis.

PHOTO KEY

1. **Olympic mullein (*Verbascum olympicum*); Zones 6 to 8**
2. **Rocket larkspur (*Consolida ambigua*, also sold as *C. ajacis*); annual**
3. **Hollyhock mallow (*Malva alcea* var. *fastigiata*); Zones 4 to 8**
4. **Feverfew (*Chrysanthemum parthenium*); Zones 4 to 8**

A Free-Seeding Cottage Garden

Easy-to-grow perennials and annuals that self-sow with abandon characterize this charming, informal planting. A mix of spiky and rounded forms intermingle to create a combination with plenty of variety, with the towering yellow olympic mulleins dominating the garden. They rise above a rounded clump of white feverfew, a fresh white daisy with a bright yellow center that echoes the mullein flowers. Pink hollyhock mallows bridge the gap between the low feverfew and the towering mullein spikes, and a sweep of self-sown rocket larkspur forms a hazy violet-blue background.

Expert Advice
for Cottage Garden Plants

&· **Enjoy delphinium colors without staking.** Larkspur (*Consolida* spp.) is an easy-to-grow annual that features spiky flowers in rich violet-blue, pale lilac, pink, or white. They have all the charm of delphiniums but require little of the work. The full flower forms of double-flowered larkspurs give a garden a sophisticated look. Unlike delphiniums, larkspurs tolerate heat and drought and bloom nonstop for months beginning in late spring. Pull the dead stems at the end of the season, making sure to shake the seed throughout the garden to ensure next years' crop of bloom.

&· **Get tough with your mallows.** Give hollyhock mallows rich, moist soil and you'll kill them with kindness. Instead, plant them in well-drained, average soil in full sun, and they'll reward you with two months or more of nonstop bloom. Like the other plants in this garden, these plants self-sow. In spring it's easy to dig up seedlings that pop up where you don't want them and transplant them to another site.

&· **Don't overfeed your mulleins.** Mulleins (*Verbascum* spp.) are familiar roadside weeds, but some make great garden plants because their showy flower spikes persist through the entire summer. The Olympic mullein in this combination is a perennial, but most mulleins are biennials. In their first year in the garden, they produce striking rosettes—enormous felted leaves that resemble giant spinach plants—and they bloom the following year. Olympic mullein is a great choice for sandy soil, because it needs good drainage. Don't enrich the soil too much before planting, or your mullein may grow up to 8 feet tall. Also try moth mullein (*V. blattaria*), which has more open flowers.

For drama in a sunny spot with lean soil, combine the slender spikes of *Verbascum phoenicium* with the red blooms of red valerian (*Centranthus ruber*) and a contrasting carpet of *Geranium clarkei* 'Kashmir White'.

205

PHOTO KEY
1. **Siberian iris (*Iris sibirica*);** Zones 2 to 9
2. **Lady's-mantle (*Alchemilla mollis*);** Zones 3 to 8

A Pleasing Duo for Moist Soil

An elegant pair of perennials that blooms in early summer changes a wet-soil site from a liability into an asset. The purple-blue flowers of Siberian irises bring rich color to this planting in early summer, while the straplike leaves are an eye-catching vertical accent. An underplanting of lady's-mantle, with lush, lobed leaves and lacy chartreuse flowers, adds rich contrast and makes this combination pop. The texture of a moss-covered rock contrasts with the lush, soft foliage.

Tips for Success
with Adaptable Perennials

🌱 **Try this adaptable, easy-to-please iris.** Siberian iris is one of my favorite early-summer perennials. It produces exquisite flowers in shades of blue, purple, yellow, and white, and its elegant foliage is attractive all season long. After the flowers fade, the leaves provide fine texture and a strong vertical accent through the entire growing season. They turn yellow to burnished gold in fall, and the dried seed capsules, which split into three sections, are an interesting feature through winter. These irises grow beautifully in rich, moist to wet soil, and adapt to most garden conditions except poor, dry soil. Divide the clumps in summer or early fall when they become crowded and bloom less. Siberian irises also are resistant to iris borers, a pest that's devastating to hybrid bearded irises.

🌱 **Keep lady's-mantle in top-notch form.** Lady's-mantle is grown for its foliage as much as its chartreuse flowers. After a rain, hairs on the rounded, scalloped leaves trap moisture and collect it into beads that sparkle in the sun. The plants need constantly moist soil but won't tolerate boggy conditions. A site with good air circulation is a plus, because the furry foliage and fine-textured flower sprays trap moisture that may lead to rot where air circulation is poor. I cut plants back to the ground after they flower to remove the brown stalks and aging leaves. This also eliminates the potential for rot and makes room for fresh foliage to appear.

🌱 **Include lady's mantles in drier sites.** Dwarf species of lady's mantle will tolerate somewhat drier conditions than *Alchemilla mollis* does. Try *A. alpina* and *A. erythropoda*, both of which thrive in average to rich, well-drained soil. They are perfect for rock gardens or along rock walls and stone paths. All lady's-mantles will self-sow, so don't be surprised if you see seedlings in unexpected places.

Lady's-mantle, with leaves that shimmer in the morning dew, along with white-edged hostas and golden corydalis (*Corydalis aurea*), fill this moist-soil site to overflowing.

PHOTO KEY
1. Daylily (*Hemerocallis*);
   Zones 3 to 9
2. 'August Moon' hosta
   (*Hosta* 'August Moon');
   Zones 3 to 8
3. 'Golden Ring' Japanese
   barberry (*Berberis thun-*
   bergii 'Golden Ring');
   Zones 5 to 8
4. Bowles' golden sedge
   (*Carex elata* 'Aurea');
   Zones 5 to 9

Bright Colors for a Shady, Wet Site

Perennials with yellow and chartreuse foliage brighten shady spots like no other colors. In this planting, the bold leaves of 'August Moon' hosta glow through a translucent veil of fine-textured sedge. The yellow leaves of the sedge and the chartreuse hosta foliage combine to create a pleasing color echo that unifies the garden. The darker green daylily foliage forms a backdrop that makes the yellow foliage in front seem even brighter. A deep purple-leaved barberry spills lazily over the yellow leaves, adding a note of contrast. Shrubs such as barberries make excellent companions for perennials, because they add valuable height to the back of a border as well as colorful flowers and foliage. This combination would be perfect for partial shade to nearly full sun, provided the soil stayed evenly moist and the barberry was planted on higher, drier ground.

208

More Plants for Wet Soil in Shade

✿ Sedges for wet spots. Bowles' golden sedge is just one of several sedges that grow in wet soil. Also try drooping sedge (*Carex pendula*), with glossy, evergreen straplike leaves, or fringed sedge (*Carex crinita*), which has narrow, chartreuse leaves. Both grow in rich, wet soil or standing water in full sun or shade.

✿ Lovely shrubs for wet soil. Try any of the following moist-soil shrubs in a mixed planting with perennials: spicebush (*Lindera benzoin*), with yellow spring flowers and red summer berries; sweetspire (*Itea virginica*), with fragrant white flowers in early summer and wine red fall color; summersweet (*Clethra alnifolia*), with fragrant spires of white flowers in midsummer and yellow leaves in fall; and swamp azalea (*Rhododendron viscosum*), also with fragrant white flowers in early to midsummer. For fall and winter interest, plant winterberry (*Ilex verticillata*), which produces an abundance of bright red berries. Remember, you need one male winterberry for each female in order to get berries.

Blue-leaved 'Buckshaw Blue' hosta and yellow-leaved sedge create a beautiful combination that echoes the plants in the photo on the opposite page. Yellow variegated periwinkle (*Vinca minor*) and 'Sutherland Gold' continue the yellow theme.

A Bold Wet-Soil Mix

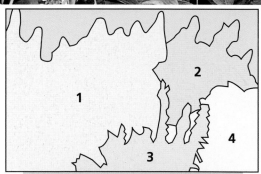

L arge, vigorous perennials with bold foliage and even bolder flowers are just the ticket for creating an eye-catching planting in a large site. Rodgersia is the showstopper in this wet-soil garden, where the bronze-tinted foliage and rose-pink flowers of the cultivar 'Superba' contrast with the lighter foliage and flowers of the species. Both plants produce mops of foamy flowers, reminiscent of cotton candy, in mid- to late summer. The bold rodgersia foliage nearly dwarfs the large leaves of hostas along the edge of this planting. The erect spikes of hosta flowers echo the shape and color of the rodgersias.

PHOTO KEY

1. **Rodgersia (*Rodgersia pinnata*); Zones 4 to 8**
2. **Rodgersia (*Rodgersia pinnata* 'Superba'); Zones 4 to 8**
3. **Wavy-leaved hosta (*Hosta undulata*); Zones 3 to 9**
4. **'Blue Moon' hosta (*Hosta* 'Blue Moon'); Zones 3 to 9**

Secrets for Wet Soil and Bog Gardens

Try bold, beautiful rodgersias. Most gardeners shy away from trying rodgersias, but these plants are easy and rewarding if you meet their need for rich, moist soil. They will grow in light to full shade, provided the soil is constantly moist. The two most commonly available species are *Rodgersia pinnata*, pictured here, and fingerleaf rodgersia (*R. aesculifolia*), hardy in Zones 4 to 7. Less easy to find but worth the hunt is bronze-leaved rodgersia (*R. podophylla*), hardy in Zones 5 to 7. Fingerleaf rodgersia and bronze-leaved rodgersia both bear large clusters of creamy white flowers.

Keep hosta crowns above water. Hostas thrive in a bog garden or at the edge of a pond. Place them where their crowns are not covered with water, but the roots have access to constant moisture. Established plants withstand occasional flooding, but prefer wet feet and dry crowns.

Make an artificial bog garden. If your soil is dry but you want to grow bog plants, like rodgersias, why not create an artificial bog garden? Making a bog garden is just like making a water garden, only you fill the "pool" with soil instead of water. Start by excavating the site. Avoid shapes with tight corners and narrow curves, because the liner will be difficult to place in these spots. (I dug an 8-foot-wide, 25-foot-long, 2½-foot-deep trench for my bog garden.) Line the site with a plastic pool liner (the 45-mm type suitable for a water garden). The liner should extend at least 1 foot beyond the hole on all sides. Spread the liner evenly, then fill the hole with rich, loamy soil and compost. Add 6-inch layers at a time, tromping each layer lightly in place to settle the soil and liner. When the

For an all-season accent in or beside a water garden, plant yellow striped 'Pretoria' canna. It has rich orange flowers in summer and looks great paired with sweet flag (*Acorus calamus*), Louisiana hybrid irises or southern blue flag, and sedges.

hole is filled, mound the soil 6 to 8 inches high in the center to allow for further settling. Water your bog well and let it settle for several weeks before planting. Trim the liner back to 6 inches above the soil. After a year of settling, trim any remaining plastic back to the soil line. The final soil level in the bog should be several inches below grade so water runs into the bog when it rains. Keep the soil wet at all times.

211

A Planting for the Water's Edge

Fiery-colored yellow flags and Japanese primroses create an eye-catching planting for the edge of a pond or stream. Ostrich fern fronds rise above a carpet of primroses and add grace and motion when compared to the stiff, erect clumps of iris leaves. The rounded leaves of marsh marigolds are all that remains of these early spring flowers, which carry their butter yellow blooms in loose clusters. The primrose and marsh marigold foliage will disappear by mid-summer, because the plants go dormant after flowering. To add summer flowers to this garden, try planting astilbes alongside it.

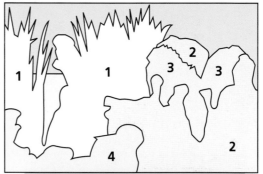

PHOTO KEY
1. Yellow flag (*Iris pseudacorus*); Zones 4 to 9
2. Japanese primrose (*Primula japonica*); Zones 5 to 8
3. Ostrich fern (*Matteuccia struthiopteris*); Zones 3 to 8
4. Marsh marigold (*Caltha palustris*); Zones 2 to 8

Secrets for Water's Edge Plantings

❧ Let primroses plant themselves.
Japanese primroses are popular plants for wet sites because of their plentiful late-spring bloom and the fact that they self-sow with abandon. Self-sown seedlings often vary in color. If you want a cultivar that will come true from seed, try 'Miller's Crimson', which has rich red flowers. 'Potsford White' has white, 1-inch-wide flowers with yellow centers.

❧ Try more candelabra primroses. The Japanese primroses in this combination are just one of several candelabra primroses, named for their tiered flower clusters. All grow in constantly moist soil in partial shade. They form large clumps if given room to spread. Some of my favorites are Bee's primrose (*Primula beesiana*), with magenta flowers; Bulley's primrose (*P. bulleyana*), which has deep burnt orange flowers; amber primrose (*P. heladoxa*),

with yellow flowers; and silverdust primrose (*P. pulverulenta*), with rich red flowers.

❧ Line stream banks with yellow flag.
Yellow flags make a wonderful edging for streams or a water garden. Many people think they're native wildflowers, but they were introduced to North America from Europe during colonial times. You can plant yellow flag in moist soil or standing water. For a change of pace, try the cultivar 'Variegata', which has yellow-striped leaves in spring but fades to lime green in summer. For a showier planting, use double-flowered 'Flore-Pleno'.

❧ Keep ferns moist for season-long greenery. Ostrich ferns grow in wet soil as well as moist, well-drained conditions. You'll enjoy their featherlike fronds most when you plant them in wet soil, because in dry soil, they go dormant in summer.

If you have a moist garden site with plenty of room, try sensitive fern (*Onoclea sensibilis*), with its unique, hand-shaped fronds. It's a fast spreader, but makes a good companion for Siberian iris, astilbes, and rodgersias.

Foliage and Flowers for a Pond's Edge

Brilliant red flowers and variegated foliage will create stunning reflections in this water garden. The secret to planting the edge of a water garden or any other wet spot is to arrange plants according to their soil moisture preferences. Here, a drift of pickerel weed makes a bold backdrop and actually extends out into the pond. A true aquatic plant, it will grow in shallow standing water. Flaming red Mexican lobelia and Japanese primroses, which are past bloom in this view, are growing in the soggy soil at the pond's edge. Rabbit-ear iris, equally at home in moist soil or shallow water, occupies the pond edge. The burgundy lobelia foliage and the green-and-white–striped iris leaves add rich color accents all summer long. In spring, before the lobelia blooms, primroses and purple-blue iris flowers add an abundance of color.

Moisture-Loving Plants for Wet Soil

❧ **A versatile moisture-lover.** Pickerel weed, named for the fish that often takes refuge in the tangle of submerged stems, is an aquatic plant that thrives in shallow water up to 1 foot deep. Throughout the summer, the plants produce rich blue flower spikes that are a favorite landing spot for dragonflies waiting for unwary insects to fly by. The narrow heart-shaped leaves are handsome in their own right. Pickerel weed is an excellent choice for artificial water gardens or natural ponds, although it will spread widely in shallow, earth-bottom ponds. In artificial ponds that have a liner, plant pickerel weed in heavy loamy or clay soil in a broad, shallow pot. Set the pot in the water so that the rim of the pot is 4 to 8 inches below the water level.

❧ **Hardy cardinal flowers.** Mexican lobelia (*Lobelia splendens*) is a striking addition to this garden, but it isn't hardy enough for many gardens. Fortunately, our native cardinal flower (*L. cardinalis*) makes an equally fine choice for wet soil and is hardy in Zones 2 to 9. It bears scarlet-red flowers, and cultivars with maroon stems are available—'Dark Crusader' is one. Both species demand constant moisture for best growth. Like most lobelias, they may be short lived. Plants self-sow profusely in suitable conditions and are easy to grow from seeds.

❧ **An iris that loves wet feet.** The moisture-loving rabbit-ear iris in this combination is equally at home in the moist soil at the edge of a pond or growing submerged in a few inches of water. Its purple-blue flowers are borne just above the foliage in late spring and early summer. Unlike Japanese iris (*Iris ensata*), which this plant resembles, rabbit-ear iris tolerates alkaline soil. It also can be grown in pots set in a water garden.

Great blue lobelia (*Lobelia siphilitica*) is a striking blue-flowered wildflower that loves moist soil. For an informal meadow combination, pair it with 'Harrington's Pink' New England aster.

A Streamside Planting for Shade

In the dappled shade and constant moisture along a slow stream, a wealth of colorful perennials blooms in early summer. In this moist-soil garden, spiky leaves and exquisite flowers of Siberian iris create a stunning focal point amid a sea of colors and textures. Bright magenta Japanese primroses have seeded themselves through a mixed planting that includes monkey flower and a frothy mass of euphorbia. Behind the swale where the land rises slightly, perennials that prefer drier conditions, including hardy cranesbills and rhubarb, form a colorful backdrop. In this location, their roots can reach moist soil, but their crowns stay high and dry so they don't rot.

PHOTO KEY
1. Rhubarb (*Rheum*); Zones 3 to 8
2. Siberian iris (*Iris sibirica*); Zones 2 to 9
3. Yellow monkey flower (*Mimulus guttatus*); Zones 5 to 10
4. Hardy cranesbills (*Geranium* spp.); Zones 3 to 8
5. Euphorbia (*Euphorbia*); Zones 3 to 8
6. Japanese primrose (*Primula japonica*); Zones 5 to 8

Plants for a Shady Streamside

❧ **Siberian irises galore.** Easy-to-grow Siberian irises will thrive in the wet soil of a bog garden as well as in the moist, well-drained conditions of the average perennial border. Your biggest problem may be deciding which cultivar to grow—each one is more beautiful than the last. Most have 1- to 2-inch flowers and broad, strappy foliage that reaches 3 feet tall after flowering. Some of my favorite selections include: 'Butter and Sugar', a yellow and white bicolor; 'Fourfold White', with pure white flowers; 'Limeheart', with creamy white flowers tainted with yellow; 'Orville Faye', with medium blue flowers; and 'Tycoon', with velvety royal purple flowers. 'Flight of Butter-flies' looks more delicate than other cultivars, with narrow leaves to 2 feet tall and small 1 inch blue flowers veined with white.

❧ **The flower with the face of a monkey.** Monkey flowers were named for their flat-faced, speckled flowers that looked like a monkey to some imaginative botanist. These charming plants are not well known to gardeners, especially in the eastern United States, but are well worth trying. Scarlet monkey flower (*Mimulus cardinalis*) bears scarlet flowers that sometimes have yellow throats, while Lewis's monkey flower (*M. lewisii*) bears pink flowers. Many hybrids are available as well. Monkey flowers thrive in heavy, wet soils and, where happy, will reseed freely to form a colorful carpet around other wetland plants. Plant them in full sun or dappled shade. They do not thrive in areas where summer nights are hot and steamy.

❧ **Cranesbills for moist soil.** This combination features a mixed planting of hardy cranesbills (also called hardy geraniums) as a colorful backdrop. Although not true wetland

The huge leaves of umbrella plant (*Darmera peltata*), which thrives in rich, wet soils, are up to 2 feet across and are just the ticket for adding drama to a collection of fine-textured irises and primroses.

plants, many cranesbills thrive in moist soil. Our native pink wood geranium (*Geranium maculatum*); European woodland cranesbill (*G. sylvaticum*); blue meadow cranesbill (*G. pratense*); and lilac geranium (*G. himalyense*) are a few species that will grow well in a moist spot.

❧ **Ornamental rhubarbs for flower gardens.** Rhubarbs make stunning foliage plants, and their huge leaves add a tropical look to gardens. Even common rhubarb (*Rheum rhabarbarum*) is attractive enough to include in perennial beds and borders. Ornamental rhubarb (*R. palmatum*) bears giant sharp-lobed leaves and sends up tall, branched spikes of tiny pink flowers in late spring.

A Sunny Perennial Garden

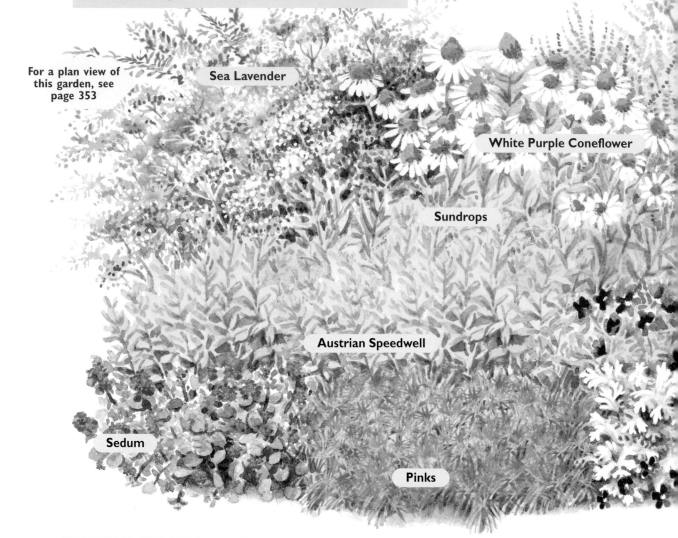

For a plan view of this garden, see page 353

Sea Lavender

White Purple Coneflower

Sundrops

Austrian Speedwell

Sedum

Pinks

Plant Names	Bloom Color and Season	Height and Spread
'Silver Brocade' artemisia	Silvery gray leaves	6" to 12" tall and 2' wide
White purple coneflower	White flowers in summer	2' to 3' tall and 1' to 2' wide
Jupiter's beard	Pink flowers in spring to summer	2' to 3' tall and 2' wide
'Emerald Cushion Blue' moss phlox	Blue flowers in spring	4" to 6" tall and 1' to 2' wide
Pinks	Pink flowers in early summer	6" to 8" tall and 1' wide
Russian sage	Blue flowers in late summer to fall	3' to 5' tall and wide

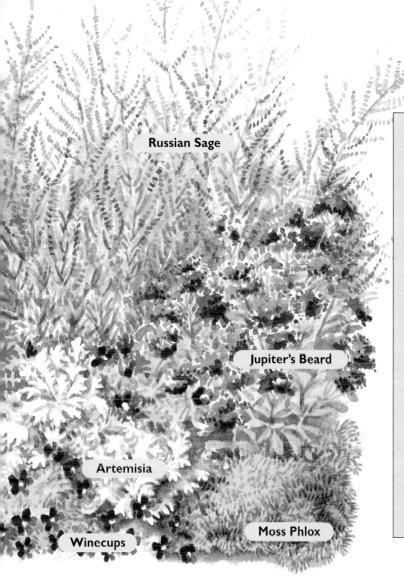

Russian Sage

Jupiter's Beard

Artemisia

Winecups

Moss Phlox

Where to Plant Your Garden

This richly colored garden is perfect for a hot dry spot where you think nothing beautiful could possibly grow. Try planting this bed along a driveway or sidewalk, or beside the wall of a house or garage, where reflected summer heat is a problem. It also works well as a border between a terrace and a lawn. If you have a large space to fill, you can double the width of the border. Just leave space for a 2- to 3-foot-wide path or stepping stones down the center for easy maintenance, and repeat the entire design back to back. The effect will be stunning, and the added foliage will help moderate the heat from the driveway or sidewalk.

Plant Names	Bloom Color and Season	Height and Spread
Sea lavender	Lavender-blue flowers in summer	2' to 2½' tall and wide
'Vera Jameson' sedum	Rose-purple flowers in late summer to fall	1' tall and 2' wide
'Crater Lake Blue' Austrian speedwell	Bright blue flowers in summer	1' to 1½' tall and 2' wide
Sundrops	Yellow flower in early summer	1' to 1½' tall and wide
Winecups	Magenta flowers in summer to fall	6" to 8" tall and 3' wide

A Partial Shade Garden

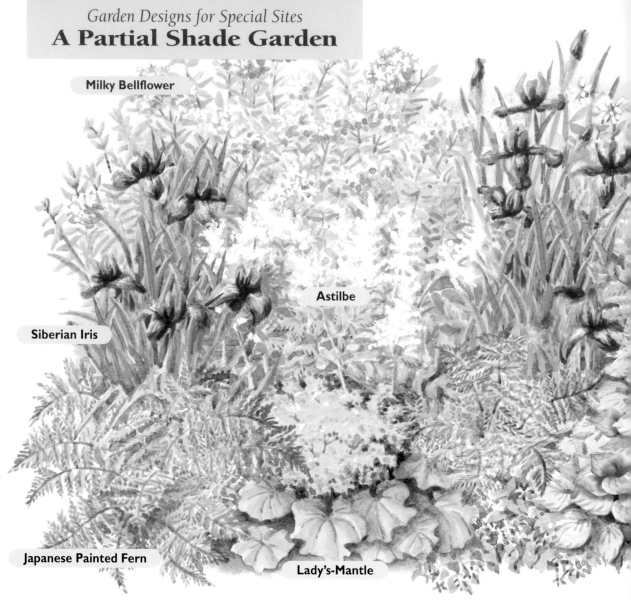

Milky Bellflower

Astilbe

Siberian Iris

Japanese Painted Fern

Lady's-Mantle

Plant Names	Bloom Color and Season	Height and Spread
'Deutschland' astilbe	White flowers in early summer	2' tall and wide
'Superba' Chinese astilbe	Rose-pink flowers in summer	3' to 4' tall and 2' to 3' wide
'Loddon Anna' milky bellflower	Pink flowers in early summer	3' to 4' tall and 3' wide
Serbian bellflower	Blue flowers in late spring to summer	8" to 12" tall and 12" wide
'Johnson's Blue' cranesbill	Blue flowers in early summer	1' to 1½' tall and wide
Japanese painted fern	Silver and pink fronds	1' to 2' tall and wide

For a plan view of
this garden, see
page 355

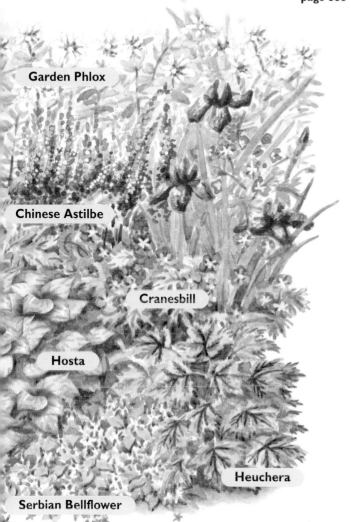

Garden Phlox

Chinese Astilbe

Cranesbill

Hosta

Heuchera

Serbian Bellflower

Enjoying Your Garden

What could be more inviting than relaxing beside a cool, shady perennial garden on a warm afternoon? This design features perennials that need full sun for part of the day to bloom their best, but that appreciate protection from the hot, burning rays of the afternoon. The plants bloom in spring and summer and have colorful foliage that will keep the garden looking bright and beautiful through fall. The strong, spiky foliage of Siberian iris and the bold leaves of heuchera and hosta are the focal points of this garden. Even though the hosta, lady's-mantle, and heuchera leaves are distinctively colored or patterned, the similar leaf shapes create a pleasing repetition throughout the bed. The predominant flower color scheme is blue and pink, with white and yellow for accent.

Plant Names	Bloom Color and Season	Height and Spread
'Dale's Strain' heuchera	Green flowers in late spring	1' to 3' tall and 18" wide
'Halcyon' hosta	Blue leaves; lavender flowers in late summer	1' to 1½' tall and 2' wide
'Orville Fay' Siberian iris	Rich blue flowers in late spring to early summer	2' to 3' tall and 2' wide
Lady's-mantle	Chartreuse flowers in early summer	1' tall and 2' to 3' wide
'David' garden phlox	White flowers in late summer	2' to 3' tall and 2' wide

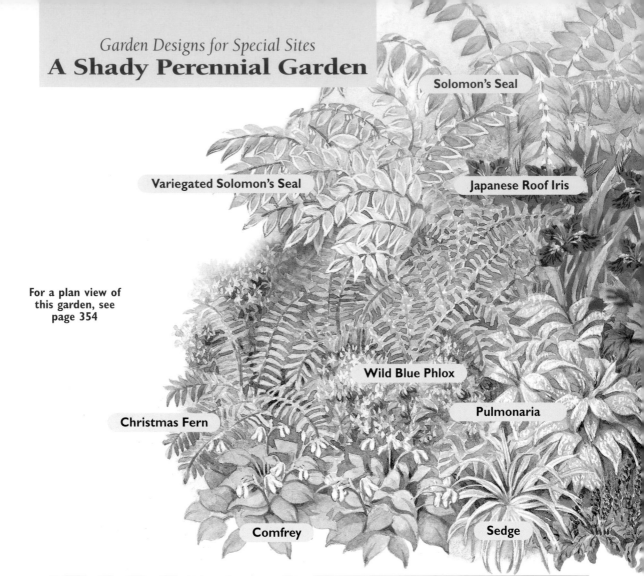

Garden Designs for Special Sites
A Shady Perennial Garden

Solomon's Seal

Variegated Solomon's Seal

Japanese Roof Iris

For a plan view of this garden, see page 354

Wild Blue Phlox

Pulmonaria

Christmas Fern

Comfrey

Sedge

Plant Names	Bloom Color and Season	Height and Spread
Ajuga	Deep blue flowers in spring	6" to 8" tall and 1' wide
Comfrey	Creamy white flowers in spring	6" to 10" tall and 2' wide
'Sulphureum' Persian epimedium	Pale yellow flowers in spring	1' tall and 2' wide
Christmas fern	Deep green fronds	1' to 2' tall and wide
Japanese painted fern	Silver and pink fronds	1' to 2' tall and wide
Maidenhair fern	Lime green fronds	2' tall and wide
'Palace Purple' heuchera	Greenish white flowers in summer	1' to 2' tall and 1' wide
'Francee' hosta	White-edged foliage	2' to 2½' tall and 2' wide
Dwarf crested iris	Blue flowers in spring	6" to 12" tall and wide

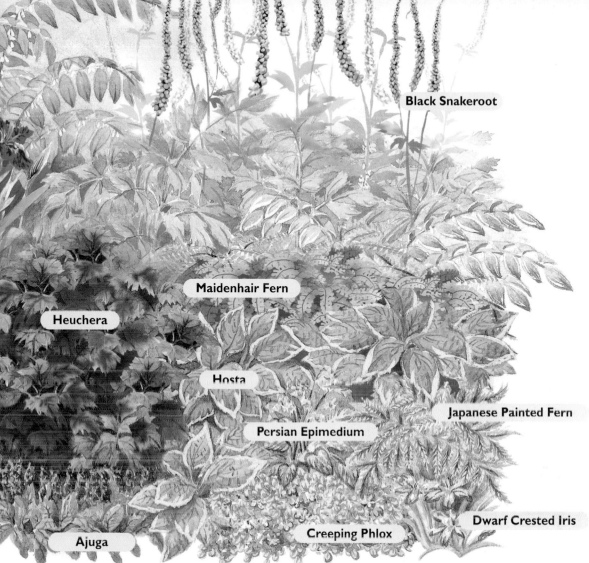

Black Snakeroot

Maidenhair Fern

Heuchera

Hosta

Japanese Painted Fern

Persian Epimedium

Dwarf Crested Iris

Ajuga

Creeping Phlox

Plant Names	Bloom Color and Season	Height and Spread
Japanese roof iris	Blue flowers in spring	1' to 1½' tall and 1' to 2' wide
Creeping phlox	Pink flowers in spring	6" to 12" tall and 12" wide
Wild blue phlox	Blue flowers in spring	1' tall and wide
'Roy Davidson' pulmonaria	Pale blue flowers in early spring	8" tall and 2' wide
Black snakeroot	White flowers in early summer	4' to 6' tall and 3' wide
Creeping variegated broad-leaved sedge	White-striped foliage	6" tall and 1' wide
Solomon's seal	Green flowers in spring	2' to 5' tall and 1' to 2' wide
Variegated Solomon's seal	White-edged leaves	1' to 2' tall and 2' wide

A Garden for Clay Soil

For a plan view of this garden, see page 351

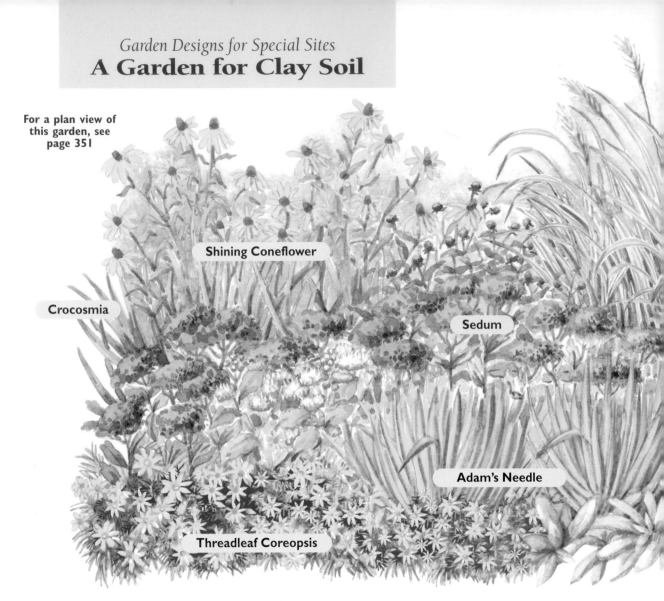

Shining Coneflower

Crocosmia

Sedum

Adam's Needle

Threadleaf Coreopsis

Plant Names	Bloom Color and Season	Height and Spread
'Gold Sword' Adam's needle	Yellow-striped leaves; white flowers in summer	4' to 5' tall and 3' wide
Hardy ageratum	Blue flowers in late summer to fall	1' to 2' tall and 2' to 3' wide
'Violet Carpet' aster	Purple flowers in summer	1' to 1½' tall and 2' wide
'Blue Stocking' bee balm	Violet-blue flowers in summer	3' to 4' tall and wide
'Herbstsonne' shining coneflower	Yellow flowers in late summer	3' to 4' tall and 2' to 3' wide
'Zagreb' threadleaf coreopsis	Yellow flowers in summer	1' to 1½' tall and 2' to 3' wide

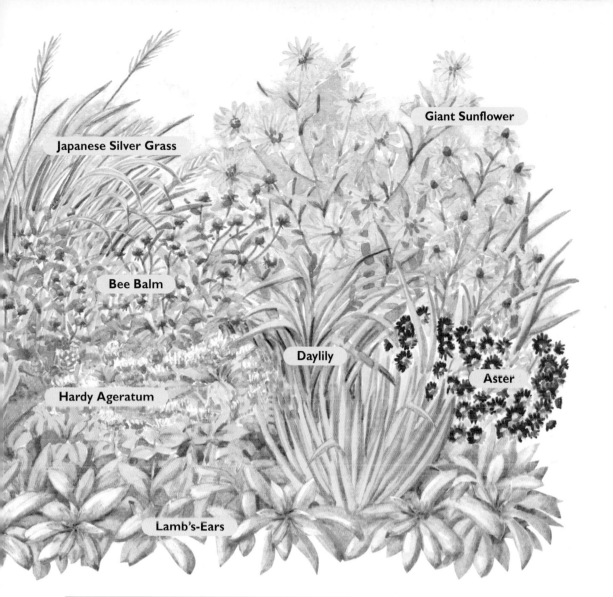

Japanese Silver Grass

Giant Sunflower

Bee Balm

Daylily

Aster

Hardy Ageratum

Lamb's-Ears

Plant Names	Bloom Color and Season	Height and Spread
'Lucifer' crocosmia	Red-orange flowers in summer	2' to 3' tall and 1' wide
Daylily	Yellow flowers in summer	3' tall and wide
'Cabaret' Japanese silver grass	White-striped foliage	3' to 5' tall and 3' to 4' wide
Lamb's-ears	Silvery foliage; rose-pink flowers in early summer	4" to 12" tall and 1' to 2' wide
'Autumn Joy' sedum	Rose-pink flowers in late summer	2' tall and wide
Giant sunflower	Yellow flowers in late summer to fall	4' to 6' tall and 3' wide

A Garden for Sandy Soil

Feverfew

Spanish Bayonet

Lavender

Penstemon

Common Chives

Mother-of-Thyme

Plant Names	Bloom Color and Season	Height and Spread
Common chives	Pink flowers in early summer	1' to 1½' tall and 1' wide
Feverfew	White flowers in early summer	1' to 2' tall and 1' wide
Lavender	Blue flowers in summer	1' to 2' tall and wide
Lily leek	Yellow flowers in early summer	8" to 12" tall and wide
Rocky mountain penstemon	Blue flowers in early summer	1' to 2' tall and 1' wide
Prairie smoke	Dusty rose flowers in spring	6" to 12" tall and 12" wide
Autumn sage	Scarlet flowers in summer and fall	2' to 3' tall and 3' wide
Spanish bayonet	Gray-green leaves; white flowers in summer	3' to 5' tall and 3' wide
Mother-of-thyme	Pink flowers in summer	4" to 6" tall and 1' wide
'Moonshine' yarrow	Soft yellow flowers in early summer	1' to 2' tall and wide

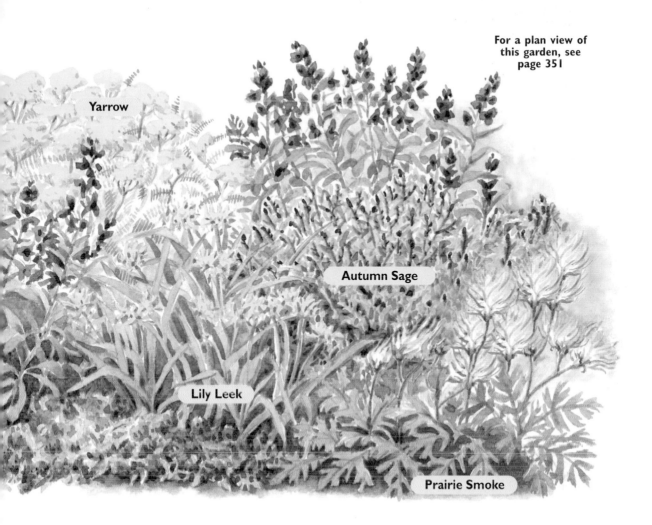

Yarrow

For a plan view of this garden, see page 351

Autumn Sage

Lily Leek

Prairie Smoke

Getting the Best from Your Garden

Yellow and blue flowers dominate this sunny border for a well-drained site. The peak of bloom comes in early summer. The spiky forms of penstemon, lavender, sage, and Spanish bayonet dominate, but they are softened by the broad mass of rounded yarrow, lily leeks, and the trailing carpet of mother-of-thyme. The seedheads of penstemon and yarrow will keep the garden interesting well into winter.

This garden is perfect for a lazy gardener, as all the plants thrive on neglect. Divide the yarrow every three years or so to prevent it from overtaking the penstemon, which will die out if crowded. For spring interest, add species tulips, such as yellow *Tulipa tarda* and scarlet *Tulipa praestans*. These tulips are a perfect choice for a well-drained, sandy bed, because they need to bake dry during the dormant season—in wet soil, they'll rot.

A Garden for Wet Soil

For a plan view of this garden, see page 350

Yellow Flag

Lobelia

Japanese Primrose

Siebold's Hosta

Plant Names	Bloom Color and Season	Height and Spread
Ostrich fern	Bright green fronds	2' to 5' tall and 3' wide
'Elegans' Siebold's hosta	Gray-blue leaves; pale lilac flowers in summer	3' tall and 3' to 4' wide
'Sum and Substance' hosta	Chartreuse leaves; lilac flowers in summer	3' tall and 3' to 6' wide
'Ruby Slippers' lobelia	Ruby red flowers in late summer	2' to 3' tall and 1' wide
Japanese primrose	Pink, rose, or magenta flowers in spring	1' tall and wide
Rodgersia	Pink flowers in early summer	2' to 3' tall and 3' wide
Bowles' golden sedge	Chartreuse and/or yellow foliage	1' to 2½' tall and 2' wide
Variegated yellow flag	Yellow flowers in early summer	2' to 4' tall and 2' to 3' wide

Ostrich Fern

Rodgersia

Hosta

Bowles' golden Sedge

Garden Color for Three Seasons

This lush garden for wet soil can transform a garden trouble spot into a colorful delight with plenty of interest from spring through fall. The sumptuous, bold foliage and colorful flowers of these moisture-loving plants are sure to please. Hostas and ferns dominate this bed, which demands a spot with humus-rich, constantly moist soil. There's dramatic contrast between the bold leaves of the hosta and rodgersia and the fine-textured ferns and sedges. Carpets of bright Japanese primroses seed freely through the hostas, adding lively touches of color in spring. The spiky foliage and rich yellow iris blooms enliven the combination in early summer, along with the frothy flower plumes of rodgersia. In late summer, the brilliant cherry red flower spikes of lobelia recall the bright primrose flowers and carry the flower display until fall.

Combinations ON THE WILD SIDE

Wild gardens, like woodland and meadow gardens, offer long-lasting color and are easy to maintain. Once you plant a wild garden, you'll also discover that it's a haven for wildlife. Its rich mix of flowers and foliage, with an emphasis on native perennials, offers plenty of nectar for butterflies as well as places for caterpillars (butterfly larvae) to feed. Birds frequently visit meadow gardens to search for insects and seeds to eat. For example, goldfinches and sparrows love the seeds of coneflowers and gayfeathers. In this section, I've profiled beautiful combinations for woodland gardens, meadow or prairie gardens, seaside gardens, and water gardens (water gardens are great habitats for frogs). And I used the best of these combinations to design complete gardens that feature many unusual or native perennials that thrive in special conditions like shady woodlands and salty seaside soil.

PHOTO KEY
1. Celandine poppy (*Sty-lophorum diphyllum*); Zones 4 to 9
2. Virginia bluebells (*Mertensia virginica*); Zones 3 to 9

Wildflowers for Shady Spring Contrast

For a bright touch of yellow-orange in a woodland garden in spring, try a combination that features celandine poppies. Here, its cheery poppy blossoms contrast with the nodding, sky blue flowers of Virginia bluebells. The complementary colors of the poppies and bluebells make an exciting garden picture that lasts for several weeks. Soon after the Virginia bluebells finish blooming, their foliage begins to turn yellow. The plants go dormant and their foliage disappears by late spring. But the lovely sea green foliage of celandine poppy persists after its flowers fade and fills the gaps left by the retreating bluebell foliage.

Virginia bluebells have a delicate scent, so if you plant this combination, be sure to take time to enjoy their perfume. Bluebells and celandine poppies both grow best in rich, moist soil in the shade of mature trees. Wild blue phlox (*Phlox divaricata*) would make a good companion for this combination. Its sky blue blossoms also appear in spring and last for about two weeks.

Secrets for Spring-Blooming Wildflowers

🌺 **Try a Colonial favorite.** Gardeners have loved Virginia bluebells since Colonial times. The historic gardens in Williamsburg, Virginia, include plenty of fragrant, sky blue Virginia bluebells in spring. The new shoots of this wildflower emerge early in spring. The flowers buds are pink, but they open into blue, nodding, bell-like flowers. Once you've planted Virginia bluebells, watch for self-sown seedlings to pop up in colorful drifts in your beds or even across the lawn. If you check carefully, you may spot an occasional lavender-, pink-, or white-flowered plant among the masses of blue.

🌺 **Plant a poppy in the shade.** Celandine or wood poppy (*Stylophorum diphyllum*) isn't a true poppy (*Papaver* is the botanical name for true poppies), but it's a close relative that belongs to the poppy family. Its four-petaled, crepe-paperlike flowers look like miniature

Iceland poppies. But unlike Iceland poppies, which need full sun, celandine poppies do best in light to full shade. Celandine poppies are prolific self-seeders that will come up happily throughout the garden. If the plants look ratty after the blossoms fade, cut them back and they'll send out new leaves.

🌺 **Let ants roam in a woodland garden.** Ants may spoil our picnics, but they're welcome guests at the banquet when the fruits of native spring wildflowers ripen. Why? Because ants disperse the seeds, which helps the wildflowers reproduce. The seeds of many native plants, including Virginia bluebells and trilliums, have a fleshy, fatty covering that's a prime food for ants. The ants carry off the seeds, eat the coverings, and cast away the seeds. Removed from the competition of the parent plant, the seedlings have room to grow and start a new colony. So hats off to the ants!

The rich humus inside a rotting stump makes a perfect seedbed for a celandine poppy. Fern fronds and the parasol-like leaves of mayapple (*Podophyllum peltatum*) accent the natural planter.

A Woodland Spring Tapestry

The snow white flowers of trilliums are one of my favorite sights when I walk in the woods in spring. Trilliums are one of the best-known native wildflowers, and their huge white flowers make a fine showing. In this combination, the deep blue flowers of wild blue phlox contrast with the stark white trilliums and the subtle, fuzzy white flower of goldenseal. Bloodroot started this combination going in very early spring, with starlike white blooms. The bloodroot foliage will remain attractive all season.

Shop carefully for these plants. Some wildflowers, especially trilliums, are collected from the wild to be sold. Ask your supplier if they propagate trilliums, and don't buy from suppliers who dig plants from the wild.

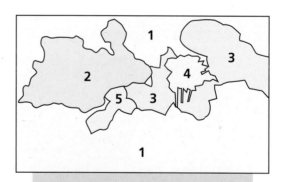

PHOTO KEY
1. White trillium (*Trillium grandiflorum*); Zones 3 to 9
2. Wild blue phlox (*Phlox divaricata*); Zones 3 to 9
3. Bloodroot (*Sanguinaria canadensis*); Zones 3 to 9
4. Black snakeroot (*Actaea [Cimicifuga] racemosa*); Zones 3 to 8
5. Goldenseal (*Hydrastis canadensis*); Zones 3 to 8

Plants for a Woodland Spring Tapestry

Collect some trillium seed. Trilliums are fairly easy to grow from seed, although it does take five to seven years to produce flowering plants. The first trick you may have to master is keeping ants from stealing the trillium seeds (the ants like to eat the fleshy covering around the seeds). To foil the ants, tie a piece of nylon stocking over the trillium seedheads in your garden after the flowers fade. Collect the protected seeds as soon as they're ripe (in early to midsummer). Sow the seeds immediately in outdoor seedbeds or in flats. If you opt for flats, leave the flats outdoors over winter. The freezing and thawing from winter cold helps overcome seed dormancy.

Be patient with trillium seedlings. Trillium seeds don't germinate all at once. Some of the seeds you sow in midsummer will germinate the following summer. (Take note:

Seedlings have only one leaf, not three.) After the second winter, more of the seed will sprout. It may take three years for all of the seedlings to appear. Keep the seedlings well watered during the growing season. By the third year, most plants will form three leaves. At this stage, you can transplant them to your garden.

Try many shades of wild blue phlox. Most cultivars of wild blue phlox are shades of sky blue or lavender, and you could try substituting any one of them in this combination. One of the most popular is 'Clouds of Perfume', with soft, sky blue flowers and a heady, heavenly scent. 'Dirigo Ice' has icy blue flowers with notched petals, while 'London Grove Blue' has deep, true blue flowers. If you want to create a single-color combination of phlox and trilliums, choose compact 'Fuller's White'.

'Blue Ridge' creeping phlox (*Phlox stolonifera*) produces showy periwinkle blue flowers in spring. It also has evergreen foliage, so it works well as a groundcover that links wildflower combinations together in a woodland garden.

Wildflowers for Hummingbirds

You might not expect to find hummingbirds in the woods, but combinations of columbines and phlox like this one are a sure hummingbird draw. These wildflowers bloom in the warmth of the early-spring sunshine. Heucheras, sedges, and ferns are good companions for this spring-blooming combo, because they tolerate dry shade, and their attractive foliage will provide summer interest after the wildflowers fade. For fall interest, add woodland asters and goldenrods and the showy berries of blue cohosh (*Caulophyllum thalictroides*) and baneberry (*Actaea* spp).

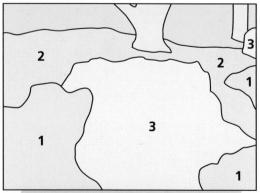

PHOTO KEY

1. **Wild blue phlox (***Phlox divaricata***); Zones 3 to 9**
2. **Whorled sedum (***Sedum ternatum***); Zones 4 to 8**
3. **Wild columbine (***Aquilegia canadensis***); Zones 3 to 8**

Growing Wildflowers for Hummingbirds

❧ **Red flowers mean a meal for hummers.** People use the color red as a warning of danger, but for hummingbirds, red is a signal that there's food to be had. So hummingbirds make a beeline to the red-orange flowers of wild columbine and sip nectar from the tubular blossoms. Wild columbines bloom early in spring, and they're often the first flowers that hungry migrating hummingbirds encounter as they head north. They help the migrating birds refuel during their journey, making it possible for them to travel from the tropics all the way to northern parts of North America.

❧ **Phlox is for hummers, too.** Phlox blossoms also provide food for migrating and resident hummingbirds. The sweet-scented flowers offer a delicious treat for the birds. While red is the color that hummingbirds find most irresistible, they'll also feed from blue, yellow, and even white flowers, especially once they've discovered nectar plants in your garden. So be sure to include some red phlox or other red flowers as the calling card, but don't stop there.

❧ **Columbines are sure to spread.** Columbines adapt to a variety of garden situations, from rich to poor soil and sun to shade. In rich soils, plants may be short-lived due to root rot. They live longer when planted in soils on the lean and dry side. In any garden, columbines are prolific self-seeders, so there will always be plenty of seedlings to transplant or share with friends.

❧ **This sedum likes the shade.** For every rule a gardener can make, such as "sedum grows best in full sun and dry soil," there's bound to be an exception. The exception to the sedum rule is whorled sedum, pictured

For variety in woodland combinations, try special cultivars of wildflowers, such as pure yellow 'Corbett' columbine and 'Barb's Choice' wild blue phlox, which has red flower centers.

here. This lovely carpet-forming sedum is native to deciduous woods where the sunshine pours in during spring, but shade rules the rest of the season. The spring soil is rich and moist, although it may dry out in summer. Like all sedums, it's delicately beautiful but tough and durable.

Pink and White Wildflower Echoes

With woodland wildflower combinations, you can have lavish color even in a shady spring garden. This scene features a color echo between the delicate sprays of pink bleeding hearts and the showy peony-flowered 'Angelique' tulips. Native white wild blue phlox adds a subtle color echo of the pale centers of the tulips. The cabbagelike leaves of the bergenia add interesting texture, and earlier in the season, the pink bergenia flowers are a graceful note of early-spring color. The tulips will die back in summer, but the arching sprays of Solomon's seal will fill the gaps nicely. Rich, moist soil and light to partial shade suit these plants to a tee.

PHOTO KEY

1. Solomon's seal (*Polygonatum biflorum*); Zones 3 to 9
2. Old-fashioned bleeding heart (*Dicentra spectabilis*); Zones 2 to 9
3. 'Fuller's White' wild blue phlox (*Phlox divaricata* 'Fuller's White'); Zones 3 to 9
4. 'Angelique' tulip (*Tulipa* 'Angelique'); Zones 5 to 8
5. Heartleaf bergenia (*Bergenia cordifolia*); Zones 3 to 9

Expert Tips for Wildflower Echoes

Treat shaded tulips like annuals. In the wild, tulips grow in arid regions that are moist in spring but dry in summer. Also, tulips need lots of sunlight to ripen their foliage so they can store enough food to promote reflowering from year to year. In the moist, shady conditions that this combination needs, the tulips are out of their element. For combinations like this, plan to treat hybrid tulips as annuals, and plant bulbs anew each fall.

Grow a four-season beauty. The luscious leaves and rich pink flowers of bergenia add color and texture from earliest spring right through fall. The evergreen leaves, tinted with shades of red by the cold, add winter color to your garden. In early spring, bergenia produces dense clusters of pink, bell-shaped flowers. The seedheads are also decorative long after the flowers fade. To get the best from this four-season beauty, plant it in rich, evenly moist soil in sun or shade.

Mix wildflowers with perennials. Native wildflowers are the mainstays of many woodland gardens, but adding woodland plants from other countries can improve your garden. The trick for combinations like this one, which combines native and non-native plants, is the same as for any plant combination—make sure the plants have the same soil and moisture requirements. Also check whether a plant is invasive: Choosing a non-native invasive can eventually ruin your garden and adjacent wildlands. Some invasives, such as goutweed (*Aegopodium podagraria*), easily take over, crowding out other plants. Invasive plants can even escape the confines of your garden, invading nearby woodlands and displacing native wildflowers. To protect your local woodlands, don't plant invasive plants such as goutweed, lesser celandine (*Ranunculus ficaria*), Japanese knotweed (*Polygonum cuspidatum*), and dame's rocket (*Hesperis matronalis*).

To enhance a wildflower garden, add bulbs like white 'Petrel' narcissus and spring perennials like primroses and starry lavender Bishop's hat (*Epimedium grandiflorum*).

A Wildflower and Perennial Garden

Pink and white with a touch of blue is the theme for this woodland garden, which combines some of the best long-flowering native wildflowers with beautiful non-native perennials. Siberian bugloss, western bleeding heart, and Allegheny foamflower bloom for nearly a month in spring, while barrenwort and creeping phlox join the show for a week or two. The bigroot cranesbill will bloom in early summer, producing bright pink blossoms. The bleeding heart continues blooming most of the summer, accented by the rich red heuchera leaves. This combination is tailor made for a spot with rich, moist soil and light to partial shade. In full shade, plants will bloom for a shorter period.

PHOTO KEY

1. Siberian bugloss (*Brunnera macrophylla*); Zones 3 to 8
2. 'Montrose Ruby' heuchera (*Heuchera* 'Montrose Ruby'); Zones 4 to 8
3. 'Pink Ridge' creeping phlox (*Phlox stolonifera* 'Pink Ridge'); Zones 3 to 8
4. Allegheny foamflower (*Tiarella cordifolia*); Zones 3 to 8
5. 'Ruby Mar' Western bleeding heart (*Dicentra formosa* 'Ruby Mar'); Zones 3 to 9
6. Barrenwort (*Epimedium diphyllum* 'Nanum'); Zones 5 to 9
7. Bigroot cranesbill (*Geranium macrorrhizum*); Zones 3 to 8

Plants for a Garden of Wildflowers and Perennials

❧ Opt for an oversize forget-me-not. To me, Siberian bugloss looks like a very large forget-me-not. The sky blue flowers cover the plant for weeks in midspring, followed by lush, heart-shaped leaves with the texture of sandpaper. The bugloss in this combination has plain green leaves, but you may want to substitute a cultivar with variegated foliage. 'Langtrees' has subtle silver leaf edgings, while 'Jack Frost' has netted silver foliage. 'Hadspen Cream' has a thin, even white edging to the leaves, and 'Looking Glass' has silver leaves with green margins.

❧ Sample hybrid bleeding hearts. Western bleeding heart has grayish leaves with rounded lobes. The plants spread to form wide patches. 'Ruby Mat' has deep cherry red flowers, and 'Alba' has snow white flowers. This combination would also work well with bleeding heart hybrid cultivars like 'Luxuriant', which has reddish flowers and blooms from spring through fall in moist soil. 'Zestful' has deep rose-red flowers over blue-gray foliage. 'Bacchanal' has rich wine red flowers and dark burgundy-stained gray leaves. 'Silversmith' has white flowers blushed with shell pink.

❧ Try some unusual epimediums. Epimediums are prized for their exquisite flowers, luscious foliage, and easy care. If you like hunting around for unusual plants, you'll find some excellent and underused species. *Epimedium diphyllum*, pictured here, is a lovely, late-flowering perennial with delicate, nodding white flowers. The dwarf selection 'Nanum' is only 4 to 5 inches tall and makes a great front-of-the-border plant among delicate wild-flowers. *E. sagittatum* has 6 inch spear-shaped leaflets on 1-foot stems and airy sprays of small white flowers. *E. × warleyense* has burnt orange flowers and heart-shaped leaflets. Use them as accents or groundcovers in rich, moist soil in partial to full shade.

A mound of wild geranium and shooting stars (*Dodecatheon amethystinum*) creates a pink color echo for a lightly shaded site, accented by blue pulmonaria blossoms, yellow 'Hawera' narcissus, and threadlike sedge leaves.

PHOTO KEY

1. **Pearly everlasting** (*Anaphalis margaritacea*); Zones 3 to 8
2. **Butterfly weed** (*Asclepias tuberosa*); Zones 3 to 9
3. **Tennessee coneflower** (*Echinacea tennesseensis*); Zones 4 to 8

A Meadow Mix for Wildlife

A duo of coneflowers and butterfly weed makes a bright start on a dazzling garden, and it will attract wildlife to your yard to boot. These native meadow perennials offer habitats for butterflies and other beneficial insects, and coneflower seeds are food for many songbirds. Pearly everlasting also has the small, daisylike flowers that attract many ben-

eficial insects. A dense planting of wildflowers like these can also shelter bird nests and small wildlife. This dry soil combination is perfect for sandy or clay soil in full sun or light shade. The plants are tough and generally disease free. Once established, they require very little maintenance. Fussy work, like dead-heading and staking, become chores of the past. To expand this combination into a full-fledged wildlife garden, you could also plant Joe-Pye weed (*Eupatorium* spp.) and pincushion flower (*Scabiosa caucasia*).

Expert Advice for Managing Meadow Perennials

❧ Start butterfly weed from seed. Butterfly weed grows from a fleshy taproot that can store water, helping established plants survive in dry soil and during long droughts. Though the taproot makes butterfly weed a good choice for some difficult garden sites, it also makes the plants almost impossible to transplant successfully. The root extends so deep into the soil that you inevitably break it while trying to dig the plant. The secret to success with butterfly weed is to set out young seedlings, before the taproot gets established. The best way to do this is to start seeds yourself. Sow the seeds and place the flat in a sealed bag. Fresh seeds germinate readily indoors or outdoors after six weeks of chilling at 40°F. Plant the seedlings in their permanent garden location when they're 2 to 4 inches tall.

❧ Be choosy when buying endangered plants. Tennessee coneflower is one of many federally listed endangered species that are grown in gardens. These plants may have little natural wild habitat left and are more common in gardens than they are in the wild. Nurseries that sell endangered plants must have a federal permit that shows they are propagating the plants themselves, not collecting them from the wild. The nurseries must publish their permit number in their catalog in order to sell the plants legally, so check your catalogs for a permit number before you place an order.

❧ Watch out for hybrid coneflowers. Purple coneflowers (*Echinacea* spp.) are notorious cross-pollinators. When you plant different species of purple coneflowers in your garden, bumblebees mix up the pollen as they travel from flower to flower. The seedlings that result will be hybrids, with petal shapes and flower forms that have some characteristics of both parents. The hybrids are often beautiful, but over time, as the original plants die off, you may no longer have any pure species plants left in your garden.

Milkweeds add a special touch to meadow combinations because their sweet nectar attracts butterflies like these fritillaries. Monarch butterflies also visit milkweeds to lay eggs.

PHOTO KEY

1. **Rosinweed (*Silphium inte-grifolium*); Zones 4 to 7**
2. **Wild bergamot (*Monarda fistulosa*); Zones 3 to 9**
3. **Gray-headed coneflower (*Ratibida pinnata*); Zones 3 to 10**
4. **Culver's root (*Veronicas-trum virginicum*); Zones 3 to 9**

A Summer-Blooming Prairie Scene

Drifts of pink wild bergamot and gray-headed coneflower mingle with dramatic Culver's root flower spikes in this lively garden of non-stop bloom. This combination looks like it could be a native prairie, but it's actually a carefully planned garden. With prairie and meadow combinations, you might want to be casual about design so the combination looks "natural." However, choosing and placing plants artistically is still important so your garden won't look *too* wild. In this combination, the spiky Culver's root is the focal point, and the drifts of coneflowers, bergamot, and rosinweed form a pleasing background. In time, the plants will self-sow and blend together to form a sea of mixed textures and colors.

Secrets for Summer-Blooming Prairie Perennials

🌿 **Try some prairie natives.** Many native meadow and prairie wildflowers are great ingredients for colorful and exuberant perennial combinations. Rosinweed, pictured here, is just one of many *Silphium* species that work well for the middle or back of a perennial border. It has glossy, oval leaves on 3- to 5-foot stems, and the flowers open for nearly two months in mid- to late summer. *Silphium* flowers resemble sunflowers in bloom, and most types have attractive leaves that encircle the plant's stem. They're easy to grow in rich, moist soil in full sun or light shade.

🌿 **Don't bother staking.** In prairie and meadow gardens, plants grow profusely, tumbling into one another. With all this enthusiastic growth, the plants form a self-supporting network of stems that hold up one another, and that means no staking. You can enjoy maximum beauty with minimum work. It's a great way to garden!

🌿 **Add grasses to the mix.** In nature, meadows and prairies include both wildflowers and grasses. To make this combination more authentic, you could try adding grasses like little bluestem (*Schizachyrium scoparium*) and Indian grass (*Sorghastrum nutans*). The grasses help support the wildflowers and contribute a green background to show off the colorful flowers. Plus, the dried seedheads of the grasses add fall and winter interest to the combination. One reason that garden designers often don't include grasses is that people think they look messy. If you're concerned that your neighbors won't like your meadow garden, start by planting wildflowers only. Once they've learned to enjoy its abundant color, you can add in some grasses.

A prairie garden is perfect for a sunny dry bank that's hard to mow. Try combining a grass, such as big bluestem, with showy flowers, such as white Culver's root, pink wild bergamot, and yellow oxeye.

Meadow Perennials for a Sunny Border

Billowing masses of flowering spurge and spotted Joe-Pye weed contrast with bold purple coneflowers and the spiky flower clusters of downy skullcap in this combination of native meadow plants. The wild bergamot bloomed earlier in the season, but its rounded seedheads still add interest to the combination.

This beautiful grouping shows that native meadow perennials can fit comfortably into a traditional garden border. It's designed just like a border of standard garden perennials would be, with the tallest plants in back and the shortest in front. This combination would look stunning at the edge of a yard in front of a backdrop of deciduous trees.

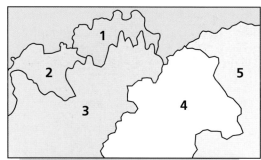

PHOTO KEY
1. 'Atropurpureum' spotted Joe-Pye weed (*Eupatorium maculatum* 'Atropurpureum'); Zones 2 to 8
2. Purple coneflower (*Echinacea purpurea*); Zones 3 to 8
3. Downy skullcap (*Scutellaria incana*); Zones 4 to 9
4. Flowering spurge (*Euphorbia corollata*); Zones 3 to 8
5. Wild bergamot (*Monarda fistulosa*); Zones 3 to 9

Native Meadow Plants for Perennial Borders

A better baby's-breath. Baby's-breath (*Gypsophila paniculata*) is a popular perennial, but it needs alkaline soil and doesn't grow well in areas with hot, humid nights. The flowering spurge in this combination, also called prairie baby's-breath, is a baby's-breath look-alike that will succeed where true baby's-breath fails. The delicate, open clusters of white spurge flowers look amazingly like baby's-breath. Flowering spurge grows in moist or dry, rich or poor soil, in full sun or light shade.

A healing plant. Purple coneflower (*Echinacea purpurea*) is a true mainstay of modern herbal medicine, used in skin creams, shampoos, toothpaste, and as a cure for the common cold. However, the boom in echi-nacea products has been hard on wild populations of purple coneflowers. If you buy echinacea products, check the label or ask your supplier for products made from plants raised especially for harvesting.

An unusual native plant. The skullcaps (*Scutellaria* spp.) are a group of exceptional but little-known native American perennials that are hard to find at local perennial nurseries. These beautiful, adaptable plants thrive in sun or partial shade in rich, evenly moist soil. Skullcaps overflow with true-blue flowers in spring or summer, depending on the species. They're called skullcaps because the flowers resemble tight-fitting, brimless hats. To find skullcaps, try shopping from mail-order nurseries that specialize in wildflowers.

Starry yellow cup plant (*Silphium perfoliatum*), lemon yellow thin-leaved coneflower (*Rudbeckia triloba*), white-flowered *Aralia spinosa*, and rosy Joe-Pye weed provide color and drama against the dark backdrop of a woodland.

A Riot of Meadow Flowers for Wet Soil

Purple asters and red cardinal flowers vie for attention in a sea of contrasting yellow in this combination of moisture-loving meadow perennials. All of these perennials bloom in late summer and fall, so they're great choices for adding color to beds and borders as the gardening season winds down. Just be sure to plant them in moist, rich soil in full sun.

When you plant meadow perennials that feature daisylike flowers such as coneflowers and asters, you'll also find plenty of butterflies and bees in your garden, as well as a range of beneficial insects that help control insect pests. The tubular flowers of the cardinal flowers and great blue lobelia will also attract hummingbirds.

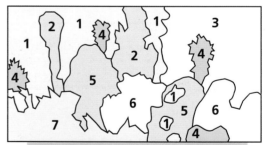

PHOTO KEY
1. **Thin-leaved coneflower (*Rudbeckia triloba*); Zones 4 to 7**
2. **Great blue lobelia (*Lobelia siphilitica*); Zones 4 to 8**
3. **Helenium (*Helenium autumnale*); Zones 3 to 8**
4. **Cardinal flower (*Lobelia cardinalis*); Zones 2 to 9**
5. **New England aster (*Aster novae-angliae*); Zones 3 to 8**
6. **Sweet coneflower (*Rudbeckia subtomentosa*); Zones 4 to 7**
7. **Canada goldenrod (*Solidago canadensis*); Zones 3 to 8**

Tips for Late-Season Meadow Color

🌿 **Get names straight before you buy.**
You may find common names of perennials easier to remember than botanical names, but when it comes to coneflowers, botanical names can be less confusing than common names. If you ask for coneflowers at a nursery, you could end up with any of several different species! *Echinaceas* have the common name of purple coneflower. Some *Rudbeckias* are also called coneflowers. And still other coneflowers are actually species of *Ratibida*. While all these flowers have a conelike center and long petals, they come in different colors and heights, and they need different growing conditions.

🌿 **Don't sneeze at helenium.** Helenium (*Helenium autumnale*) is also called sneezeweed, but the flowers won't make you sneeze. It's the roots of the plant that tickle your nose—people used to dry helenium roots and grind them into a powder that was used as snuff. You'll enjoy showy yellow helenium flowers, which also make long-lasting cut flowers. To keep helenium prospering, plant it in rich, evenly moist soil in full sun or light shade.

🌿 **Plant lobelias for hummers.** Hummingbirds respond most strongly to red, but they're also attracted to blue, yellow, and orange. So blue lobelia and cardinal flower, both pictured here, are terrific hummingbird attractors. To get the best from lobelias, plant them in rich, evenly moist soil in full sun or partial shade. They reseed freely in bare areas, so they often sprout in garden paths or compost piles. In winter, keep the rosettes free of mulch, because they may rot if they're covered.

Pink and purple asters, tall goldenrod (*Solidago altissima*), and white snakeroot (*Eupatorium rugosum*) provide a lively mix of late-summer color for a sunny backyard meadow garden.

PHOTO KEY

1. **Tall tickseed (***Coreopsis tripteris***); Zones 3 to 8**
2. **Cup plant (***Silphium perfoliatum***); Zones 5 to 9**
3. **Inkberry (***Ilex glabra***); Zones 5 to 9**
4. **Swamp milkweed (***Asclepias incarnata***); Zones 3 to 8**
5. **Boneset (***Eupatorium perfoliatum***); Zones 3 to 8**

A Low-Maintenance Butterfly Meadow

Rich textures, bright colors, and a variety of flower sizes make this meadow combination a real winner. It flowers just when summer populations of butterflies reach their peak, and the butterflies will flock to the plants to feed on nectar. Just remember, in order to have butterflies in your garden, you'll have to feed some caterpillars, too. But a little caterpillar grazing on your perennial foliage won't harm the plants, so welcome both the butterflies and the caterpillars to your garden.

Like a natural meadow, once established, this combination is a great low-maintenance alternative to a lawn or traditional border. Tree seedlings and perennial weeds, such as quackgrass and dock, are the main foes for meadow plants. As the meadow matures, its thick vegetation will suppress all but the most aggressive weeds. You'll need to mow or cut back your meadow combinations each year to control woody growth such as trees and shrubs. Spring mowing is ideal, so you can enjoy the dried flowers and grasses all winter.

Perennials for a Butterfly Meadow

❧ **A magnet for butterflies.** The rosy pink flowers of swamp milkweed, pictured here, are irresistible to butterflies, and its foliage is prime food for the caterpillars of the monarch butterfly. (Monarch caterpillars will eat all types of milkweed foliage.) Unlike its cousin butterfly weed (*Asclepias tuberosa*), swamp milkweed needs rich, moist soil to thrive. It will even grow submerged in the water of a garden pond. Choose a site for this plant carefully, because the plants spread by underground stems and may quickly take over a small bed.

❧ **Joe-Pye weed's cousin.** The boneset in this combination is a lovely native plant of wetlands and low meadows. Though its pure white flowers put on quite a show in summer, it's often overlooked in favor of its gaudier cousin Joe-Pye weed (*Eupatorium purpureum*). Plant boneset in rich, moist to wet soil in full sun. The plants mature into multistemmed clumps up to 3 feet tall that seldom need dividing. In late summer, the plants are smothered with white flowers—and with butterflies!

❧ **A plant for birds and butterflies.** Cup plant (*Silphium perfoliatum*) really does provide cups from which birds can drink. The plant has two opposing leaves at intervals along the stems. The blades of these leaves join around the stem, forming a solid "cup" that can gather dew or rainwater. I've seen goldfinches and chickadees drinking from these small pools. Cup plants also produce large amounts of seed that finches, sparrows, chickadees, and other birds eat with gusto. The tall tickseed in this combination produces lots of seeds too, but only nimble, lightweight birds, like chickadees and finches, can pick out the seeds without toppling the tall, slender flowerstalks. The flowers of both species are magnets for butterflies.

If you have a large sunny spot with wet soil, try some tall, moisture-loving meadow and prairie plants. This enormous yellow-flowered cup plant dwarfs the 6-foot-tall Joe-Pye weed and the white asters beside it.

A Rosy Combo
for a Seaside Site

Clear air and cool sea breezes keep seaside combinations like this mix of shrub roses and perennials in prime vigor, even at the height of summer. But because placid summer weather can turn into a raging gale, plants for seaside gardens need to be tough. Jupiter's beard and Jerusalem sage can tolerate salt spray and salty soils. While meadow rues do best in rich, moist soil, the columbine meadow rue in this combination can tolerate seaside conditions. Adding shrubs to perennial combinations can help buffer perennials against storms. In this garden, a mixed planting of shrub roses serves as a living windbreak to catch the wind and salt spray before it hits more delicate flowers. The roses also add height and permanent winter structure to the garden.

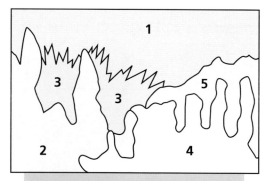

PHOTO KEY

1. Shrub rose (*Rosa* sp.); Zones 4 to 8
2. White Jupiter's beard (*Centranthus ruber* var. *albus*); Zones 4 to 8
3. Pacific coast iris (*Iris douglasiana*); Zones 6 to 8
4. Jerusalem sage (*Phlomis russeliana*); Zones 4 to 9
5. Columbine meadow rue (*Thalictrum aquilegifolium*); Zones 4 to 8

Secrets for Success with Seaside Plants

🌿 Try Jerusalem sage for cut flowers.
Jerusalem sage forms a neat groundcover of felted, heart-shaped leaves that remain attractive all season. The 2- to 3-foot flower spikes arise in early summer. Tiers of soft yellow flowers open in succession from bottom to top. The unusual flower spikes make dramatic additions to cut flower arrangements. You can also let the flowers go to seed. The stems punctuated with buttonlike dried seedheads are a unique addition to dried flower arrangements.

🌿 Extend the bloom of Jupiter's beard.
Jupiter's beard is an early-spring bloomer. The buds push out of the ground in spring along with the new leaves. The spring display is just the beginning of the show, however. The plants stay in full bloom for several months.

How? The branched stems continually produce side shoots with new buds that keep the plant looking great into early summer. If you cut the spent stems back, the plants will produce even more flowers.

🌿 Give Pacific coast iris dry soil. Pacific coast iris, pictured here, is a tough, drought-tolerant plant. Even in poor, dry soil, it will produce mounds of medium blue, grape-scented flowers in late spring.

🌿 Use conifers for contrast. The dark green foliage of conifers can be an effective backdrop for perennial plantings. Pines like Scott's pine (*Pinus sylvestris*) are fairly salt-tolerant. They're often used in seaside plantings to block salt spray and add height to the garden, just as the shrub roses do here.

For a salt-tolerant edging along a lawn or path, combine drifts of red-flowered Jupiter's beard with blue catmint (*Nepeta* × *faassenii*).

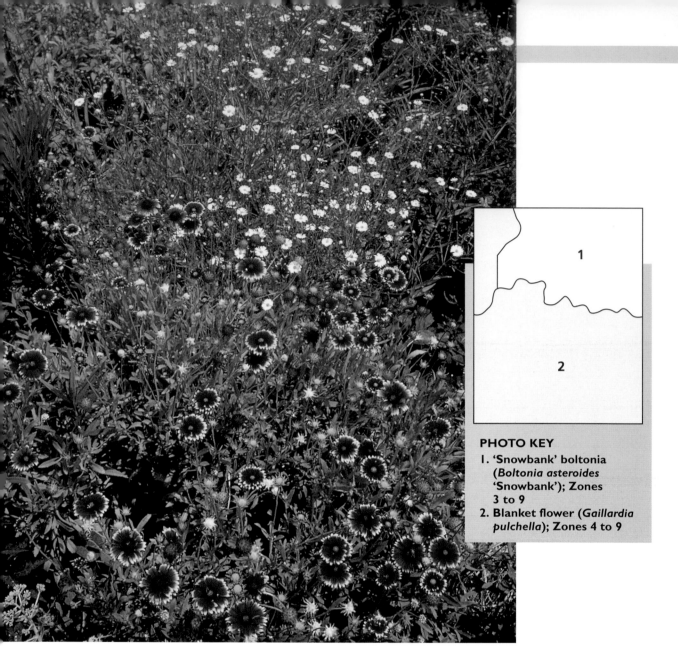

A Blanket of Seaside Flowers

Fiery red and yellow contrast with icy white in this bright combination for a sunny seaside spot in sandy or clay soil. The blanket flowers bloom tirelessly all summer, producing new flowers from rambling stems that sprawl outward in a loose tumble. The white daisies of 'Snowbank' boltonia bloom in late summer. After the boltonia fades, the swamp sunflowers will bloom, bearing yellow flowers with yellow centers. To add more early-season bloom to this combination, you could plant coreopsis, prickly pear (*Opuntia humifusa*), and butterfly weed (*Asclepias tuberosa*).

Expert Tips for a
Seaside Blanket of Flowers

❧ Keep blanket flowers in bloom.
Blanket flowers get their name from the three rings of color in each blossom that resemble the intricate patterns in handwoven Navajo blankets. Blanket flowers are easy to grow in well-drained soil, but they live for only a few years. To keep blanket flowers blooming reliably in your garden, you'll need to set out new plants each spring or fall. In sandy, open soil, the plants may self-sow prolifically, doing the replanting for you. If you want a longer-lived substitute for the blanket flowers in this combination, try *Gaillardia* × *grandiflora*. 'Burgundy', which has rich red flowers, is one of my favorite cultivars.

❧ Grow a marsh plant in dry sand.
Although it grows lushly in rich, moist soils, boltonia also thrives in drier sites in sand and clay. Boltonia has adapted to the changing moisture levels of its native habitats—wet ditches and the edges of wetlands. Ditches and wetlands can become very dry in summer as the groundwater level drops, and the plants that grow there can survive the annual cycles of wet winters and springs and dry summers. So unless the soil bakes bone dry, boltonia is at home in sand or clay.

❧ Feed the birds with sunflowers.
Cheery perennial sunflowers add bold splashes of late season color when most of the garden is winding down for the season. The rich yellow flowers of swamp sunflower, pictured here, open in September and may last into November in areas where frost comes late. Leave the seedheads in place after the flowers fade. The stiff stems will remain standing in winter, and chickadees, goldfinches, and other birds will visit to pick out the ripened seeds.

Silver feather maiden grass (*Miscanthus sinensis* 'Silver Feather') and colorful blanket flowers are a good combination for a garden near the sea, but also for a hot, southern garden with clay soil.

Sedum and Thyme for the Seaside

Sedums and the seaside are a natural combination. These durable, adaptable plants tolerate heat, drought, and salt spray. This simple, bright combination is perfect for a finishing detail in a seaside garden. Try planting it atop a decorative stone, in the crevice of a wall, or between the pavers in a walkway. As long as they have good drainage, both the thyme and sedum will quickly take off and weave their stems around the rocks, pavers, or whatever else is close by. Even after their flowers fade, the foliage will remain attractive all season.

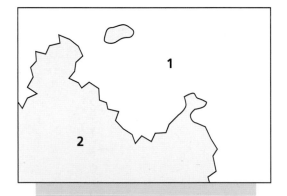

PHOTO KEY
1. Kamschatka sedum (*Sedum kamtschaticum*); Zones 3 to 8
2. Creeping thyme (*Thymus serpyllum* var. *coccineus*); Zones 4 to 9

Planting Tips for Sedum and Thyme

❧ **Cover the ground with creeping sedums.** Creeping sedums are tough groundcover plants that have a place in every yard because they tolerate a wide range of conditions, from full sun to partial shade. Under all the bright yellow flowers of Kamschatka sedum, pictured here, there's a carpet of elongated, rich green leaves that turn orange-yellow in the fall. Two-row sedum (*S. spurium*) has wider spatula-shaped leaves and pink flowers. The cultivar 'Dragon's Blood' has deep maroon foliage and dark rose-pink flowers. October daphne (*S. sieboldii*) has blue-gray leaves and pink flowers in fall.

❧ **Include thyme in many ways.** Each species of thyme has its own distinctive scent, texture, and flower color. Of course, the culinary thymes are the most pungent. Their rich green leaves and white flowers are attractive in herb or ornamental gardens, as well as in containers. Creeping thyme is excellent as a groundcover among larger herbs and ornamental plants. Give plants rich but well-drained soil in full sun or light shade. They'll also thrive in poorer, sandy soils as well as between paving stones. Shear the taller species back in early spring to encourage fresh, compact growth.

❧ **Try a thyme lawn.** If mowing the lawn bores you as much as it does me, try converting part of your lawn from grass to thyme. A thyme lawn is perfect for a small- to medium-size area that gets light foot traffic. Unlike turf grasses, thyme plants can't withstand repeated trampling, but the occasional romp on the fragrant carpet does no harm. Try planting a thyme lawn in the open space around a lushly planted container, around a fountain, or in the light shade of a single tree. If you interplant several species and colors, you'll have a crazy-quilt of living color.

Yellow-flowered gold-moss sedum (*Sedum acre*) and hens-and-chickens (*Sempervivum tectorum* and *S. arachnoideum*) would be at home in many places in a seaside garden—atop a rock wall, along a path, or in a container.

Combine the Colors of Sun and Sea

A bright mix of yellow sundrops and blue catmint reflect the colors of the sun and the sea—a perfect pair for a seaside garden. These two perennials bloom for more than a month in early summer, and they thrive in well-drained, average to rich soil in full sun or light shade. To add height to this combination, you could plant Asiatic lilies; to extend the bloom season, add blazing-stars and veronica for midsummer and asters and goldenrods for fall. If you cut the catmint back after flowering, you will get a second flush of bloom in mid-summer.

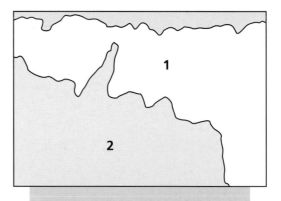

PHOTO KEY
1. Evening primrose (*Oenothera fruticosa*); Zones 3 to 8
2. 'Blue Wonder' Persian catmint (*Nepeta* × *faassenii* 'Blue Wonder'); Zones 3 to 8

Plants for the Sun and Sea

A selection of sundrops. Evening primroses (*Oenothora* spp.) are also called sundrops, because the flowers open in the evening, persist through the night and next morning, then fade away in the heat of the day. *Oenothora tetragona*, sometimes listed as a separate species, is the same as *O. fruticosa*. Some of the best cultivars include long-blooming 'Fireworks', with red buds that open to 3-inch flowers on 18-inch stalks; 'Golden Sunray', which reaches 2 feet tall; 'Summer Solstice', which flowers a month later than most cultivars; and 'Yellow River', noted for its burgundy fall color.

Spreading sundrops. Ozark sundrops, also called Missouri evening primrose (*Oenothera macrocarpon*), are altogether different from other sundrops. The plants form large, sprawling clumps of silvery green, lance-shaped foliage accented by huge, lemon yellow flowers throughout the summer. The clumps start the season compact, but by season's end may be several feet across. Place them at the front of the border where the stems can weave together with other edging plants such as verbenas and cranesbills. The cultivar 'Greencourt Lemon' is more delicate and has softer yellow flowers.

The best of the catmints. 'Blue Wonder' catmint, pictured here, is the most popular catmint for gardens, but there are other cultivars and species you can substitute if you like variety. 'Six Hills Giant' is an oversize version of 'Blue Wonder', growing three times as tall. Use it at the center or rear of a garden rather than as an edging. Siberian catmint (*Nepeta siberica*) is a striking plant with erect spikes of 1-inch flowers all summer long. Veined catmint (*N. nervosa*) thrives in poor, dry soil and tolerates heat. It's also particularly well-suited to seaside conditions.

In this seaside garden, the delicate flowers of Mexican daisy (*Erigeron karvinskianus*) echo the pink Mexican evening primrose (*Oenothera mexicana,* sometimes listed incorrectly as *O. berlandieri*), while rich blue Pacific coast iris and magenta penstemon add color contrast.

PHOTO KEY
1. Sea thrift (*Armeria maritima*); Zones 3 to 8
2. Sun rose (*Helianthemum nummularium*); Zones 6 to 8
3. Dutch iris (*Iris* Dutch hybrid); Zones 6 to 9
4. Rock soapwort (*Saponaria ocymoides*); Zones 3 to 7

Pastel Colors for a Seaside Site

Cool blues and pinks in this combination capture the colors of a sunset over a calm ocean. The foliage and flowers of Dutch iris form a dramatic exclamation point for this grouping. Dutch iris is an old-fashioned bulb more widely grown as a cut flower than as a border plant. The rock soapwort nestles against a rock that echos the pink of its flowers. Bands of rosy sea thrift and silvery sun rose foliage create a lively background. Despite the heat of a sunny bed in sandy soil, this combination thrives, and provides a colorful display for a month in early- to mid-summer.

Expert Advice for a Seaside Site

&❧ **Help sandy soil with humus.** Even perennials that are adapted to sandy soils like those common near the ocean often benefit from a little soil improvement. Sand is easy to dig, so amending it is a snap. Add a 3- to 4-inch layer of well-rotted compost or manure over the top of the soil, and spade it in to a depth of 10 to 12 inches. Turn the soil thoroughly and let the bed settle for a week or two before planting. Even the most drought-tolerant plants will benefit from the added nutrients and the extra water the humus will hold.

&❧ **Let soapwort weave its own way.** Soapwort (*Saponaria* spp.) is an excellent weaver for the front of a perennial border. Its trailing habit plus its tendency to self sow allow it to spread through the garden. It comes up readily between other plants but is never a nuisance. It forms extensive mats smothered in flowers for a month or more in summer.

&❧ **Add contrast with 'Max Frei'.** If you'd like to increase the contrast in this combination, try a larger form of soapwort. *Saponaria* × *lempergii* 'Max Frei' has 1-inch, starry pink flowers that smother the clumps in mid-summer. This soapwort thrives in cold areas but will languish in the heat south of Zone 7.

&❧ **Try some international iris.** Dutch irises are charming garden plants that often get forgotten when we think about iris choices. Set the bulbs out in fall or early spring, and they will bloom in late spring and early summer. Give Dutch irises full sun in a spot that bakes in summer, and they will re-bloom for several years. Some of the species that were combined to create the Dutch iris hybrids are enchanting and long-lived garden plants as well. Try Spanish iris (*Iris xiphium*),

Sea thrift (*Armeria maritima*) is a classic choice for the salt and wind of the seaside garden. While it's native to windswept ledges, it thrives equally well in a sunny, well-drained spot near the ocean or in an inland garden. It's a great companion for sedums and soapworts (*Saponaria* spp.).

with its rich blue, white, or yellow flowers, and English iris (*I. xiphioides*) with blue, purple, or white flowers. These irises will go dormant after flowering, so they work well in combination with weaving plants like rock soapwort.

PHOTO KEY

1. Cinnamon fern (*Osmunda cinnamomea*); Zones 3 to 8
2. Variegated yellow flag (*Iris pseudacorus* 'Variegata'); Zones 4 to 9
3. Golden club (*Orontium aquaticum*); Zones 6 to 11

Spikes of Gold and Green

The yellow-striped leaves of variegated yellow flag create a classic color echo with the "clubs" of golden club in this early-spring water garden combination that accents foliage and unusual flowers. Both of these plants need rich, loamy soil and thrive in standing water, though the yellow flag is equally at home simply in wet soil. The cinnamon fern in the background does best at the water's edge or in shallow water in light to full shade.

To build a complete picture around this combination, you could add lacy royal ferns (*Osmunda regalis*), marsh marigold (*Caltha palustris*), pink Japanese primroses (*Primula japonica*), and bold, textured rodgersias.

Growing Golden Clubs and Water Irises

Bizarre and beautiful golden club. The "clubs" of golden club, pictured here, are a collection of tightly packed flowers called a spadix. They're similar to the "Jack" inside the flower of a Jack-in-the-pulpit. Golden club needs to grow in wet soil or standing water in full sun or light shade. If you want to grow golden clubs in a water garden, you can plant them in heavy loam soil in a container and submerge the container in the water.

Now it's yellow, now it's not. The most striking feature of the variegated yellow flag iris in this combination is the bold yellow stripes that grace its dramatic, swordlike leaves. The yellow color is very intense as the leaves emerge in the spring, but as the flowers open, the color begins to fade. By summer, the stripes almost disappear. Don't be alarmed: Next spring, the new foliage that appears will have those yellow stripes. For the best bloom, you'll want to plant yellow flag in full sun or light shade, but if you're mainly growing them for foliage interest, partial shade is fine (they also do well in partial shade in the South). In favorable conditions, yellow flag can spread aggressively, forming clumps 4 to 5 feet across.

More irises for water gardens. Yellow flag isn't the only iris that likes wet feet. Rabbit-ear iris (*Iris laevigata*) thrives in wet soil or standing water, as does *Iris hexagona*. They have deep purple-blue flowers in late spring and early summer. Blue flag irises (*I. virginica* and *I. versicolor*) are also at home in standing water or soil that stays moist all season. Some of the most unusually colored water irises are classified as Louisiana hybrids. Japanese irises (*I. ensata*) are the most impressive water irises, with large, flat flowers of 5 inches or more across.

When yellow flag irises come into full bloom, the golden yellow flowers wave like flags at a victory parade. For a triumphant effect, try repeating clumps of yellow flag all around the edge of a water garden.

PHOTO KEY

1. **Evergreen miscanthus** (*Miscanthus transmorriso-nensis*); Zones 7 to 10
2. **Gunnera** (*Gunnera manicata*); Zones 7 to 10
3. **Tropical water lily** (*Nymphaea* sp.); Zones 10 to 11
4. **Water canna** (*Thalia dealbata*); Zones 7 to 11
5. **Variegated rabbit-ear iris** (*Iris laevigata* 'Variegata'); Zones 4 to 9
6. **Scouring rush** (*Equisetum*); Zones 3 to 9

Water Lilies and Waving Grasses

Floating water lilies, spiky rushes and irises, and bold-textured gunnera and water canna make a serene and rather formal display in this water garden. The huge clump of evergreen miscanthus in the background echoes the grassy forms of the iris and scouring rush. If you want to create a water garden combination like this one and you have a water garden with a plastic liner, you'll need to grow the water plants in pots sunk to the rim in the water. (Check "Secrets for Potted Water Garden Plants" on the opposite page for details on preparing potted plants for water gardens.) Even if you have a pond with an earthen bottom, planting in a pot is the best choice for the scouring rush, which is a rapid spreader.

You can leave the hardy plants—scouring rush and iris—in the water over winter. The tropical water lilies and more tender perennials must be lifted out of the water in the fall and stored in a frost-free cellar or greenhouse over the winter.

Secrets for Potted Water Garden Plants

✦ Pot water plants in heavy soil. When you pot up most plants, you use a light, airy potting mix. Not so with aquatic plants; the heavier the soil, the better. You need a mix that will stay in the pot and keep the plants well anchored, rather than a mix that will sift into the water. You don't need to put drainage holes in the bottom of the container, because it will be filled with water anyway once it's in place. I always put a 1-inch layer of pea gravel over the soil in the pot. This helps prevent the soil from washing out while I'm sinking the pot to the bottom of the pond.

✦ Try tropical water lilies. Tropical water lilies are popular water garden plants because of their huge, brilliantly colored flowers. Night-flowering varieties have fragrant flowers. 'Wood's White Knight' is a prolific bloomer with pure white flowers, and it spreads across a large area. Tropical water lilies are heat and light sensitive and need full sun for best bloom. They grow slowly at first in the spring until the water warms above 70°F. If you don't want to bother with lifting these water lilies out of your water garden and storing them over winter, you can treat them as annuals and order new plants at the start of each growing season.

✦ Don't forget the hardy water lilies. If you're willing to settle for fewer blooms in exchange for less maintenance, try hardy water lilies instead of tropical. They have flowers that range from white and pale yellow to pink, rose, and red. You can leave hardy water lilies in a water garden over winter, but lift and repot them in spring if their roots have filled the container.

✦ Treat gunnera tenderly. While the gunnera in this water garden grows happily outdoors year-round in the Pacific Northwest, in the North, it needs to be stored indoors during the winter. Umbrella plant (*Darmera peltata*) is a great substitute that's hardy in Zones 4 to 7.

Hardy white water lily (*Nymphaea odorata*) and yellow floating heart (*Nymphoides cordata*) are enthusiastic spreading plants that can cover the entire surface of a garden pool.

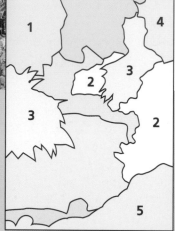

PHOTO KEY

1. Mountain fleece
   (*Persicaria amplexicaulis*);
   Zones 5 to 8
2. Yellow corydalis
   (*Corydalis lutea*);
   Zones 5 to 8
3. Lady fern (*Athyrium
   filix-femina*); Zones 3 to 9
4. Astilbe (*Astilbe*); Zones
   3 to 8
5. European wild ginger
   (*Asarum europaeum*);
   Zones 4 to 8

A Stream's Edge Combination

A slow-moving stream lined with plants adds movement to a garden, but it also creates a quiet, contemplative feeling. The plants in this combination aren't true aquatic plants, but they thrive in light to full shade in the moist, rich soil just above the waterline. A carpet of golden corydalis is the mainstay of this combination.

Its first flowers emerge in early spring and the plants bloom nonstop until frost. Even in the deep shade of my garden, this powerhouse bloomer never goes a day without flowers. The bold texture of the shiny wild ginger leaves contrasts beautifully with the delicate corydalis. The large masses of ferns dip their fronds lazily into the water, enhancing the relaxing feeling of the garden. This combination would work equally well planted along a lightly shaded edge of a water garden or pond.

Moist-Soil Plants for a Stream Edge

❧ A gentle spreader. Corydalis self-sows prolifically, filling in spaces around larger plants beautifully but never overwhelming them. And corydalis seedlings are easy to weed out, so controlling its spread isn't a problem. If yellow isn't your color, substitute *Corydalis ochroleuca* for the yellow corydalis in this combination. It has creamy white flowers and the same nonstop bloom as its yellow cousin.

❧ Another nonstop bloomer. Mountain fleece is another perennial that doesn't know when to quit. The first of its cherry red spikes emerges above the spinachlike leaves in early summer. From the moment the first flowers open, the plant is covered nonstop with pencil-thin flower spikes until a hard freeze kills it back. Plants thrive equally well in sun or shade. Moist, rich soil is best, but I've seen this perennial growing in sunbaked, dry clay.

❧ A versatile fern. Lady fern is one of the best ferns for gardens. It thrives almost anywhere and has graceful, lacy fronds that grow 1 to 3 feet long. Plants do best in rich, moist soil and light to partial shade. The multicrowned clumps can become quite large with age. In midsummer, if the early fronds begin to look tattered, just cut them back and new fronds will quickly fill in.

❧ A shining carpet. The European wild ginger in this garden is an easy-to-grow groundcover that creates a shining carpet of rounded leaves. Wild gingers like moist, woodsy soil, but they aren't wetland plants, so be sure to position them well above the water's edge. Other wild gingers include 'Callaway' mottled wild ginger (*Asarum shuttleworthii* 'Callaway'), arum wild ginger (*A. arifolium*), and Virginia wild ginger (*A. virginicum*).

For something lush and lovely, try combining cottage garden perennials with a water garden. Here, lilies, cattails, irises, and rushes grow in the water, while billowing clumps of lady's-mantle (*Alchemilla mollis*) adorn the edge.

Bold Leaves and Bright Color beside the Water

The enormous leaves of the umbrella plant add high drama to this streamside garden. A carpet of sunny yellow monkey flower lines the edges of the stream, accenting the flowing lines of the rocky channel. The delicate leaves of the maple contrast perfectly with the gigantic, coarsely toothed leaves of the umbrella plant. Small trees like the maple can be great companions for perennials, because they add year-round interest with foliage, branches, and bark. Red-leaved Japanese maples are a dramatic choice because of their elegant foliage and rich color. The fine-textured stems and curving trunks create a living sculpture in the winter landscape. Shrubs can serve the same purpose, and even rocks or garden sculpture can be part of your perennial combinations.

268

Plants with Bold Leaves and Bright Colors

🦋 **The tropical beauty of umbrella plant.**
Umbrella plant, pictured here, blooms early in spring, long before the foliage appears. Bloom stalks rise from the ground to a height of 1 to 3 feet. The soft pink flowers look like spirea blossoms. The leaves, which begin to emerge as the flowers fade, look like crepe paper parasols blown inside out by a brisk wind. As they emerge, the leaves flatten out to an impressive size. Umbrella plant thrives in standing water or constantly moist, humus-rich soil in light to full shade. It spreads by thick, creeping underground stems to form broad, dramatic clumps. Divide plants in early spring or fall, keeping at least one large eye (the point from which new leaves emerge) per division.

🦋 **A dwarf umbrella plant.** If you have a small garden where a 4 × 6-foot clump of umbrella plant is out of the question, don't despair. There's a dwarf form available, and it's small enough for a tiny bog or water garden. The plants form 1- to 2-foot clumps.

🦋 **Try monkey flower.** Monkey flowers (*Mimulus* spp.) are an unusual sight in American gardens, even though they're native plants. The monkey flower we grow most often is a hybrid that's treated as an annual, but the plants hate summer heat and often grow poorly. Not yellow monkey flower, though. It's a prolific self-sower where conditions suit it, and it blooms for most of the summer. If the weather gets too hot, the plants go dormant and start reblooming in fall, when the weather cools down.

🦋 **Substitutes for Japanese maple.** If you don't have room for a full-size Japanese maple but love the effect of its red foliage in this combination, try one of the slower growing, weeping selections, such as threadleaf Japanese maple (*Acer palmatum* 'Dissectum Atropurpureum'), which grows 4 to 6 feet tall and wide. If that's still too big, try a red- or purple-flowered astilbe, such as 'Fanal', which also has red tinged foliage.

In this moisture-loving garden, heart-shaped leaves of Imperial taro (*Colocasia esculenta* 'Illustris') contrast with delicate bleeding heart and stiff clumps of Dixie wood fern (*Dryopteris* × *australis*).

Fancy Flowers and Foliage for the Pond

Water gardens that stand out from the crowd combine both aquatic plants and bog plants. This garden features the floating heart-shaped leaves of fragrant water lily beside iris, monkey flower, and astilbe. The perennials at the water's edge frame the pond and help to blend it into the larger landscape. Free-seeding primroses, shown here past bloom, add early-season color in shades of rose, pink, and white.

This combination uses hybrid monkey flowers, which tend to fade out in hot gardens. You can substitute scarlet monkey flower (*Mimulus cardinalis*), which goes dormant in summer heat but flowers prolifically all season where summers are cool. Though short-lived, it seeds freely in moist soil, so you should always find it somewhere in the garden.

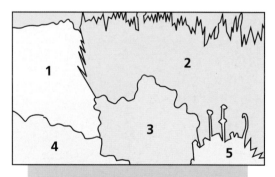

PHOTO KEY

1. **Astilbe (*Astilbe × arendsii*); Zones 3 to 9**
2. **Siberian iris (*Iris sibirica*); Zones 2 to 9**
3. **'Wisley Red' monkey flower (*Mimulus × hybridus* 'Wisley Red'); Zones 6 to 8**
4. **Fragrant water lily (*Nymphaea odorata* hybrid); Zones 3 to 9**
5. **Primrose (*Primula* sp.); Zones 4 to 8**

Plants with Fancy Foliage and Flowers

🏵 **Proper placement for Siberian irises.**
Siberian irises like wet feet but not standing water. Unlike true water irises, such as Japanese iris, these plants need to be a little above the waterline, where the crowns are dry and the roots have access to water. They also thrive in rich garden soil away from water.

🏵 **The right way to grow astilbes.**
Though astilbes grow fairly well in perennial gardens in the cooler northern zones, they really grow best in mucky soil at the water's edge. Where the soil dries out in summer, the plants never achieve their full potential—the flower spikes aren't as tall or full. Worse yet, the foliage may turn brown and crispy in dry summer weather. If summers are hot and your soil just won't stay wet all season, try one of the Chinese astilbes (*Astilbe chinensis*). They

don't seem to mind the heat, and the soil can get a little dry from time to time without ruining the flower and foliage display. Plants have rose-pink flowers and range in height from the 3- to 4-foot variety *taquettii* 'Superba' to the diminutive 6- to 12-inch 'Pumila'.

🏵 **Primroses by the pool.** Japanese primroses, also called candelabra primroses, are the most common primroses for wet conditions. They come in a variety of shades of pink and rose, as well as coral and white. There are other worthwhile moisture-loving primroses, too. Florinda primrose (*Primulas florindae*) has sweet-scented yellow flowers on 2- to 3-foot stems above wide, straplike leaves. It's hardy in Zones 6 to 8. *P. pulverulenta* has magenta flowers and is hardy in Zones 5 to 8.

In rich, wet soil along the bank of a stream or pond, Japanese primroses will self sow to form multicolor drifts that bloom for weeks in spring. Upright, feathery royal fern (*Osmunda regalis*) and bold ostrich fern (*Matteuccia struthiopteris*) make excellent companions.

A Woodland Wildflower Garden

Christmas Fern

Virginia Bluebells

Umbrella Plant

Wild Blue Phlox

Celandine Poppy

Plant Names	Bloom Color and Season	Height and Spread
White baneberry	White flowers in spring; white berries in fall	1' to 3' tall and 2' to 3' wide
Bloodroot	White flowers in early spring	6" to 12" tall and wide
Virginia bluebells	Sky blue flowers in spring	1' to 2' tall and 1' wide
Celandine poppy	Orange flowers in spring	1' to 2' tall and 1' wide

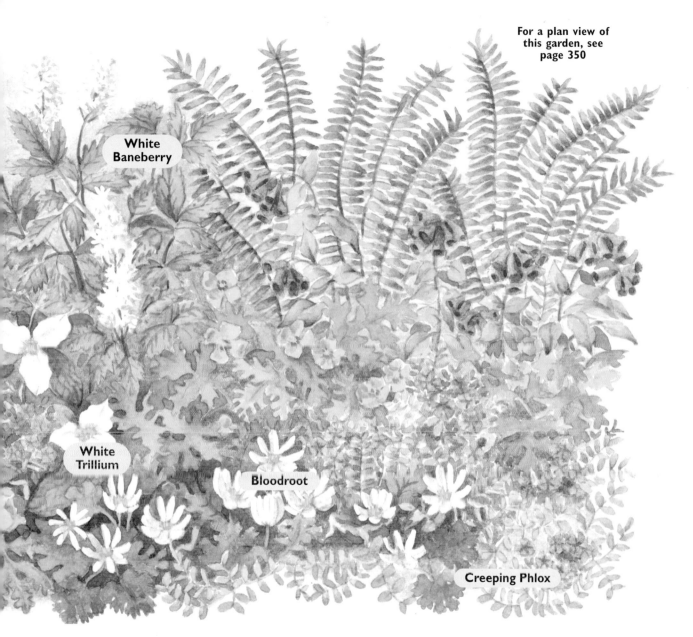

For a plan view of this garden, see page 350

White Baneberry

White Trillium

Bloodroot

Creeping Phlox

Plant Names	Bloom Color and Season	Height and Spread
Christmas fern	Deep green fronds	1' to 2' tall and wide
'Blue Ridge' creeping phlox	Blue flowers in spring	6" to 12" tall and 12" wide
Wild blue phlox	Blue flowers in spring	1' tall and wide
White trillium	White flowers in spring	1' to 2' tall and 1' wide
Umbrella plant	White flowers in spring	2' to 3' tall and wide

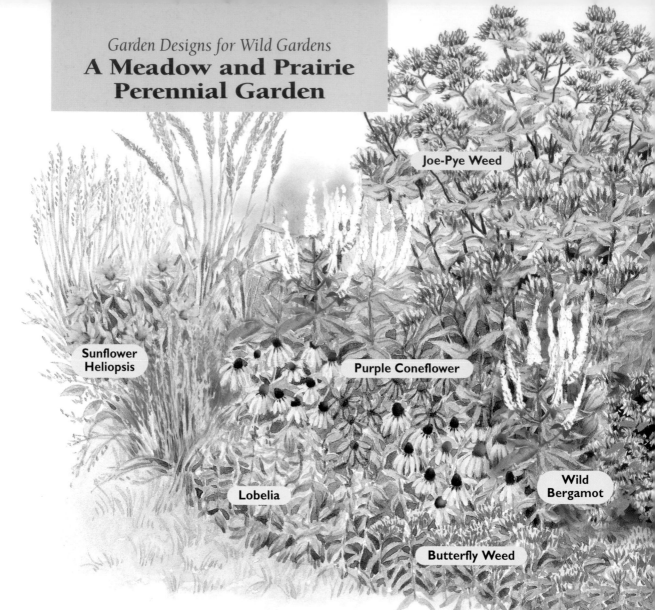

Garden Designs for Wild Gardens
A Meadow and Prairie Perennial Garden

Joe-Pye Weed

Sunflower Heliopsis

Purple Coneflower

Lobelia

Wild Bergamot

Butterfly Weed

Plant Names	Bloom Color and Season	Height and Spread
New England aster	Purple flowers in late summer to fall	3' to 4' tall and 3' wide
Wild bergamot	Lavender flowers in summer	2' to 3' tall and wide
Little bluestem	Red foliage and silvery flowers in fall	1' to 3' tall and 1' wide
Butterfly weed	Orange flowers in summer	1' to 2½' tall and 1' to 2' wide
Gray-headed coneflower	Yellow flowers in summer	2' to 4' tall and 1' wide
Purple coneflower	Rose-purple flowers in summer	2' to 4' tall and 1' to 2' wide

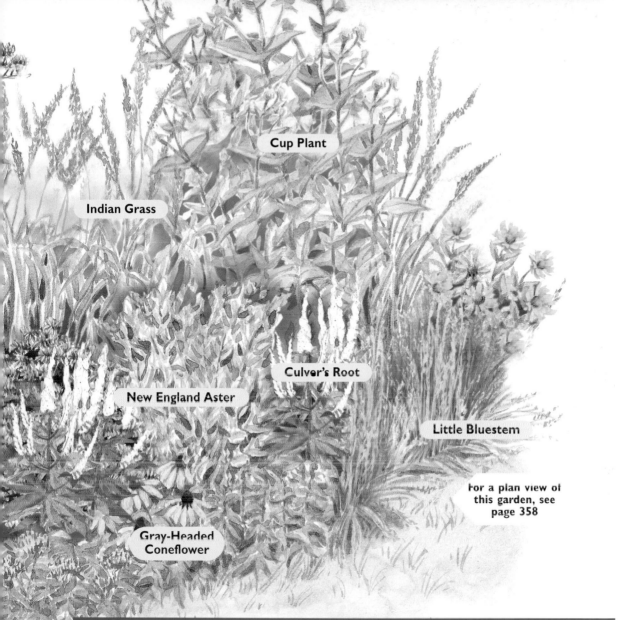

Cup Plant

Indian Grass

Culver's Root

New England Aster

Little Bluestem

Gray-Headed
Coneflower

For a plan view of
this garden, see
page 358

Plant Names	Bloom Color and Season	Height and Spread
Culver's root	White flowers in summer	2' to 4' tall and 1' wide
Cup plant	Yellow flowers in summer	3' to 6' tall and 3' to 4' wide
Sunflower heliopsis	Yellow flowers in early summer	2' to 3' tall and wide
Indian grass	Blue-green leaves, golden flowers in summer	2' to 5' tall and 1' wide
Spotted Joe-Pye weed	Rose-pink flowers in late summer	4' to 6' tall and wide
Great blue lobelia	Blue flowers in late summer to fall	1' to 3' tall and 1' wide

Garden Designs for Wild Gardens
A Seaside Perennial Garden

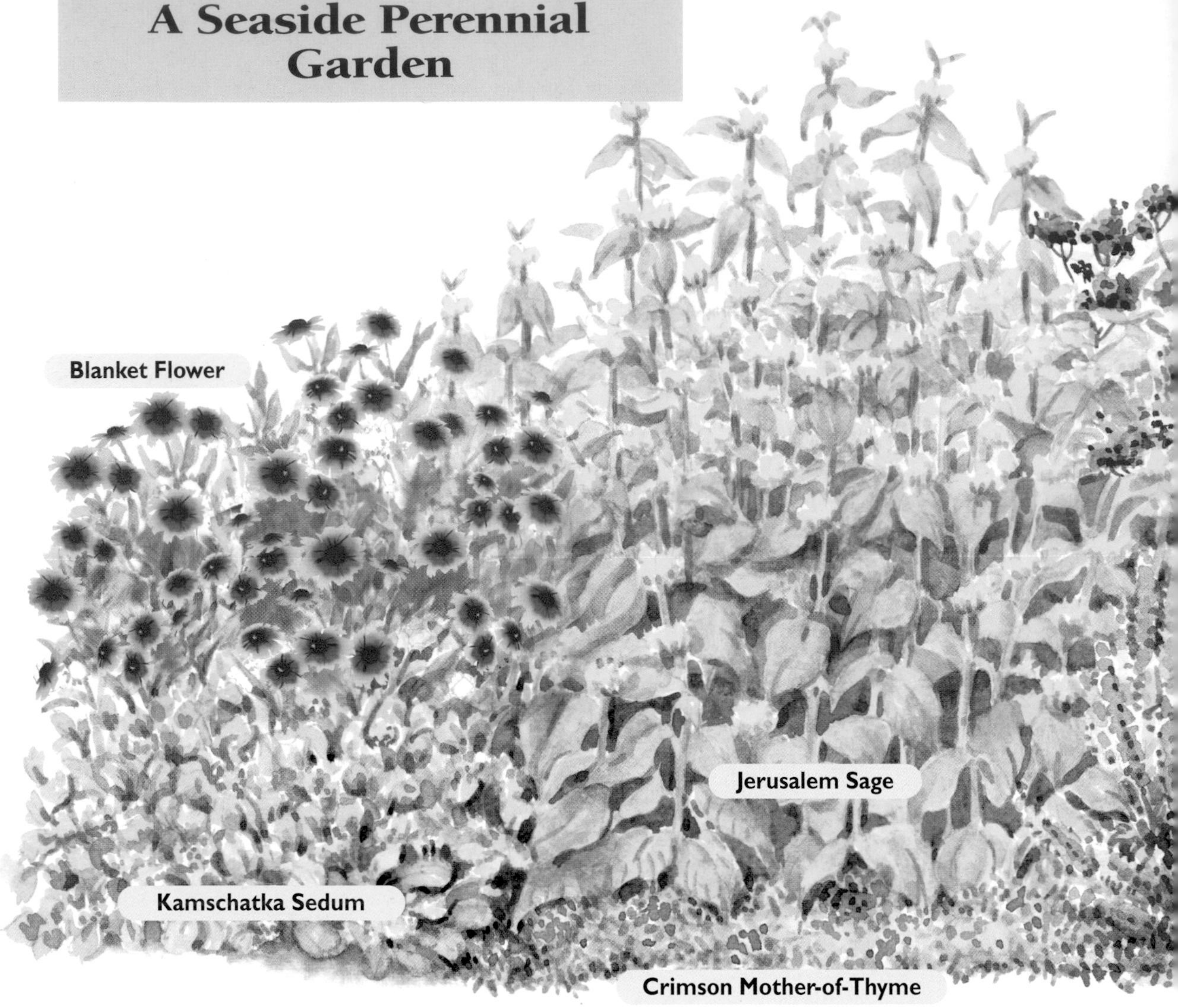

Blanket Flower

Jerusalem Sage

Kamschatka Sedum

Crimson Mother-of-Thyme

Plant Names	Bloom Color and Season	Height and Spread
Blanket flower	Red-and-yellow flowers in summer	1' to 2' tall and 1' wide
Catmint	Blue flowers in early summer	1' to 1½' tall and 2' to 3' wide
Jerusalem sage	Yellow flowers in summer	3' to 4' tall and 3' wide
Jupiter's beard	Pink-red flowers in spring to summer	2' to 3' tall and 2' wide
Kamschatka sedum	Yellow flowers in summer	4" to 6" tall and 1' wide
Sundrops	Yellow flowers in early summer	1' to 1½' tall and 1' to 2' wide
Crimson mother-of-thyme	Rose-red flowers in summer	4" to 6" tall and 1' wide

For a plan view of this garden, see page 354

Jupiter's Beard

Sundrops

Catmint

Enjoying Your Seaside Garden

This colorful garden is as refreshing as a cool sea breeze. In fact, it's the cool summer breezes that keep seaside gardens looking so fresh. Cool nights extend the blooming season and keep plants from looking bedraggled by summer heat and drought. This garden features a pleasing, complementary color scheme of orange, yellow, and blue. The bright orange-and-yellow blanket flowers bloom almost all summer, along with the lavender-blue catmint. Kamschatka sedum, sundrops, and Jerusalem sage join the summer display. The mother-of-thyme and Jupiter's beard add a touch of contrast. In the fall, the seedheads of Jerusalem sage will accent the last of the blanket flowers.

Garden Designs for Wild Gardens
A Perennial Water Garden

For a plan view of this garden, see page 361

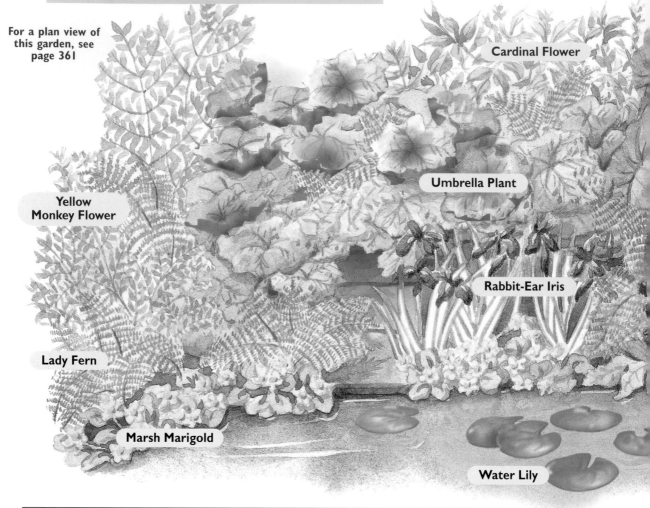

Cardinal Flower

Umbrella Plant

Yellow Monkey Flower

Rabbit-Ear Iris

Lady Fern

Marsh Marigold

Water Lily

Plant Names	Bloom Color and Season	Height and Spread
Cardinal flower	Scarlet flowers in late summer	1' to 3' tall and 1' wide
Lady fern	Bright green fronds	2' to 3' tall and 2' wide
Royal fern	Sea green fronds	3' to 5' tall and 3' to 4' wide
Golden club	Yellow flowers in spring	1' to 2' tall and wide
Variegated rabbit-ear iris	Blue flowers in early summer	2' to 3' tall and 1' to 2' wide
Marsh marigold	Yellow flowers in spring	1' to 2' tall and wide
Evergreen miscanthus	Tan flowers in fall	3' to 4' tall and 4' wide
Scarlet monkey flower	Red-orange flowers in early summer	2' to 3' tall and 2' wide

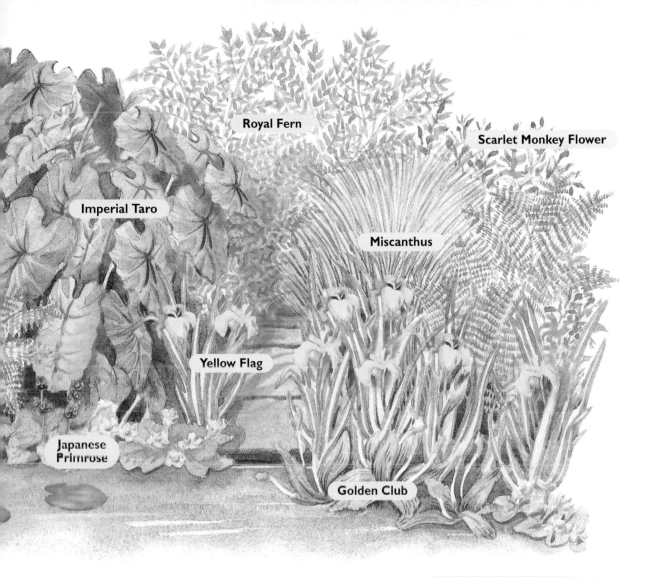

Royal Fern

Scarlet Monkey Flower

Imperial Taro

Miscanthus

Yellow Flag

Japanese Primrose

Golden Club

Plant Names	Bloom Color and Season	Height and Spread
Yellow monkey flower	Yellow flowers in early summer	6" to 12" tall and wide
Japanese primrose	Pink, rose, and magenta flowers in spring	1' tall and wide
Imperial taro	Black and green foliage	2' to 3' tall and wide
Umbrella plant	Pink flowers in spring	2' to 4' tall and 3' wide
Fragrant water lily	White flowers in summer	Floating, 3' wide
Variegated yellow flag	Yellow flowers in early summer	2' to 4' tall and 2' to 3' wide

Combinations
FOR EXTRA FUN

Creating a beautiful garden is the top priority when we combine perennials, but it's not the only one. Perennials offer pleasures that go beyond a garden that's pleasing to view. You can choose perennials with nectar-rich flowers that attract butterflies and hummingbirds to create a garden full of fascinating life and activity. Gardeners who work away from home during the day can experiment with silvery combinations that glow in the moonlight and fragrant combinations to enjoy whether it's daytime or evening. Creating perennial combinations with flowers that are good for cutting and drying will give you a garden that has beauty and color you can literally bring inside your house. Enjoy these combinations and garden designs that feature a special touch of gardening fun.

PHOTO KEY
1. **Wild bergamot (*Monarda fistulosa*); Zones 3 to 8**
2. **Globe thistle (*Echinops ritro*); Zones 3 to 8**

A Perfect Pair for Hummingbirds and Butterflies

Bergamot is a favorite summer treat for hummingbirds, and it makes a dashing combination with globe thistle, another hummer favorite. Hummers relish the sweet nectar that they sip from the scarlet, purple, or pink tubular flowers of bergamot. Bergamot and globe thistle flowers attract butterflies and bees, too. There are dozens of bergamot cultivars available, including 'Blue Stocking' and 'Marshall's Delight'. The silvery spheres of the globe thistle open to rich blue flowers in midsummer. To keep this combination happy, plant it in well-drained soil in full sun to light shade. Bergamot is more drought-tolerant than its cousin bee balm (*Monarda didyma*), which prefers evenly moist soil. Globe thistle, on the other hand, doesn't like to grow in wet soil and can tolerate drought, so you can skip it when you're watering.

Tips for Attracting Hummingbirds and Butterflies

🐦 Rely on red and purple flowers.
Hummingbirds love red flowers, which is why many hummingbird feeders have red plastic flowers around each opening. Purple, blue, and pink also attract hummingbirds, and I've seen them visit white and yellow flowers, too. Butterflies are also attracted to red flowers, but purple is actually their favorite color. So the best lure for hummingbirds would be a vivid red bee balm like 'Gardenview Scarlet', while butterflies may like purplish 'Violet Queen' best.

🐦 Keep your hummers healthy. Even with a garden filled with hummingbird flowers, it's hard to resist hanging a nectar feeder in the garden. Though many people put red food coloring in the sugar solution to help attract the birds, it's not necessary or advisable to do so. Hummers have very keen eyesight, and the red decorations around the feeder openings are sufficient to attract them. Research indicates that the red food coloring may be harmful to the hummers. So put out clear sugar solution in a well-designed feeder, and the healthy hummers will find you.

🐦 Divide bee balm; don't bother globe thistle. To keep bee balm (*Monarda* spp.) in top condition, spread compost around the base of the plants every year, and divide plants when the clumps begin to die out in the center. Lift the plants in early spring or after flowering, remove the old woody crowns, and replant the vigorous divisions into soil that's been amended with compost. When you're tending bee balm, try not to disturb your globe thistles—they do best when left alone. If you want to propagate globe thistles, just use a shovel to cut a section away from the rest of the plant.

Bee balm and yarrow (*Achillea millifolium*), two fast-spreading perennials, make great companions for a butterfly garden. They're each aggressive enough to hold their ground against the other.

Brilliant Colors
for Butterflies

Brilliant hot-colored flowers are magnets for butterflies, bees, and many other beneficial insects. This hot-color combination of coreopsis and butterfly weed sizzles in midsummer, and the masses of coreopsis will remain in bloom for a month or more. These perennials need full sun or light shade and soil that's moist but well drained. The plants can tolerate drought, but they won't bloom as long when the soil is dry.

Butterflies will visit the flowers to drink nectar, while bees and other insects feed on both nectar and pollen. The presence of the insects will also attract birds to the garden.

PHOTO KEY
1. 'Zagreb' threadleaf coreopsis (*Coreopsis verticillata* 'Zagreb'); Zones 3 to 9
2. Butterfly weed (*Asclepias tuberosa*); Zones 3 to 9

Secrets for Bringing in Butterflies

🦋 **Substitutes for a wet site.** If you love this combination of coreopsis and butterfly weed but want to plant a moist to wet spot instead of a well-drained one, just plant some moisture-loving substitutes. Substitute the rose-pink-flowered swamp milkweed (*Asclepias incarnata*) for butterfly weed. It has 2- to 4-foot stems with large, lance-shaped leaves. The plants form open clumps and spread by running stems. For coreopsis, choose the rose-flowered *Coreopsis rosea*, which delights in moist, rich soil.

🦋 **Parachutes away!** After the flowers of milkweed fade, elongated, upright green seedpods form. When the seeds ripen, the pods split open, and the seeds sail out on silken parachutes and float away in the breeze. If you want to collect the seed for propagation, gather the pods when they begin to dry but before they split. The best way to test them is to squeeze them; they should feel slightly papery and somewhat hollow. Open one pod and check to make sure the seeds are brown, not green. If the pods are ready, pull them off the plants and let them dry for a day or so. Open them and grab the tips of the silk in one hand. Use your other hand to rake off the brown seeds. Discard the parachute, and sow or store the seeds.

🦋 **Milkweed and caterpillars.** When you're admiring the milkweed flowers in your garden, look along the plant's stems and under the leaves, too. You may spot small black-and-yellow caterpillars, which are the larvae of monarch butterflies. The caterpillars feed on the foliage for about two weeks, then form a chrysalis from which the butterfly emerges. If you're lucky, you may spot the transformation in process.

Butterfly weed is a type of milkweed, and milkweeds are a mainstay of butterfly gardens. Fritillary butterflies and many others will drink nectar from the flowers, and caterpillars of monarch butterflies feed exclusively on milkweed foliage.

A Perfect Red-and-Purple Duo

Some gardeners may find a combination of red and purple flowers like this one a little garish, but hummingbirds and butterflies love it. The starry blooms of fire pink open for a month in late spring and early summer. They seem to float above the ever-blooming carpet of verbena. To extend the bloom season and enrich this combination, you could add penstemons, prairie phlox (*Phlox pilosa*), sundrops (*Oenothera* spp.), and winecups (*Callirhoe digitata*). All of these plants thrive in average to rich, moist but well-drained soil in full sun or partial shade. Once they're established, the plants are drought tolerant.

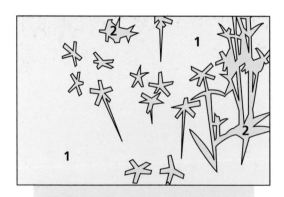

PHOTO KEY
1. Rose verbena (*Verbena canadensis*); Zone 4 to 10
2. Fire pink (*Silene virginica*); Zones 4 to 9

More Plants for Butterflies and Hummers

❧ **Verbenas by the van load.** Rose verbena is a lovely native wildflower that's been hybridized with other species to form some fantastic garden plants. 'Homestead Purple', with violet flowers, is one of the most popular cultivars. 'Appleblossom' is pale pink and 'Sarah Groves' has medium pink flowers that darken with age. 'Gene Cline' has deep rose-red flowers, and 'Snowflurry' is pure white. These verbenas are easy-care plants that tolerate almost any soil as long as it's not too wet. They'll also tolerate partial shade, but they bloom fuller and longer in full sun. If you deadhead the old stems or shear the plants back in midsummer, they'll bloom nonstop from spring through frost.

❧ **Even more verbenas.** Rose verbena is just one of the carpet-forming verbenas that are perfect for the front of a perennial border. Moss verbena (*Verbena tenuisecta*) has deeply divided, threadlike leaves, and the plants form wide, matlike clumps that are smothered in violet flowers for the entire growing season. 'Alba' is a lovely white-flowered form. 'Edith' has soft pink flowers. 'Sissinghurst' is coral rose. Rigid verbena (*V. rigida*) has white, pink, or purple flowers and forms mounded, open clumps up to 1 foot high. Moss verbena is hardy only to Zone 7, and rigid verbena, only to Zone 8, but you can grow them as annuals in colder zones.

❧ **Pretty pinks.** The stunning red flowers of fire pink start opening in spring and continue without stopping for at least six weeks. The inflated seedpods are loaded with seeds, and the plants self-sow easily in bare soil. Wild pink (*Silene caroliniana*) is a close relative with rich pink flowers. Royal catchfly (*S. regia*) is a giant version of fire pink that carries its scarlet

The flattened flowers of maroon knautia (*Knautia macedonica*) and lavender pincushion flower (*Scabiosa caucasica*) make perfect landing pads for busy butterflies in search of sweet nectar.

flowers atop 2- to 3-foot stems. They make a dramatic showing in a dry soil perennial or prairie garden. All three of these *Silene* species form thick, deep taproots, so they don't transplant well. Set out young plants before the taproot gets too big.

PHOTO KEY
1. Spotted Joe-Pye weed (*Eupatorium maculatum*); Zones 2 to 8
2. Early phlox (*Phlox maculata*); Zones 4 to 8
3. Mealy-cup sage (*Salvia farinacea*); Zones 8 to 10
4. Prairie dropseed (*Sporobolus heterolepis*); Zones 3 to 9
5. 'Homestead Purple' verbena (*Verbena* 'Homestead Purple'); Zones 5 to 7

A Beautiful Butterfly Border

Massive clumps of Joe-Pye weed and tall early phlox form the backdrop for a drift of everblooming mealy-cup sage in this 6-foot-deep butterfly border. A carpet of bright verbena blooms all summer at the front of the border, while the feathery dropseed foliage provides contrasting textures.

This well-planned combination of rich foliage textures and long-blooming plants makes a great garden, and its complexity also makes it an attractive habitat for butterflies and a variety of wildlife. Gardens with lots of diversity are generally more interesting to wildlife than very uniform, neat gardens. So if you want lots of wildlife in your yard, plan for plenty of combinations, like this one, that provide food and cover for insects, birds, and animals.

Plants for a Beautiful Butterfly Border

Fragrant early phlox. Gardeners love fragrant early phlox blossoms because they bring the beauty of phlox to a garden weeks before the familiar garden phlox (*Phlox paniculata*) blooms. Early phlox is resistant to powdery mildew, which mars the foliage of many other kinds of phlox. Enjoy them in the garden or indoors as long-lasting cut flowers. 'Miss Lingard' is a lovely pure white selection.

Long-blooming mealy sage. Mealy-cup sage, pictured here, is a showy plant with silvery flower spikes that start opening in May and continue all summer. Most gardeners know mealy-cup sage as an annual, because it's hardy only to Zone 8. In addition to the lovely white form, there are three lovely blue forms. 'Blue Bedder' is a compact grower to 2 feet, while 'Victoria' is taller (to 3 feet), with rich blue flowers. 'Indigo Spires' is a hybrid cultivar that grows 3 to 4 feet tall and is hardy to Zone 7.

A native ornamental grass. While native grasses won't attract butterflies to your garden, they're a food source for seed-eating birds like juncos. The prairie dropseed (*Sporobolus heterolepis*) in this combination is a native grass that produces airy seedheads coated in a fragrant oil that smells like ripe peaches. Its fall color varies from golden yellow to bright pumpkin orange. In fall, the seedheads drop grain that is eaten by juncos and other sparrows

Bulb plants for butterflies and hummingbirds include rich blue lily-of-the-Nile (*Agapanthus* 'Ben Hope'), yellow-orange *Crocosmia* 'Canary Bird', and lavender-pink *Allium cilicium*, all of which thrive in rich, well-drained soil and full sun.

Early-Summer Butterfly Blossoms

Color abounds in this early-summer display of easy-care perennials that butterflies will find irresistible. There's a pleasing mix of flower sizes and textures, but there's also repetition in the rounded plant forms of bee balm and heliopsis. The tall clump of lilies and the bright yellow heliopsis flowers give the combination an exciting punch, and the curious nodding heads of gooseneck loosestrife lend a humorous touch. The upright stems of long-blooming spike speedwell add a vertical accent. To be at its best, this combination needs rich, evenly moist soil and full sun. Daylilies and chrysanthemums would be good choices to plant with this combination for late-season color.

PHOTO KEY
1. 'Miss Alice' Asiatic lily (*Lilium* 'Miss Alice'); Zones 3 to 8
2. 'Blue Charm' spike speedwell (*Veronica spicata* 'Blue Charm'); Zones 4 to 8
3. 'Violet Queen' bee balm (*Monarda didyma* 'Violet Queen'); Zones 3 to 8
4. 'Karat' sunflower heliopsis (*Heliopsis helianthoides* 'Karat'); Zones 3 to 9
5. 'Zagreb' threadleaf coreopsis (*Coreopsis verticillata* 'Zagreb'); Zones 3 to 9
6. Gooseneck loosestrife (*Lysimachia clethroides*); Zones 3 to 8

Techniques for Butterfly-Attracting Blooms

🙣 Give gooseneck loosestrife a second chance. Gooseneck loosestrife is a charming old-fashioned perennial that's often passed over in favor of newer, more glamorous plants. But it's well-worth growing, because it offers lots of garden interest. The lush green foliage is gorgeous all season and turns yellow in fall. The curvy flower spikes bloom profusely, and after the flowers fade, the seedheads add summer and fall interest. The only drawback to this plant is that it spreads rapidly, but it's easy to pull or dig from spots where it's not wanted.

🙣 Control spreading perennials. Many spreading perennials are lovely garden plants, but people shy away from them because they're concerned that the plants will overtake their gardens. If you love the old-fashioned rompers, like gooseneck loosestrife, bee balm, and obedient plant (*Physostegia virginiana*), but don't want to spend time keeping them inbounds, plant them in a large plastic pot or other container with the bottom cut out. Sink the container into the garden bed, leaving the lip of the container about an inch above the soil to keep roots from escaping. Top dress the container with manure or compost each year. Divide the plant when it gets so crowded that bloom starts to decline.

🙣 Plant Asiatic lilies in spring or fall. Asiatic lilies are a glorious addition to the summer garden. Bulbs are offered for sale in fall through nurseries and mail-order catalogs. But if you forget to order and plant bulbs in fall, don't worry. Most nurseries sell the bulbs in spring, too. Plant them out as soon as you can work the soil, and they will bloom that summer. Set the bulbs at least two to three times as deep as the size of the bulb.

Phlox is a butterfly favorite, and flamboyant 'Starfire' garden phlox has the perfect color for butterfly-attracting combinations. It's an early-blooming cultivar and has red-tinged foliage.

🙣 Keep your oxeyes straight. Sunflower heliopsis, also called oxeye, is a native prairie perennial with 2-inch daisylike flowers resembling sunflowers. It blooms for up to three months, starting in early summer. Cultivars such as 'Karat' have 3-inch flowers on 3- to 3½-foot stalks. 'Golden Plume' has double flowers, and 'Summer Sun' has 3-inch flowers on 2- to 3-foot stems. Don't confuse sunflower heliopsis with oxeye daisies (*Chrysanthemum leucanthemum*), which have white flowers with yellow centers.

PHOTO KEY
1. Variegated giant dogwood (*Cornus controversa* 'Variegata'); Zones 5 to 8
2. Spurge (*Euphorbia characias* subsp. *wulfenii*); Zones 8 to 9
3. 'Mariesii' doublefile viburnum (*Viburnum plicatum* var. *tomentosum* 'Mariesii'); Zones 5 to 8
4. Jerusalem sage (*Phlomis russeliana*); Zones 4 to 9
5. Italian bugloss (*Anchusa azurea*); Zones 3 to 8
6. Catmint (*Nepeta*); Zones 3 to 8

A Garden That Glows in the Dark

Silvery foliage plants and chartreuse spurge flower spikes highlight this garden that's designed to be enjoyed in the evening. If you like sitting outside on summer evenings, you'll enjoy creating a garden of plants like these that enliven a garden without relying on artificial light. At its best, garden lighting enhances gardens by accentuating special features, like the dramatic outlines of a tree trunk. But unless it's subtle, garden lighting can ruin the hushed, restful quality of a garden at night. In this garden, the combination of perennials and woody plants makes the best of natural light. White-edged dogwood leaves shimmer in the moonlight. The spurge, which looks quite solid in this daytime view, takes on a ghostly glow in the evening and moves softly when there's a breeze. This combination needs full sun and would thrive in dry, gravelly soil that has good drainage.

Secrets for Gardens That Glow in the Dark

꙾ Use a euphorbia that suits your zone. The bottlebrush flower spikes of the spurge used in this combination are dramatic in both the day and evening. However, this species is hardy only in Zone 8 and warmer areas. If you garden north of Zone 8, you can substitute a hardy spurge, such as *Euphorbia sikkimensis* or *E. palustris*. They're not quite as dramatic looking, because they have flattened flower clusters instead of tall spikes, but the chartreuse to acid yellow flowers create the same haunting luster in the evening garden.

꙾ Mix flowering trees with bold perennials. Tall and bold perennials often look out of proportion in a garden, especially in a narrow bed. One way to balance the coarse texture and large size of perennials like the spurge in this combination is to use flowering trees as a backdrop. The height and solid branch structure of the trees help bring the spurge into scale with the rest of the garden. For added evening interest, use variegated trees with white, cream, or yellow in the leaves. The pale colors reflect light and brighten up the garden.

꙾ Discover perennial anchusas. Summer forget-me-not (*Anchusa capensis*) is a popular annual grown for its true blue flowers. Perennial species of *Anchusa*, like the Italian bugloss used in this combination, aren't as well known, but they offer the same rich blue flowers as the annual forms. The 3- to 4-foot plants have rather coarse textured leaves, but the flower spikes are showy in the spring and early summer. Hardy in Zones 3 to 8, Italian bugloss thrives in lean soil in full sun. 'Dropmore' is a popular cultivar. 'Loddon Royalist' is more compact, to 3 feet, with rich gentian blue flowers. 'Little John' is an 18-inch dwarf type.

Chartreuse is one of the most reflective colors for an evening garden. A frothy tumble of chartreuse lady's-mantle lights up a mass of pale blue *Geranium pratense* flowers, which also glow in the evening.

PHOTO KEY
1. **Everlasting flower (*Helichrysum italicum*); Zones 7 to 10**
2. **Garden sage (*Salvia officinalis*); Zones 3 to 9**
3. **Common chives (*Allium schoenoprasum*); Zones 3 to 9**

Fragrance from Flowers and Foliage

A rose and violet color echo with silver highlights softens this combination of fragrant perennials. The sweet-smelling flowers and pungent chive foliage are both beautiful and edible. The sage leaves are fragrant when crushed, as are the felted, silvery leaves of everlasting plant. This combination is perfect for well-drained, sandy soil in full sun. If you want to create an entire fragrant garden based on this combination, try adding pale pink *Verbena canadensis* 'Appleblossom' or *Verbena tenuisecta* 'Edith'. For both fragrance and evening interest, plant evening primroses (*Oenothera speciosa*) and pale pink baby's-breath (*Gypsophila paniculata* 'Pink Fairy'), and for contrast, add pale yellow golden marguerite (*Anthemis tinctoria* 'Moonlight').

Enjoying Fragrant Flowers and Foliage

❧ Plants to rub and sniff. We all enjoy looking at beautiful perennial combinations, but if you plant fragrant combinations, remember to pick a flower or two and smell its perfume. You have to lift a delicate flower to your nose to capture its scent. Rub pungent herb leaves and sniff your fingers to appreciate the scent. I often pick a leaf or flower to carry around with me as I walk through the garden. I enjoy the lingering fragrance even after I've left the garden and gone indoors.

❧ The charms of chives. A mass of chives in full bloom is a glorious addition to the early summer garden. Though the flowers have a slight scent, it's the pungent leaves that add the real fragrance. Of course, you can also enjoy chives in the kitchen by using the chopped leaves to season soups and salads. The flowers are also edible and make a colorful and tasty garnish for salads.

❧ More edible onions. We tend to divide the *Allium* species into ornamental onions for flower gardens and culinary onions (including garlic) for the vegetable garden. But there's no reason why you can't grow some edible types of *Allium* with your perennials. For example, garlic chives (*Allium tuberosum*) have showy white flowers, and both the leaves and flowers are edible. They lend a spicy zest to salads and soups. Even garlic, with its curious snaky flowerheads, is ornamental enough to include in a flower border.

❧ The scent of sage. The garden sage in this combination is most noted for its early summer spikes of purple or blue flowers. But when you trim back the plants, you'll notice that the leaves are extremely pungent. If you enjoy the somewhat musty but spicy scent, trimming the plants after they flower will be a delight. If you don't, hold your nose and trim away. The plants will reward you with a fresh round of flowers.

Try placing a garden bench near fragrant plants like lavender (*Lavandula angustifolia*), one of the most popular scented perennials. Lavender has such pungent essential oils that a generous clump can add fragrance to the air all around it.

A Ghostly Silver and Gray Garden

Fragrance and evening appeal combine in a garden of scented white flowers and silver foliage. Fragrant spires of phlox give off a sweet perfume both day and night. The foliage of the white sage is also strongly scented, and it's delightful to rub the soft leaves to release the scent. At night, the silvery foliage captures the moonlight and seems to glow. All the white flowers, along with the metallic foliage of Miss Willmott's ghost, capture the moonlight. To make the show of fragrant flowers last longer, you could add 'Mt. Fuji' garden phlox for midsummer bloom and 'David' phlox for late summer. Annual angel's trumpet (*Datura meteloides*) would provide fragrance and summer-long bloom.

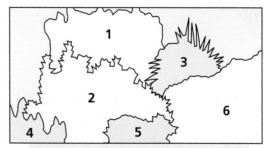

PHOTO KEY
1. **'Miss Lingard' early phlox (*Phlox carolina* 'Miss Lingard'); Zones 4 to 8**
2. **White sage (*Artemisia ludoviciana*); Zones 3 to 9**
3. **Blue wheat grass (*Agropyron magellanicum*); Zones 5 to 8**
4. **Common snapdragon (*Antirrhinum majus*); Zones 5 to 9**
5. **Miss Willmott's ghost (*Eryngium giganteum*); Zones 4 to 8**
6. **Bowman's-root (*Gillenia trifoliata*); Zones 4 to 8**

Secrets for a Silver and Gray Garden

❧ **Watch out for white sage.** If you plan to plant white sage in your garden, keep in mind that it will spread to form a huge clump in just a few seasons. The best way to control its spread is to plant it with other aggressive perennials. Packed tightly in among its neighbors, there is little room for the sage to spread. Another simple way to control white sage is to dig and divide it whenever it gets too big. The only problem you may have is finding ways to get rid of the extra divisions!

❧ **Extend the season with snapdragons.** Snapdragons add elegance and long-season bloom to this evening combination. Snapdragons are a great choice for extending color in many perennial combinations, not just evening combinations. Their flowering spires add height and lift to the garden, and they come in a variety of colors from white to yellow, red, and pink. Plant them toward the middle or back of the bed with low, rounded plants in front.

❧ **Try a new ornamental grass.** Blue wheat grass (*Agropyron magellanicum*), featured here, has the same silvery blue color of ornamental fescue (*Festuca* spp.), but it's much easier to grow than fescue. Most gardeners know *Agopyron repens*—it's quackgrass, an annoying weed. Fear not, for unlike its rampant cousin, blue wheat grass forms tidy clumps that stay where they're planted.

❧ **Meet Bowman's-root.** Bowman's-root, also called Indian physic, is a native perennial that was once used as a cure-all. The plants form beautiful, vase-shaped to rounded clumps of wiry stems covered in three-lobed, toothed leaves. In late spring and early summer, the plants are smothered in white flowers with four twisted petals. The buds are tinged with red, giving the plant a bicolor effect. In autumn, the leaves turn bright yellow. To get the best from Bowman's-root, give it rich, well-drained but moist soil in full sun or partial shade. The plants will self-sow but won't become invasive.

For fragrance, drama, and evening interest, nothing beats single white peonies. Bold leaves of garden rhubarb (*Rheum rhabarbarum*) help set off the 8-inch flowers of 'Lotus Queen' peony.

PHOTO KEY
1. Oregano (*Origanum laevigatum*); Zones 7 to 10
2. 'Powis Castle' artemisia (*Artemisia* 'Powis Castle'); Zone 4 (with winter protection) or Zones 5 to 8

A Simple Duo of Fragrant Herbs

A simple pair of perennial herbs with fragrant leaves makes a superb combination for both a container and a garden border. The silvery mounds of the artemisia add a delicate lacy texture and ghostly glow in an evening garden. The foliage also gives off a pungent fragrance when rubbed. Delicate oregano flowers weave through the artemisia, creating a soothing cool color combination that would look lovely in a pastel garden.

Both of these plants thrive in light but fertile, well-drained soil in full sun. For more evening interest, you could plant silvery lamb's-ears or lavender with this duo. Artemisia and oregano do beautifully in a container in a light soil mix, and they won't need heavy watering. If you plant this combination in a container, add a soft edge by planting a pale-flowered trailing verbena around the rim. Some good choices include 'Sarah Groves' or 'Appleblossom' rose verbena (*Verbena canadensis*), which have pink flowers, or white 'Snowflurry'. You could also use some white-flowered 'Alba' moss verbena (*V. tenuisecta*) or pale pink 'Edith'.

Perennial Herbs
for Fragrant Combinations

☙ **A shrubby artemisia.** After a year or two of growth, the stems of 'Powis Castle' artemisia, featured in this combination, can get rather woody, and the plants may reach 3 to 4 feet tall and wide. If you plant 'Powis Castle' in a small garden, cut it back by half every other year to keep it from getting too big. In my Zone 4 garden, severe winter cold sometimes kills the stems, but the plants come back after this "shearing" by Mother Nature. In Zone 3, treat this artemisia as an annual—set out new plants each spring.

☙ **Excellent oreganos.** We tend to think of oregano as an ordinary kitchen garden herb, but there are several oreganos that are fragrant and beautiful, as well as edible. The true oregano (*Oregano heracleoticum*) has excellent flavor and is a superb garden plant, hardy to Zone 5. Sweet marjoram (*Origanam marjoranam*) has a stronger, more musty flavor. The oregano (*O.*

laevigatum) featured in this combination is more ornamental than edible. The leaves have the traditional pungent scent, but they're more bitter tasting. The flowers are the real selling point of this plant. They bloom all summer, especially if you shear the plants once or twice during the season to encourage new growth. Give oregano sandy but nutritious, well-drained soil in full sun.

☙ **The hardiest oregano.** The hardiest *Origanum* species is wild or pot marjoram (*O. vulgare*), which thrives even in Zone 3 gardens. Plants spread quickly to form broad clumps and may be a little hard to control in a small garden. The plants produce pale lavender flowers all summer. You can use either fresh or dried pot marjoram leaves for seasoning. The pungent, fuzzy leaves have less flavor than culinary oregano, but they're still a nice addition to soups and other dishes.

For both fragrance and evening interest, let pink-flowered chives (*Allium schoenoprasum*) mingle with the silvery foliage of white sage (*Artemisia ludoviciana*).

A Day-and-Night Combination

For a garden you can enjoy both during the day and at night, combine ghostly white, fragrant oriental lilies with richly colored daylilies, Siberian meadowsweet, and blood-red cranesbills. The lilies are showstopper flowers that make a terrific centerpiece for a perennial garden in high summer. Culver's root has grass foliage, and its creamy white flower spikes will last until fall. The Siberian iris, shown past bloom, also has white flowers that shine in the evening. All of the plants in this beautiful combination thrive in rich, evenly moist soil in full sun or light shade. Place this combination near a terrace or along a sidewalk so you can easily enjoy its beauty and heavenly fragrance.

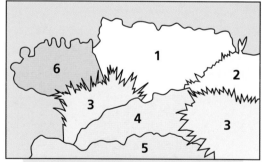

PHOTO KEY
1. **'Casablanca' oriental lily (*Lilium 'Casablanca'*); Zones 4 to 7**
2. **Culver's root (*Veronicastrum virginicum*); Zones 3 to 9**
3. **Siberian iris (*Iris sibirica*); Zones 2 to 9**
4. **Siberian meadowsweet (*Filipendula palmata*); Zones 3 to 8**
5. **Blood-red cranesbill (*Geranium sanguineum*); Zones 3 to 8**
6. **Daylily (*Hemerocallis* hybrid); Zones 3 to 9**

Secrets for a Day-and-Night Combination

❧ **Select white lilies for the evening garden.** The reflective quality of white lilies is unparalleled in the moonlit summer garden. Asiatic hybrids, such as 'Sorbet', 'Mont Blanc', and 'Top Hit', are silvery white. *Lilium auratum* is white-and-yellow striped and intensely fragrant. Other excellent scented oriental hybrids include pure white 'Siberia'; 'Arena', which has a yellow band that turns red toward the tips of the petals; and 'Belle Epoque', which is pale shell pink. 'Mount Everest', a vigorous cultivar of Easter lily (*L. longiflorum*), has snowy white, fragrant trumpets in midsummer.

❧ **Perfume the garden around the clock.** Many lilies add fragrance to the garden in the day or evening. Try the heady scent of 'Black Dragon', a trumpet lily with petals that are rosy on the inside and rich purple on the outside. 'Star Gazer' is a classic pink Oriental, while 'Acapulco' is raspberry pink, and 'Marco Polo' is blushed with pink.

❧ **Add grasses for intriguing evening effects.** While ornamental grasses are spectacular when the sun lights the foliage from behind, they also contribute wonderful special effects in the evening garden. To extend this perennial combination, you could add blue oat grass (*Helictotrichon sempervirens*), which has pale, light-reflecting leaves that glow in the moonlight. The pale plumes of grasses such as fountain grass (*Pennisetum* spp.) and Japanese silver grass (*Miscanthus* spp.) also reflect light. They're even more beautiful when they're highlighted by artificial light, such as a spotlight or flood light, and they cast elegant shadows. Use back-

Iris, phlox, lilies, and roses fill the air with heady perfume in this sumptuous bed of white- and cream-colored flowers and foliage. To add contrast to a bed like this one that includes lots of white, mix in annuals and perennials with purple foliage.

lighting to accentuate the silhouette of the leaves and plumes. Use low lights in front of a planting to cast intriguing shadows on a wall or fence.

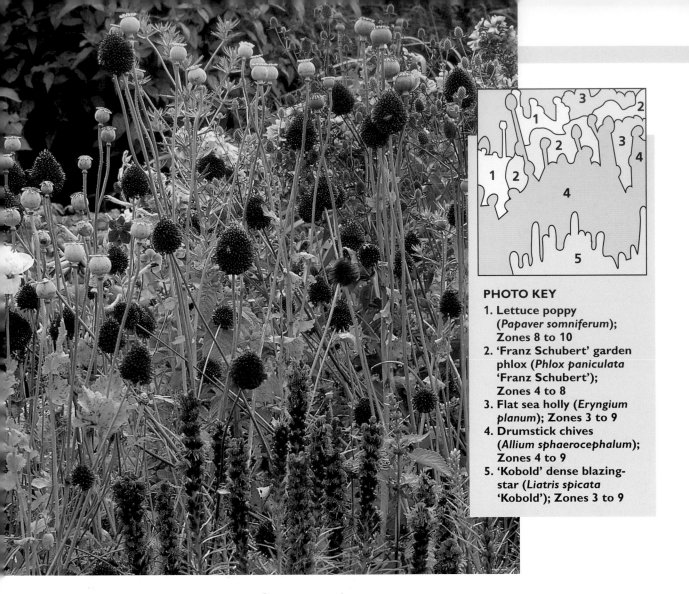

PHOTO KEY

1. Lettuce poppy
   (*Papaver somniferum*);
   Zones 8 to 10
2. 'Franz Schubert' garden
   phlox (*Phlox paniculata*
   'Franz Schubert');
   Zones 4 to 8
3. Flat sea holly (*Eryngium
   planum*); Zones 3 to 9
4. Drumstick chives
   (*Allium sphaerocephalum*);
   Zones 4 to 9
5. 'Kobold' dense blazing-
   star (*Liatris spicata*
   'Kobold'); Zones 3 to 9

Intriguing Informal Flowers for Cutting

While tradition may rule that a cutting garden should have stiff, formal rows of plants, this dramatic combination of cutting flowers proves tradition wrong. I don't believe in keeping a separate cutting garden any more than I think it's necessary to have separate gardens for herbs or wildflowers. It makes sense to use a variety of plants in your garden, and it offers you the maximum potential for creating new and exciting combinations.

This combination offers a wealth of long stems and tall flower spikes that are perfect for cutting fresh or for drying. It also has an exciting mix of textures and forms. The rich burgundy drumstick chives accent the cool colors of the other flowers. Phlox offers delicious fragrance. Crepe-paperlike poppy flowers, which show as globe-shaped seedheads in this view, provide spring and early-summer interest. In the fall, the drying, spiny seedheads of sea holly will add interest until frost.

Plants for Intriguing Arrangements

Use sea hollies fresh or dried. The spiny, stiff petal-like leaves of sea holly last longer than most cut flowers because these specialized leaves (called bracts) are more durable than flower petals. Cut the flowerheads when the bracts are fully colored and the tiny flowers in the head begin to open. Use them fresh or hang them in a cool place to dry. They will retain the blue color when dried, although the intensity of the color will fade.

Enjoy the ease of drying poppy pods. Poppies are lovely in flower but are short-lived as cut flowers. The pods, however, are very decorative and easy to dry. Keep an eye on the seedpods as they plump up. They're ready to cut when they're fully expanded and turn milky blue. Bundle the stems together and hang them in a cool, dry place. They will shrivel slightly but will retain their blue color.

Cut and cure some onions. The tall stems of drumstick chives are perfect for cutting. Harvest the flowerheads just as the sheath that covers the flowerhead begins to peel back, revealing the maroon buds inside. Cut the stems in the morning, and sink them immediately into warm water. Store them in a cool, dark place for a few hours to cure before placing them in the vase.

Try this prairie flower in a vase. Blazing-star is a star among flowers for cutting, and you can easily produce your own supply. Plant blazing-stars in rich, moist soil in full sun. The flower spikes emerge from a crown of grassy foliage in early summer, and the flowers open soon after the stalks elongate. Blazing-star has the curious habit of opening its flowers from the top of the spike down. Cut the spikes after the first flowers open. They will continue to bloom for up to two weeks indoors.

Colorful oriental poppy (*Papaver orientale*) flowers are stunning in fresh arrangements. They're short-lived, so cut flowers just before a special occasion, and sear the stems to keep them from bleeding.

PHOTO KEY
1. **'Connecticut Yankee' Asiatic lily** (*Lilium* 'Connecticut Yankee'); **Zones 3 to 8**
2. **Balloon flower** (*Platycodon grandiflorus*); **Zones 3 to 8**

Blue and Gold Cutting Combination

Bright blue and gold flowers offer a cheery greeting whether they're growing together in your garden or on display in a vase in your front entryway or living room. Asiatic lilies and blue balloon flowers are happy sharing space both indoors and out. The starry flower shapes create an interesting variation on a theme, and the brilliant yellow of the lilies accentuates the richness of the blue balloon flowers. Both plants grow well in fertile, well-drained soil in full sun or light shade. Keep in mind that balloon flowers emerge late in the spring, so be patient. They bloom for a month or more in midsummer. To create a cut flower garden based on this combination, try planting it with bee balm, phlox, yarrow, and artemisias.

Secrets for Sensational Cut Flowers

❧ Curing cut flowers. Fresh cut flowers must be cured or seasoned before you add them to arrangements, or they'll wilt quickly and never recover. Cut the stems in the morning when their water content is at its highest. Use a sharp knife to get a clean cut. Plunge the stems immediately into warm water. Place them in a cool, dark place overnight. Cut the stems again before they go into the vase. Add a drop of bleach and a teaspoon of sugar to the water. The sugar feeds the plant, and the bleach slows the growth of bacteria. Change the water daily.

❧ Lilies as cut flowers. Lilies are a popular cut flower, but when you cut a stem that's long enough to use in a vase, you'll end up removing most of the foliage from the plants. This weakens the plants, and they won't have enough energy to produce good flowers the following season. So if you grow lilies for cut flowers, treat the plants like annuals. Plant them in dense drifts so you can cut every other stem and not ruin the garden display. In arrangements, remove the stamens from the lily flowers because the pollen leaves stains when it drops.

❧ Planting lilies. Plant lily bulbs in the fall or early spring in light, rich but well-drained soil in a spot with full to partial sun. Full sun is best for strong, straight stem development. Plant the bulbs two to three times as deep as the bulb is tall. A 4-inch bulb should be 8 to 12 inches deep.

❧ Preparing balloon flowers for the vase. When you cut balloon flowers, a milky sap drips from the cut stems. To prepare the stems for arranging in a vase, cut them in early morning or evening, when their water content is highest, and sear the bottom of each stem

'Cerise Queen' yarrow and Asiatic lilies provide plenty of possibilities for fresh flower arrangements. Yarrows are also easy to preserve for dried arrangements. Cut the stems just as flowers open, and hang them upside down in loose bunches to dry.

with a lighted match. Hold the match under the cut end for 5 seconds to seal the opening and stop the bleeding. Properly seared stems will last for a week or more indoors.

PHOTO KEY
1. 'Moonshine' yarrow (*Achillea* 'Moonshine'); Zones 3 to 8
2. Common chives (*Allium schoenoprasum*); Zones 3 to 9
3. Mexican daisy (*Erigeron karvinskianus*); Zones 5 to 7

A Sunny Trio for Flower Arranging

Here's a trio of bright blooms that will work equally well in fresh or dried flower arrangements. Lavender chive flowers contrast beautifully in color and form with flat-topped yellow yarrow. Small Mexican daisies trail through the planting. This trio thrives in full sun in rich, light soil that has good drainage. Yarrow is one of the most popular cut flowers, though it's seldom seen in florist shops except when dried. Yarrow is fast growing and easy to establish. A two-year-old clump will offer dozens of stems for cutting. To keep these plants vigorous and productive, dig and divide the plants every three to four years. Yarrow and Mexican daisies are both vigorous spreaders, so be sure to choose a site carefully for this combination.

Growing Yarrow and Chives

🐛 **Cut yarrow for continued bloom.**
'Moonshine' yarrow is a free-blooming hybrid. In the garden, it will rebloom if you cut back the flowers after they fade. If you cut the flowers for arrangements while they're still fresh, the plants will still send up additional shoots from the clump and rebloom. So you can enjoy your yarrows indoors and in the garden at the same time.

🐛 **Rely on fernleaf yarrow for drying.**
Tall-stemmed fernleaf yarrow (*Achillea fillipendulina*) is an excellent plants for dried flower arrangements. The rich yellow, flat clusters bloom on erect, unbranched stalks in early summer. The deep yellow color holds well even after the flowers are dry. There are several excellent fernleaf yarrow cultivars, including the hybrid 'Coronation Gold', which grows 2 to 4 feet tall and has 3- to 4-inch flower clusters. 'Parker's Variety' is 3 to 4 feet tall with 4-inch flower clusters on sturdy stems; 'Cloth of Gold' is 3 to 4 feet tall and has bright yellow flowers.

🐛 **Enjoy culinary cut flowers.** Chive flowers aren't good for flower arrangements, but fresh chive blossoms make a beautiful, edible garnish for salads. You can also cut the leaves any time during the growing season to flavor soups and stew or to spice up salad greens.

🐛 **Divide chives easily.** Chives grow from a small, pungent bulb that reproduces quickly to form dense clumps. If clumps get too crowded, or if you want to propagate the plants, you can divide them in early spring or after flowering. Lift the plants with a trowel or shovel and knock away the excess dirt so you can see the bulbs. The roots will be tangled, but the individual bulbs will be easy to separate. Pull the clump into sections, or if you want to produce lots of new plants, divide them down to single bulbs. Replant the bulbs into amended soil, and water well.

'Heidi' yarrow and 'Butterpat' helenium (*Helenium autumnale* 'Butterpat') make an attractive late-summer bouquet in the garden or indoors.

Flowers Aplenty for Cutting

For flower arrangements both large and small, grow combinations of small flat flowers and spiky flowers, like this pairing of white feverfew and purple betony. Perennials like these that produce plenty of flowering stems allow for selective harvesting for arrangements without ruining the appearance of your garden. Flat flowers, like feverfew, make nice nosegays, while flowers with tall stems, such as wood betony, make dramatic arrangements. You can also use small flowers, like feverfew and baby's-breath, to add finishing touches to an arrangement of large flowers.

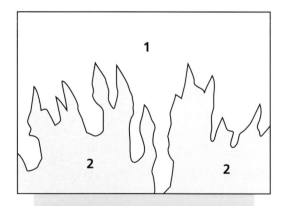

PHOTO KEY
1. Feverfew (*Tanacetum [Chrysanthemum] parthenium*); Zones 4 to 8
2. Wood betony (*Stachys officinalis*); Zones 4 to 8

Secrets for Flowers Aplenty

❧ Rely on an old-fashioned favorite.
Feverfew, pictured here, is an old-fashioned
flower that you'd trade over the garden gate
rather than buy at a nursery. Now it's a popular nursery plant because it rewards gardeners with months of flowers with little or
no care. Plants reseed freely and will come up
throughout the garden wherever space allows. They excel as cut flowers and have a
long vase life.

❧ Try this daisy in the shade. Feverfew
thrives in sun or shade. Use its bright white
daisylike flowers to brighten up a dull spot in
your garden in early summer. For extra color,
try the cultivar 'Aurea', which has bright chartreuse foliage. The only drawback to growing
feverfew in the shade is that the plants won't
flower as heavily or as long.

❧ Grow plenty of daisies for cutting.
Daisies have always been popular cut flowers.
Try growing white-flowered oxeye daisy (*Leucanthemum vulgare* [*Chrysanthemum leucanthemum*]) and the similar but larger-flowered
hybrid Shasta daisies (*Chrysanthemum maximum*). For rose pinks and reds, try
pyrethrum daisies (*Chrysanthemum coccineum*). Yellow- or white-flowered mar-
guerites (*Anthemis frutescens*), grown as
annuals in most gardens, are more delicate
and blend well with large flowers in a vase.

❧ Cut betony at the base. Wood betony,
featured here, has a long history as a medic
inal herb, but it's also a beautiful and garden-
worthy plant. The quilted, lance-shaped
leaves form an attractive rosette in winter and
spring. The narrow flower spikes emerge in
summer, and the bloom period lasts for over a
month. Plants thrive in sandy or rich, well-

To enjoy your astilbes both in the
garden and in arrangements, grow
several clumps, and cut flowering
stems selectively from each clump.
The astilbe flowers here are just
starting to open—the perfect time to
cut them.

drained soil in full sun. For arrangements, cut
the stems all the way to the base after the first
flowers open.

PHOTO KEY
1. 'Alba' great bellflower (*Campanula latifolia* var. *alba*); Zones 3 to 7
2. 'Bowl of Beauty' peony (*Paeonia* 'Bowl of Beauty'); Zones 3 to 8
3. 'Purple Rain' lilac sage (*Salvia verticillata* 'Purple Rain'); Zones 6 to 8

A Bowl of Beauty Combination

Sumptuous, fragrant peonies are elegant in the vase or in the garden. This garden combination features a cool color scheme with the shrub-sized 'Bowl of Beauty' peony as the focal point. A supporting cast of starry white bellflowers contrasts with the bold peony flowers. The mounding clumps of lilac sage add a finishing touch at the front of the bed. Both single- and double-flowered peonies are perfect for making generous arrangements in a large vase. You can make a single color arrangement or mix several colors.

Secrets for Blooming Beauty

🌿 Time it right when cutting peonies. Peonies last the longest if they're cut just as the buds begin to open. If you cut them too soon, they'll never open fully. But if you cut the flowers too late, the petals will drop after a day or two. Single-, double-, and anemone-flowered peonies are all good for cutting. Even under the best conditions, cut peonies are a short-lived pleasure. The average vase life is three to four days, but they're gorgeous while they last.

🌿 Plant peonies in the fall. Though we enjoy peony flowers in the spring, fall is the best time to plant these border beauties. The least expensive way to buy peonies is as bare root divisions from a specialty nursery. Order in the spring, when you can visit the nursery and see the plants in bloom. The earlier you order, the better the selection will be. Plants will be shipped in September to the North and in October to the South. Set the fleshy roots in a well-prepared bed with the buds 1 to 2 inches below the surface. Don't bury them too deeply or they won't flower well. You may get a bloom or two the first year, but it takes at least three years for the plants to settle in and bloom well.

🌿 Grow a great bellflower. The great bellflower in this combination has dramatic trusses of blue or white flowers, but you don't see them often in gardens. Why? Sadly, it's because the flowers are short-lived and plants seldom rebloom. But I love the plant and enjoy growing it anyway. The flowers open in late spring atop 2- to 5-foot stalks and last for about two weeks. The seedheads are undistinguished, so I cut the stems back after the flowers fade. To enjoy the flowers in fresh arrangements, cut the spikes when about one-quarter of the individual flowers are open.

🌿 Shear to stimulate more Purple Rain. 'Purple Rain' lilac sage turns heads wherever it's grown because of its curved spikes of brilliant purple flowers that last for most of the summer. When flowering wanes, or if plants get too leggy, shear the clump back by half. Side shoots will produce successive flushes of bloom.

Fragrant blue milky bellflowers (*Campanula lactiflora*) are a must for cut flower arrangements, and the stiff silver heads of *Eryngium giganteum* add a bold dash to almost any arrangement.

Garden Designs for Extra Fun
A Butterfly and Hummingbird Garden

For a plan view of this garden, see page 360

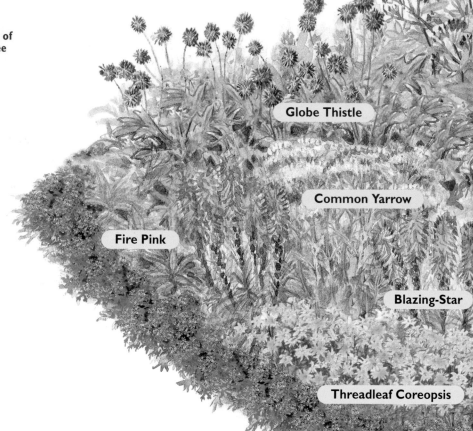

Globe Thistle

Common Yarrow

Fire Pink

Blazing-Star

Threadleaf Coreopsis

Plant Names	Bloom Color and Season	Height and Spread
Allium	Lavender flowers in summer	1' to 2' tall and 1' wide
'Marshall's Delight' bee balm	Pink flowers in summer	2' to 3' tall and wide
'Kobold' dense blazing-star	Violet flowers in summer	1' to 2' tall and 1' wide
Butterfly weed	Orange flowers in summer	1' to 2½' tall and 1' to 2' wide
'Zagreb' threadleaf coreopsis	Yellow flowers in summer	1' to 1½' tall and 2' to 3' wide
Globe thistle	Blue flowers in summer	3' to 4' tall and 2' to 3' wide
'Karat' sunflower heliopsis	Yellow flowers in summer	2' to 4' tall and 2' to 3' wide

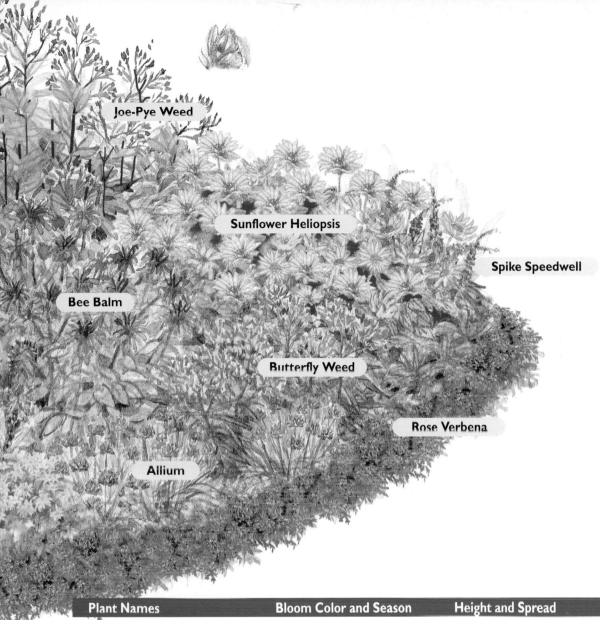

Joe-Pye Weed

Sunflower Heliopsis

Spike Speedwell

Bee Balm

Butterfly Weed

Rose Verbena

Allium

Plant Names	Bloom Color and Season	Height and Spread
Atropurpureum' Joe-Pye weed	Rose-pink flowers in late summer	4' to 6' tall and wide
'Rosalinde' early phlox (not visible above)	Deep pink flowers in early summer	2' to 2½' tall and 1' wide
Fire pink	Red flowers in spring and summer	1' tall and wide
'Blue Charm' spike speedwell	Blue flowers in summer	2' to 3' tall and 1' wide
Rose verbena	Violet flowers in spring and summer	6" tall and 2' to 3' wide
Common yarrow	White flowers in summer	1' to 3' tall and 2' wide

A Fragrant Garden for Evening Enjoyment

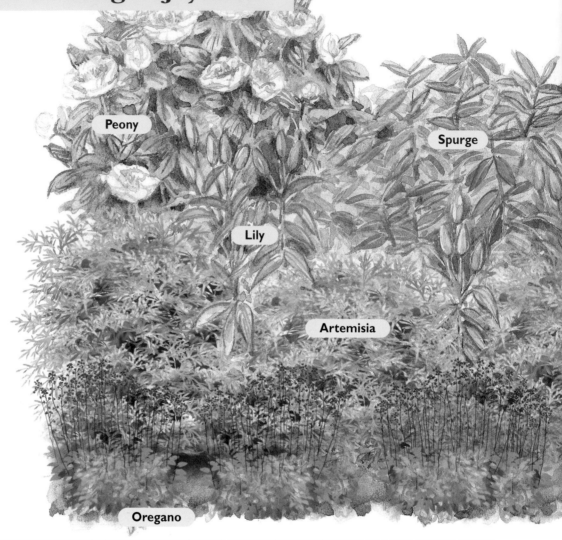

Peony

Spurge

Lily

Artemisia

Oregano

Plant Names	Bloom Color and Season	Height and Spread
'Powis Castle' artemisia	Silver foliage	2' to 5' tall and wide
Wood betony	Rose flowers in early summer	1½' to 2' tall and wide
Common chives	Pink flowers in early summer	1' to 1½' tall and 1' wide
Showy geranium	Blue-purple flowers in early summer	1½' to 2' tall and wide
Lady's-mantle	Chartreuse flowers in early summer	1' tall and 2' to 3' wide
'Casa Blanca' lily	White flowers in summer	2' to 3' tall and 1' wide

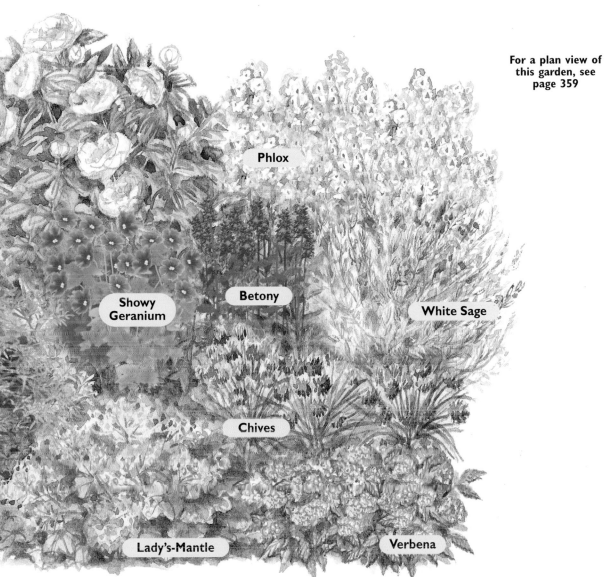

For a plan view of this garden, see page 359

Phlox

Showy Geranium

Betony

White Sage

Chives

Lady's-Mantle

Verbena

Plant Names	Bloom Color and Season	Height and Spread
'Herrenhausen' oregano	Violet flowers in summer	1' to 2' tall and wide
Peony	White flowers in early summer	3' tall and wide
'Miss Lingard' early phlox	White flowers in early summer	2' to 2½' tall and 1' wide
White sage	Silver foliage	1' to 3' tall and wide
Spurge	Chartreuse flowers in late spring	2' to 3' tall and 1' to 2' wide
Verbena	White, pink, red, or blue flowers in early summer to late fall	8" to 12" tall and 12" wide

A Garden of Flowers for Cutting and Drying

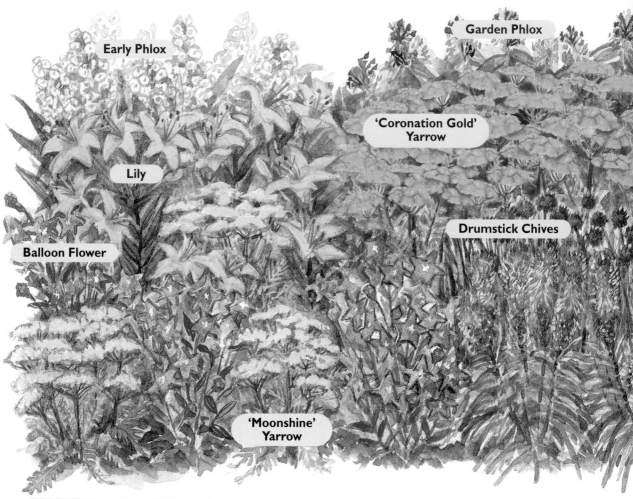

Early Phlox

Garden Phlox

'Coronation Gold' Yarrow

Lily

Drumstick Chives

Balloon Flower

'Moonshine' Yarrow

Plant Names	Bloom Color and Season	Height and Spread
Balloon flower	Rich blue flowers in summer	2' to 3' tall and 2' wide
White great bellflower (not visible above)	White flowers in early summer	3' to 5' tall and 3' wide
'Kobold' dense blazing-star	Violet flowers in summer	2' to 3' tall and 1' wide
Drumstick chives	Maroon flowers in summer	2' to 3' tall and 1' wide
Asiatic lily	Yellow flowers in early summer	2' to 3' tall and 1' wide
Miss Willmott's ghost	Silver-and-green flowers in summer	3' to 6' tall and 4' wide

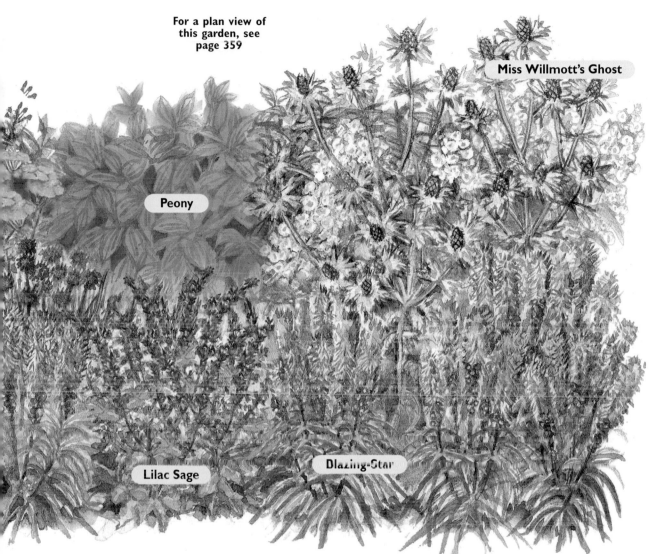

For a plan view of
this garden, see
page 359

Miss Willmott's Ghost

Peony

Lilac Sage

Blazing-Star

Plant Names	Bloom Color and Season	Height and Spread
Peony	Pink flowers in early summer	3' tall and wide
'Miss Lingard' early phlox	White flowers in early summer	2' to 2½' tall and 1' wide
'Franz Schubert' garden phlox	Lilac-and-white flowers in summer	2' to 3' tall and 2' wide
'Purple Rain' lilac sage	Purple flowers in summer	2' tall and wide
'Coronation Gold' yarrow	Yellow flowers in early to midsummer	3' tall and 2½' wide
'Moonshine' yarrow	Soft yellow flowers in early summer	1' to 2' tall and wide

Combinations
FOR DRAMATIC EFFECT

Contrast is the key to exciting garden pictures. Artful compositions, whether on canvas or in the garden, depend on dramatic focal points to create a place for the viewer's eye to come to rest. Without drama, the eye wanders and can easily overlook the details of a composition. In a painting, a spot of color, a piercing ray of light through the darkness, or a commanding form holds the gaze. In a garden bed, it may be a brilliant flower, decorative urn, brightly painted wall, or the dramatic form of a green goliath. Transform a garden from mundane to magnificent with a bold plant situated where you can view it from a window surrounded with contrasting forms. Use foliage and flower color for lasting impressions. Accessories complete any ensemble, and garden combinations are no exception. Place objets d'art such as pots, jardinieres, sculpture, or found objects to stop the eye in a bed and border. Water adds a unique dimension to a combination. Like a mirror, the glassy surface reflects the blue of the sky and shifting clouds above. Let your imagination run wild.

PHOTO KEY
1. Bigleaf ligularia (*Ligularia dentata* 'Britt-Marie Crawford'); Zones 3 to 8
2. Ostrich fern (*Matteuccia struthiopteris*); Zones 3 to 8
3. Fireweed (*Chamerion [Epilobium] angustifolium*); Zones 2 to 8

A Fabulous Foliage Frolic

Size matters where foliage is concerned. Big, colorful leaves like this handsome ligularia or groundsel beg to be noticed. They satisfy our craving for the exotic and appeal to the theatrical side of our nature. Bold foliage is sculptural and easily serves as an exclamation point in a combination or garden scene. In this simple composition, a single eye-catching perennial provides the perfect foil for the finer foliage of fireweed and the arching vases of os-

trich fern. The spring leaves of *Ligularia* 'Britt-Marie Crawford' emerge deep purple-black, ultimately expanding into rich ink-stained green as they age. The kidney-shaped leaves with pinked margins reach 2 feet long and 1½ feet wide. In summer, large trusses of ragged golden daisy-shaped flowers of this aster relative open for several weeks, adding to the dramatic display. With maturity, the crowns become enormous, and a single clump makes a lasting impression. Other popular cultivars like 'Othello' and 'Desdemona' also have dark purple leaves that fade to deep green-black where summer nights are hot.

More Bold and Beautiful Ligularias

❧ Growing ligularia. Ligularias thrive in moist to soggy sites with deep, fertile organic or loamy soils. Drying winds, hot sun, and insufficient moisture make the plants wilt miserably. Though not fatal, huge leaves hanging limp on their petioles certainly spoil the effect. In the cool of evening, foliage quickly recovers its composure. Prolonged wilting and insufficient moisture ultimately compromise the plants; leaves languish and plants decline in size and substance.

❧ Discover a wealth of choices. *Ligularia* is a large genus of bodacious perennials that excels in both foliage and flower. *L. × palmatifolia* is a hybrid with deeply cut leaves and tall stems crowned with orange daisies in wide, flat clusters (Zones 6 to 8). The ragged spear-shaped leaves of Shavalski's ligularia (*L. przewalskii*, Zones 3 to 8) are easily upstaged by the tall spires of yellow, early-summer flowers. In concert, they create a dramatic display. The broad arrowhead-shaped foliage of *L. stenocephala* forms a broad skirt around erect spikes of starry yellow summer flowers. 'Zepter' is a massive hybrid with wilt-resistant foliage and bold yellow lance-shaped inflorescences. *L. veitchiana* has broad, heart-shaped leaves and lemon yellow flowers arrayed in tall, narrow pyramidal spikes; *L. wilsoniana* is similar but the leaves are kidney-shaped (Zones 4 to 8). All species have flowers with reflexed rays (petals) and fuzzy central disks.

❧ Big leaves for warm climates. Unlike other ligularias, the kidney-shaped evergreen leaves of *Farfugium japonicum* (syn. *Ligularia tussilaginea*, Zones 7 to 9) are valuable in the winter as well as summer landscape. This beauty tolerates warm, humid summers and exhibits moderate drought tolerance once

This beautiful medley of spring woodlanders has as its centerpiece the woolly emerging leaves of tattered umbrellas (*Syneilesis aconitifolia*), which, in time, reach a foot across and turn deep lustrous green. European wood and buttercup anemones and blue corydalis will go dormant while the foliage of epimedium and twinleaf support the summer display.

established. Multiple ornate leaf forms are available, including 'Argenteum' with oversized leaves irregularly washed with white and sea green. 'Aureo-maculatum', called leopard plant, has pleated leaves splashed with yellow blotches. 'Cristata' is like an old-fashioned ruffled petticoat. 'Giganteum' has waxen leaves 2 feet or more wide. 'Kin-kan' has deep green frost-resistant foliage rimmed in gold. Choose a protected site in light to full shade with well-drained but consistently moist soil. The autumn flowers are lemon yellow.

PHOTO KEY
1. **Bamboo muhly (*Muhlen-bergia dumosa*); Zones 8 to 9**
2. **English boxwood (*Buxus sempervirens* 'Suffruti-cosa'); Zones 5 to 8**
3. **Scarlet sage (*Salvia splendens*); Zones 9 to 11**
4. **Violet taro (*Xanthosoma violacea*); Zones 9 to 11**
5. **Big blue lilyturf (*Liriope muscari*); Zones 6 to 9**

Evergreen Foliage for Lasting (Year-Round) Impact

Gargantuan greenery punches up this dramatic combination, but the evergreen foliage of groundcovers and shrubs carries the garden through all four seasons. In high summer, the two conspire against a backdrop of fine textures to create a persuasive garden picture. Few plants offer the dramatic contrast imparted by the large leaves of violet taro. Among the fine textures of airy bamboo muhly, the luscious purple leaves grab the eye. The exuberance of this planting is tempered by a pair of beautifully clipped boxwoods, which provide a year-round frame for the garden and hold the border long after the frost-tender taro has disappeared for the season. Bamboo muhly adds the softness required to punch up the contrast. Velvety purple flowers of the long-blooming selection of scarlet sage echo the color of the taro foliage.

Tips for More Fabulous Foliage

🌺 **Plant evergreen foliage for winter interest.** As the last of the deciduous ferns and late-blooming flowers succumbs to frost, evergreens steal the show. Evergreen leaves have a luminescent quality seldom seen in deciduous foliage. I compare the luster of these leaves to paint samples, which are classified as high gloss, semigloss, and matte. On a sunny day, the glossiest leaves seem to glow from the garden.

🌺 **Serviceable cast-iron plant.** More than simply serviceable, an exciting array of cultivars stands out in the garden. 'Okame', meaning "decorative fan," ('Variegata') is the popular white-striped barber shop plant. Each leaf of 'Akebono' (meaning "daybreak") has a bold yellow stripe down its center. 'Hoshi Zora' (meaning "starry sky") has broad leaves speckled in yellow, while 'Amanogawa' (meaning "river of stars") is heavily mottled like the winter sky on a cloudless night. Aspidistras creep from rhizomes roughly the thickness of a pencil. Plants produce two rounds of fresh leaves per season: the first in summer and a second flush in autumn. The odd basal flowers are overlooked by most gardeners. Aspidistras thrive outdoors in the ground or in containers. Mass plantings are effective under flowering shrubs or in drifts in the open shade of large trees. The variegated forms add color and light to shaded recesses.

🌺 **Timing your spring cleanup.** Late winter foliage invariably shows signs of wear and tear. Some leaves are routinely burned from severe weather. As winter cold moderates, plants like hellebores and epimediums begin blooming. Nothing spoils the show like delicate flowers tangled in last year's shriveled leaves. Remove all tattered old foliage in January or

Cast-iron plants have been parlor favorites since Victorian times, but in warm zones south of Zone 7 they thrive outside with little care. The white leaf tips of the distinctive selection called 'Asahi', or "sunrise" in English (*Aspidistra elatior* 'Asahi') glow in the shade.

February to make way for spring's fresh growth.

🌺 **When to prune boxwood.** Shear boxwood to increase compactness or to maintain a specified size or shape. During the first few years after planting, shear them after each flush of growth to encourage a full crown. Thereafter, you only need to shear as often as is necessary to maintain a desired shape or form. However, be aware that continuous shearing causes a thick outer shell of foliage that creates dense shade on the interior branches. Do not shear boxwood in late summer since this might force new growth that will not have sufficient time to harden before frost. Pruning of selected branches, usually to remove diseased, injured, dying, or dead ones, is preferred to shearing to maintain a natural shape and to keep plants at a desired size. Also, as plants get older, you may need to remove older branches so that light can get to the inner shoots.

PHOTO KEY

1. Astilboides (*Astilboides tabularis*); Zones 4 to 8
2. Ostrich fern (*Matteuccia struthiopteris*); Zones 3 to 8
3. Wild azalea (*Rhododendron* species); Zones 5 to 8
4. Blue-leaf hosta (*Hosta* hybrid); Zones 3 to 8
5. Doublefile viburnum (*Viburnum plicatum* var. *tomentosum*); Zones 5 to 8

Tropical Drama with Temperate Ease

You don't have to use high maintenance tropicals to create dramatic effects. Hardy plants with distinctive foliage give you tropical drama with the ease of hardy perennials. In this waterside scene, astilboides demands your undivided attention. The giant circle-saw leaf blades vary in size from a modest 2 feet across to a whopping 4 feet wide where moisture is ample and the soil is rich. The leaves are supported by an infrastructure of impressive veins that radiate like spokes from stout petioles. In spring, huge trusses of creamy white flowers nod above the expanding foliage. Mature leaves are bright green with a surface rougher than sandpaper. This breathtaking Himalayan perennial dominates any setting. Choose fine textures like ferns and contrast the brilliant foliage with deep evergreen leaves such as these rhododendrons. Complete the picture if you can by reflecting the dramatic combination in still water.

Plants for Dramatic Effect

ᘓ Keeping astilboides happy. Plant astilboides in deep, humus-rich consistently moist loam. Choose a site beside a pond, along a slow stream, or in a bog garden where fine sedges and delicate ferns provide contrast. A low spot that never dries completely is another suitable site. Plants need shade where summers are hot, but in northern zones they thrive with just a little afternoon shade. A solid backdrop of dense shrubs or a brilliant stucco wall will set off the leaves to best advantage.

ᘓ Adaptation. Big leaves are as functional as they are fanciful. They serve as vast solar collectors. The bigger the leaf, the greater the surface area for photosynthesis; the more photosynthesis, the more growth. Leaves spread wide in the shadows to maximize the surface available to trap the sun's elusive rays and convert solar energy into food. There are trade-offs, however. Big leaves take a lot of water to keep them in prime condition. As a result, many large-leaved plants, whether tropical or temperate, are native to moist or wet sites, often in the shade. Their deep, thick roots assure that sufficient water is absorbed to keep pace with water loss.

ᘓ Meet Chinese mayapple. Chinese mayapple (Zones 6 to 8) is pure eye candy. The deep green leaves of this unusual perennial have a lacquered surface that reflects light like a mirror. When paired with matte finishes, it is always the dominant player in the composition. The stem leaves are paired, one slightly higher than the other, and they shield the exotic, nodding maroon flowers borne in April and May. This Asian woodlander requires rich, consistently moist soil. The thick, waxy leaves have wilt resistance, though the plant is not for dry sites. Plants emerge early in spring and are often damaged by late freezes.

Form and color conspire to make this exotic grouping stand out. Sheltered among the stems of Japanese fiber banana (*Musa* 'Basjoo'), bold, dark Chinese mayapple (*Podophyllum pleianthum*) is electrified by a glowing carpet of dwarf sweet flag (*Acorus gramineus* 'Ogon'). Smoky purple 'Red Dragon' knotweed (*Persicaria microcephala* 'Red Dragon') punches up the contrast for high drama.

ᘓ A clumping knotweed. 'Red Dragon' knotweed (*Persicaria microcephala* 'Red Dragon') is a recent introduction that forms a well-behaved, nonaggressive clump with spectacular foliage. The purple leaves with bicolor cream and charcoal chevrons keep good color through summer, even where summers are hot. Foamy white flowers appear in summer in open clusters at the stem tips.

A Taste of the Tropics

A garden of tropical delights can be as festive as Mardi Gras or as restful as a hammock under swaying palm trees. This lush terrace planting recalls a shaded jungle retreat and is a plant collector's paradise. Lush elephant ears set the tone of this scene, framing the picture and dancing on the breeze as if begging to be noticed. A carpet of chartreuse sweet potato vine knits the composition together. For accent, potted century plants add vertical lift to the grouping in a variety of forms and leaf colors. A simple wooden chair beckons the gardener to sit and enjoy this oasis. In the background, a hardy sweet bay magnolia adds fragrance and a tropical note with its lustrous leaves. In spring, containers of tulips and other bulbs start the season, giving way to the tender plants as temperatures moderate.

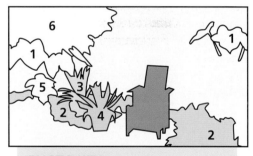

PHOTO KEY

1. Black stem elephant ear (*Colocasia esculenta* 'Fontanesii'); Zones 8 to 10
2. 'Marguerite' sweet potato vine (*Ipomoea batatas* 'Marguerite'); Zones 10 to 11
3. Century plant (*Agave americana*); Zones 8 to 10
4. Variegated century plant (*A. americana* 'Marginata'); Zones 8 to 10
5. Lava fig (*Ficus petiolaris*); Zones 10 to 11
6. Sweet bay (*Magnolia virginiana*); Zones 5 to 10

Tips for Working with Tropicals

✿ Hardier than you think. Many tropical plants are remarkably hardy with minimal winter protection. Gardeners in Zone 7 and warmer enjoy a vast array of plants without having to lift them each season. Cannas, dahlias, hardy bananas, elephant ears (*Colocasia*), and ginger lilies (*Hedychium*) are a few of the choices. North of Zone 8, add a generous covering of mulch for winter insurance. Cover the clumps with 2 to 6 inches of compost, sawdust, or other dense material after the first hard frost. Be sure to remove the mulch after the coldest weather has past.

✿ Take cuttings of tender perennials. Try overwintering tender perennials such as sweet potato vine, coleus, salvias, plectranthus, and alternatheras by taking cuttings in early September. Don't wait too late, as cool weather reduces success. Most will root in water, and you can keep rooted sweet potato vines in water all winter. Once rooted, pot up your plants in a porous soil mix and treat them like houseplants. Give them a sunny window and fertilize them to keep them healthy. If they get too large before warm weather returns, take another set of cuttings and start over.

Where conditions are right and space is sufficient, these drama queens make exciting additions to summer beds and borders. Huge Japanese fiber banana (*Musa* 'Basjoo') and the drooping cerise flowers of *Canna* × *ehemanii* tower over colorful tender perennials like dahlia 'Fascination' and silver-leaved *Melianthus major,* making a spectacular combination for a sunny spot.

✿ Overwintering tropical bulbs. Dig ginger lilies, elephant ears, and bananas before frost damages foliage if you plan to grow them as houseplants. Place them in bright light in a warm spot, and be sure to water and fertilize regularly to keep them in optimum condition. If you plan to dry them off and store them, lift them after frost browns the foliage. Cold weather signals to the plant that it is time to go dormant. Cut the stems back to about 6 inches and carefully dig the plant up. One of the more successful storage techniques includes washing the soil from the bulbs and allowing them to air-dry. Place the dry bulbs in containers that are well ventilated, such as milk crates, or similar containers; line with cheesecloth. Pack the bulbs with peat moss, small bark chips, or sawdust. This material holds just enough moisture to keep the bulbs from shriveling. Store them in a dark place where the temperature is around 40° to 50°F. Basements, cellars, and crawl spaces work great. Check on the bulbs monthly to look for signs of rotting or shriveling. Discard any rotten bulbs and spray those that are shriveled with a little water to plump them back up.

Spring Flower Drama in Shade

Springtime gardens are easy to fill with color. Bulbs, perennials, shrubs, and trees burst into bloom with the advent of warm weather. This combination features a suite of plants with bold flowers and prepossessing forms that create an elegant tapestry. The copious flowers of garden hybrid hellebores open in winter when few other plants except snowdrops dare to bloom. The flowers persist right through spring when they are joined by a variety of wildflowers. Fine-textured corydalis accents the coarser textures of its companions. An elegant color echo of flowers in shades of red soon gives way to a quiet carpet of foliage. High-gloss kidney-shaped leaves of durable European wild ginger, with tight, mat-forming clumps, offer year-round beauty, as does the hellebore foliage.

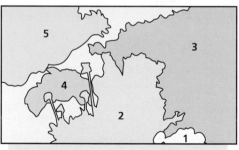

PHOTO KEY
1. **European wild ginger (*Asarum europaeum*); Zones 4 to 7**
2. **Corydalis (*Corydalis edulis*); Zones 6 to 8**
3. **Garden hybrid hellebore (*Helleborus* × hybridus); Zones 4 to 9**
4. **Giant trillium (*Trillium chloropetalum*); Zones 5 to 8**
5. **Daphne (*Daphne* species); Zones 6 to 9**

Secrets for Season-Long Beauty in Shade

New hybrid hellebores. The soft ruddy, purplish tones of old-fashioned hellebores have been replaced with tones of rich burgundy, plum, and deep purple-black. Deep apple greens, many of which are gorgeously spotted with deep red, are particularly exciting. The purity of the pinks, from soft shell pink to deep rose, is unbelievable. Perfectly shaped flowers with overlapping, rounded sepals, deep, pure colors, and above all, voluptuous double flowers transform the hellebore.

Extending the season. Shaded areas are often underwhelming after peak spring bloom is past. But if you have ample foliage, the garden will stay interesting long after flowers have faded. Include plenty of ferns, sedges, and shrubs with brilliant berries and outstanding autumn color. Hardy bold perennials bring tropical elegance without the bother of digging and storing them at the end of the season.

More evergreen groundcovers. As ephemeral spring flowers like trillium and corydalis begin to fade, the rich colors of evergreen leaves steal the show from their waning deciduous companions. Persistent foliage has a luminescent quality shared by few deciduous leaves. Try the upright vases of sacred lily (*Rohdea japonica*), lustrous wood spurge (*Euphorbia amygdaloides*), delicate partridge-berry (*Mitchella repens*), carpeting foamflower (*Tiarella cordifolia*), or blousy Allegheny spurge (*Pachysandra procumbens*). Low shrubs like Russian arborvitae (*Microbiota decussata*), *Cotoneaster* species, and sweet box (*Sarcococca* species) are additional choices.

The sweet scent of daphne. Several daphnes scent the late winter and spring air. The undisputed queen of the winter garden is

Bold color contrast elevates the excitement of this elegant combination when glowing salmon 'Beauty Queen' tulip fronts a backdrop of 'Louisiana Purple' wild blue phlox (*Phlox divaricata* 'Louisiana Purple').

Daphne odora, joined in warmer regions by the more upright *D. bholua*. Increased hardiness is the hallmark of the deciduous daphne species. The deep purple flowers of *D. mezereum*, Zones 5 to 9, open in late winter and early spring on mounding shrubs to 4 feet tall and wide. Combine them with plum-colored double hellebores for a showstopping display. Showy but poisonous red fruits follow the flowers. The selection 'Alba' has snowy white flowers. Temperamental but lovely is *D.* × *burkwoodii* 'Carol Mackie'. Small, deciduous leaves edged with creamy yellow emerge with the starry, fragrant pale pink flowers in early spring. Green-leaved 'Somerset' flowers equally well. Medium purple *Daphne genkwa* draws you in, but the flowers offer no scent.

329

PHOTO KEY
1. 'Pretoria' canna (*Canna* 'Pretoria'); Zones 8 to 10
2. Zinnia (*Zinnia elegans*); half-hardy annual
3. Black-eyed Susan (*Rudbeckia hirta*); Zones 4 to 8
4. Coral pompon dahlia (*Dahlia* hybrid); Zones 8 to 10

Bold Flower Colors That Sizzle

Big flowers in bright colors are real drama queens. Summer-hot areas call for summer-tough plants that take the heat in stride. If your plantings lack color in high summer, add some tropicals to jazz things up. Topping the list are cannas, which combine flamboyant foliage with outrageous flowers for an in-your-face display. Sweeps of 'Pretoria' canna punctuate this hot-colored summer bedding scheme, unified by carpets of orange zinnias that echo the canna flowers and masses of glowing black-eyed Susans. Coral-colored pompon dahlias add variety in form, texture, and color. Cannas and dahlias don't reach full steam until midseason, but they continue unabated until frost. Ginger lilies (*Hedychium*) are another excellent tropical, adding vertical lift with their ladders of stiff foliage on upright stalks. In late summer and autumn, they scent the garden with a unique blend of citrus and gardenia. A little extra mulch helps all these plants through winters that drop close to 0°F.

Secrets of Sizzling Borders

❧ Start from the ground up. Most gardeners want beautiful borders with minimal effort. To have a thriving, colorful garden in the heat of summer, good bed preparation and careful plant choice are imperative. Choose hardy and tender plants adapted to your soil, moisture, and exposure. Work with the positive qualities of your soil's texture and make minor adjustments to improve its structure, water-holding capacity, and fertility. Incorporate organic matter to a spade's depth and organic fertilizer as recommended by a soil test. Use mulches and drip irrigation as necessary to help plants through the hottest, driest heart of summer. Keep plants well watered during dry spells.

❧ Pinching and deadheading your dahlias. If you want exhibition-quality flowers, June is the time to begin to pinch and disbud. Pinch out the first set of buds to encourage bushy rather than tall growth. Thereafter, leave only one bud in each cluster for large flowers on sturdy stems. Deadheading— the removal of fading or dead flowers— encourages new blooms by redirecting energy that would otherwise go to making seeds. Cut the spent flowers below the closest node to encourage lateral branches with new buds.

❧ Choose noninvasive grasses. Japanese silver grass (*Miscanthus sinensis*) is the most widely planted ornamental grass, but it is also the most invasive. To its credit, it forms luscious silvery plumes in summer that dry to tawny shades and persist well into winter. The foliage is widely variable, from narrow and green to wide and beautifully streaked with white or yellow. On the darker side, this plant has become a serious pest in many areas of the country where it escapes cultivation and dom-

In this oversize container, orange, purple, and yellow make a scintillating hot color complement. The upright dahlia 'Salmon Rays' is balanced by cascading sweet potato vine and spreading lantana. The ascending branches of smoke tree (*Cotinus coggygria* 'Velvet Cloak') accentuate the strong vertical lines of the combination, and elegant white striped Japanese silver grass cools it all down.

inates natural areas. 'Cabaret' and 'Cosmopolitan' belong to the species *condensatus* and have dramatically white-striped leaves on plants to 7 feet tall. Both bloom late and are seed sterile, so they are preferable to invasive selections.

In and Out of Bloom

One of the joys of tropical plants is their long bloom period. Many remain in full bloom throughout the frost-free months, providing color and excitement. But even the longest-blooming plants rest from time to time, so there are going to be periods when foliage holds sway in your garden. In this southern garden, subtropical plants mix with hardy roses for a provocative autumn display. Mexican gold bush fills the garden with color and scent, its fine texture in direct contrast to the huge leaves of tropical princess flower. Despite the wealth of flowers, the velvety princess flower leaves create the essential punctuation in the combination, proving that foliage is indispensable in every combination. Mexican bush sage is a true autumn bloomer; it doesn't reach its peak bloom until September and continues until frost. The entire garden drama plays out against a backdrop of colorful Mexican bush sage.

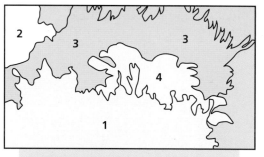

PHOTO KEY
1. **Mexican gold bush (*Galphimia glauca*); Zones 8 to 10**
2. **Hybrid tea rose (*Rosa* hybrid); Zones 6 to 9**
3. **Mexican bush sage (*Salvia leucantha*); Zones 8 to 10**
4. **Silver leaf princess flower (*Tibouchina heteromalla [grandifolia]*); Zones 9 to 11**

More Tips for Extending the Season

&. **Let foliage work for you.** Most perennials only flower for a few short weeks. Even long bloomers have their season. At any one time, most of the plants in your border offer foliage instead of flowers. Choose plants as much for their look in leaf as well as in flower. Good foliage is essential for a good-looking border. Limit the number of plants that decline after flowering. You need good placeholders to keep the garden full and provide a backdrop for the ever-changing parade of flowers.

&. **Dealing with dead spots.** Anyone can make a garden look good in June. It's easy with geraniums, irises, peonies, catmints, and roses. Imagine how sobering it is when the brilliance fades and green settles over the garden with unrelenting resolve. A walk around the garden often reveals unfortunate gaps, or worse, gaping holes. When a section of a bed looks temporarily dull and uninteresting due to too much green or too much fine texture, add drama with decorative containers, objets d'art, or tropicals.

&. **Try something new each summer.** Keep your garden lively by trying new combinations each season. Where last year's dahlia leaves a gap, try an elephant ear for bold accent. If the elephant ear you tried was overpowering, add a night-fragrant angel's trumpet (*Brugmansia*) in a decorative container. If you have been lucky at an antique store or flea market, drop in a sculptural element like a statue or a lightning rod.

&. **Your garden may need an overhaul!** If you can't easily fix a dull spot in the garden, you may need an overhaul. Don't look to the exotic, but instead consider garden stalwarts that thrive and quickly reach voluminous proportions. Daylilies are one such unlikely helpmate. With drought and deluge, clay and clamminess, you may need to develop a new appreciation for such durable mainstays. Despite flouncing foliage and the need for indefatigable deadheading, daylilies are dependable doers. Patch holes toward the front or middle of the beds with short cultivars like 'Bitsy' and 'Happy Returns', surrounded by low groundcover plants. Even the rear of the border can boast tall beauties like 'Autumn Minaret' and 'Challenger', which peek up in the bare spots between shrubs.

This long border is awash with waves of color throughout the season. In late summer, dazzling cannas vie for attention among garden phlox, yarrow, and ornamental grasses. Sweeps of bergenia foliage unify the front of the border and hint at flowers long past.

PHOTO KEY

1. Japanese anemone
   (*Anemone* × *hybrida*);
   Zones 5 to 9
2. 'Professor Van der
   Wielen' astilbe (*Astilbe
   thunbergii* 'Professor Van
   der Wielen'); Zones 3 to 9
3. Golden variegated hakone
   grass (*Hakonechloa macra*
   'Aureola); Zones 5 to 9
4. Fragrant hosta (*Hosta
   plantaginea*); Zones 3 to 8
5. 'Tokyo Delight' hydrangea
   (*Hydrangea* 'Tokyo Delight'); Zones 6 to 9

A Mixed Border Combination

Mixed borders offer the widest latitude in plant choice and enable you to build exciting combinations that utilize a wealth of annuals, tender tropicals, perennials, and shrubs. Don't be bound by rules. Shrubs help reduce maintenance by cutting the number of perennials you need to fill your space, and they have year-round presence. Hydrangeas are perfect partners for perennials. The gorgeous lacecaps of 'Tokyo Delight' hydrangea fill this border with pastel color above a blanket of yellow variegated hakone grass. The frothy mass of astilbe contrasts with the solid flowers and foliage. Hybrid Japanese anemones promise late season color, and the hosta foliage will soon be joined by fragrant flowers. This combination is equally compelling in the evening, when the luminescent whites and pale yellow glow in the waning light, and the heady scent of hosta permeates the night air.

Tips for Maintaining Mixed Borders

❧ Enjoy a wealth of hydrangeas. Whether you prefer lacecaps or hortensias (mop-heads), hydrangeas are the queens of summer shrubs. They thrive in humus-rich soil that stays consistently moist in summer. Large-leaf selections wilt shamelessly when the soil is dry and easily spoil an otherwise beautiful combination. *Hydrangea serrata* and its hybrids have smaller leaves, are more cold-hardy, and seem more tolerant of dry conditions. Where possible, choose mildew resistant cultivars. Limited bud hardiness reduces the range over which hydrangeas are grown, but new selections, such as 'Endless Summer', that bloom on new wood, allow northern gardeners to enjoy the glorious heads.

❧ Prune hydrangeas properly. Pruning is important for keeping hydrangeas vigorous and free-blooming. They bloom from buds formed on the previous season's growth, so conventional wisdom says to prune and shape plants after flowering. This timing removes the showy heads, which dry beautifully in the garden or in the vase. Instead, prune in spring, before the buds break. Remove any dead or damaged stems just above healthy buds. To encourage larger flowers, cut each stem that has flowered. Winter dieback is common, even where plants are fully hardy.

❧ Invasive ivy. English ivy can be extremely invasive, and it is illegal to sell it in several states. Ivy spreads vegetatively as a vine, but also by seeds. When ivy climbs a wall or tree trunk, this familiar plant transforms to its adult form and the vine blooms. Copious seed set allows ivy to spread uncontrolled and invade wild lands. If it is not outlawed in your state and you can find no other vine, plant only slow-growing, small-leaved, and variegated selections, and never let them flower.

Against a backdrop of colorful roses, this romantic combination of soaring foxgloves spires, spiky New Zealand flax (*Phormium tenax*) foliage, and boldly variegated 'Axminster Gold' giant comfrey (*Symphytum × uplandicum* 'Axminster Gold') celebrate the floral bounty of an early summer mixed border.

❧ Substitute hardy spikes. North of Zone 8, use New Zealand flax as a container plant and place it in your bed for summer in a decorative pot. For less work, plant hardy iris, which offers strong vertical structure that lasts throughout summer. Try Siberian iris or southern blue flag (*Iris virginica* 'Contraband Girl'). This prodigious cultivar is tall and vigorous, offering stiff, weatherproof foliage to 3 feet tall and lavender-blue flowers in spring. For colorful stripes, try a variegated yucca such a 'Bright Edge', 'Gold Sword', or 'Color Guard'.

PHOTO KEY
1. Shaggy shield fern (*Dryopteris cycadina*); Zones 5 to 8
2. Golden variegated hakone grass (*Hakonechloa macra* 'Aureola'); Zones 5 to 9
3. Japanese pittosporum (*Pittosporum tobira*); Zones 8 to 10

Water, Water Everywhere

Stone, water, and plants are perfect partners. In this cool, shaded site, a simple stone basin, set among dramatic ferns and grasses, is the focus. The elegant tropical lushness of evergreen shaggy shield fern forms a perfect vase at the base of the stone pillar. A flowing carpet of hakone grass strikes a strong horizontal line to anchor the combination. The overlapping blades are reminiscent of water sheeting over rocks on its downhill journey. Colorful flowers would disrupt the tranquility of this summer scene, but spring bulbs are welcome. Japanese pittosporum provides year-round structure, and the sweet fragrance of its inconspicuous flowers greets spring visitors. Water is an intrinsic part of every garden on the island nation of Japan. In Japanese gardens, a basin at the entrance to a teahouse is for ritual cleansing. The same placement of simple water basins at the entrance to homes is now found in gardens around the world.

Plants to Frame a Water Feature

More hakone grasses. Hakone grass is popular in gardens for its small stature and elegant spreading vaselike form. Plants tolerate cold and heat and grow freely in moist, humus-rich soil. Natives of Japan, these woodland grasses thrive in light to full shade but endure sun where temperatures are cool and moisture is abundant. The wild form, with lustrous green leaves, is the hardiest and resembles bamboo. 'Albo-striata' is a group of white-variegated selections of easy culture. Yellow-leaf selections are heat and moisture sensitive. 'All Gold' has stunning lemon yellow leaves. The foliage tints red in autumn and turns tawny brown after hard frost.

Hardy substitutes for pittosporum. Tender Japanese pittosporum has a lovely texture, whorled evergreen leaves, and horizontal branching structure, but limited cold hardiness. In colder zones, try deep green inkberry holly (*Ilex glabra*), bayberry (*Myrica*), Japanese andromeda (*Pieris japonica*), or daphne. Both green leaved and variegated forms are effective.

Rhubarb is good for more than pies. Ornamental rhubarb has among the boldest textures available to temperate-zone gardeners. This goliath is grown for its enormous clawed leaves up to 4 feet long as much as for its tall, imposing 6-foot clusters of small creamy white flowers. Rhubarbs are voracious feeders. Give them sun and humus-rich, loamy soil that stays evenly moist all season. They delight in boggy spots, with the crowns above water and the roots in the damp soil. Top-dress annually with compost or rotted manure to keep the soil rich and light. Plants take several years to mature, but it is worth waiting.

Other ways to add water. No garden is too small for water. Iron kettles, urns, and

A simple birdbath brings the light of the sky down where colorful glass balls shift with the whims of the breeze. In dramatic contrast to the small orbs, huge crinkled leaves of ornamental rhubarb (*Rheum palmatum* var. *tanguticum*) add focus to this simple scene. Delicate 'Lavender Mist' meadow rue (*Thalictrum rochebrunianum* 'Lavender Mist') completes this vignette.

glazed pots all make great containers for water. Smaller water features such as bird baths, watertight pots, and troughs make elegant water gardens. Place your water feature as an accent in a bed and border, or at the end of a vista. Set a basin where you can view it from a window and surround it with contrasting plant forms. Float glass balls on the water's surface as a mobile sculpture. Turn a watertight jardiniere into a simple reservoir of still water or add a bubbler for sound and motion. Add a small pump to your pool to mitigate the roar of traffic along a busy street.

PHOTO KEY

1. Globe thistle (*Echinops ritro*); Zones 3 to 8
2. Sweet pea (*Lathyrus odoratus*); hardy annual
3. 'Globemaster' ornamental onion (*Allium 'Globemaster'*); Zones 4 to 8
4. Persian onion (*A. aflatunense*); Zones 4 to 8 (past bloom)
5. Chinese delphinium (*Delphinium grandiflorum*); Zones 4 to 8

A Sculptural Combination

Orbicular forms repeat to unify this combination of contrasting colors. Fiesta-bright blown glass objects enhance cool colors and alluring fragrance in early summer. Fragrant sweet peas climb the spiny struts of globe thistle, whose pincushion orbs promise metallic blue flowers for color continuity after the ultramarine delphiniums are but a memory. Soft rose pink and dusty lavender sweet peas scent the air only in areas where nights are cool and must be planted early to beat the heat. Showy alliums carry the theme through, both in flower and as they fade and dry in the summer garden. Cool-colored hues of flowers and foliage soothe the eye while the hot-colored glass leaps from the garden to meet your eye. The tension between colors creates this garden's unique ambience.

Secrets of Successful Ornamentation

🐚 **Classic or contemporary?** It takes more than a hammer and nails to make a home and more than shrubs and perennials, albeit beautiful ones, to make a garden. An artistic garden requires ornaments, the personal touches that make the garden uniquely yours. Taste is so personal that every gardener will choose different art and display it in unique ways. To accessorize your garden, all you need is a little imagination and a sense of adventure. Whether you choose a classic Greek figure, a modern masterpiece, a gazing ball, or an architectural artifact, when it comes to accessorizing your garden, your own taste or sense of humor are the only constraints.

🐚 **Placing art in the garden.** Ornaments may be focal points or may be subtly woven into the garden fabric. Traditional pieces such as statues and sundials make a statement in a lawn or incorporated into a garden bed, and they also work well at the end of a vista or in the center of an open space. Urns, vases, and planters can combine plants and ornament or stand alone. A single, unplanted container adds a dramatic focus to a bed of fine-textured plants.

🐚 **Art among the flowers.** Exuberant plants often veil sculpture by early summer. No fear. Art is often at its best when nested among summer's excess. In autumn and winter, the sculptural form holds sway but most often it shares the summer spotlight with the perennials that mold its perfect setting.

🐚 **Let color run wild.** Color creates memories, so use it wisely and deliberately when you design. Purples, blues, greens, as well as pale pinks and light creamy yellows are referred to as "cool colors." Cool colors retreat from the eye. In other words, they appear far-

Tucked into a lush bed filled with exuberant foliage and colorful flowers, a modern interpretation of the female form melds with pheasant's tail grass (*Anemanthele lessoniana* [*Stipa arundinacea*]) and New Zealand flax (*Phormium tenax* 'Maori Maiden'). Sassy orange 'First Crown' lilies nearly upstage this sculptural combination for a few weeks in early summer.

ther away from you than they are. This is especially true of blues and purples. In contrast, bright yellows, oranges, reds, and deep magentas are called "hot colors." They are festive and visually they foreshorten distances. Use them to create in-your-face excitement in the garden. In mass or as accents, they incite you to say wow!

PHOTO KEY

1. **Common monkshood (*Aconitum napellus*); Zones 3 to 7**
2. **Adult English ivy (*Hedera helix* Adult Form); Zones 5 to 10**
3. **Fragrant hosta (*Hosta plantaginea*); Zones 3 to 8**
4. **Bigleaf ligularia (*Ligularia dentata*); Zones 3 to 8**
5. **Purple hairy loosestrife (*Lysimachia ciliata* 'Purpurea'); Zones 5 to 8**
6. **Snakeweed (*Persicaria bistorta* 'Superba'); Zones 3 to 8**
7. **Lungwort (*Pulmonaria saccharata*); Zones 3 to 8**
8. **English yew (*Taxus baccata*); Zones 6 to 8**

An Artful Focal Point

This artful combination boasts a wealth of varied forms and colors. While exciting, the variety is almost overwhelming. The secret of this vignette's success is the simplicity of an unplanted jardiniere, which is the prefect accent in this garden overflowing with a variety of flowers and foliage. With so much detail, the simple form allows your eye to focus, so that the intricacy of the planting can be discerned.

Tips for Incorporating Artistic Elements

Consider placement of garden elements. Extreme care goes into selecting the artwork we hang on our walls. No less attention should be paid to composing the pictures we see outside our windows. You can easily use classical proportions when positioning a focal point within a space. A quick way to think of this proportion is to use the rule of thirds. You can manipulate the feeling of depth with the placement of artistic pieces. Place your object one-third of the way down the axis from your viewing point for an intimate feel. For a more expansive view, accentuate the perspective by placing an object two-thirds of the way into the space from the viewing point. This establishes a sense of depth, while creating a proportion of space that is pleasing to the eye.

Try some functional art. Tables, chairs, and benches, whether permanent or portable, are decorative as well as functional. A single chair is a piece of sculpture when not in use and a welcome place to sit and read or to admire the garden when it's needed. A bench placed at the end of a vista or allée stops the eye and helps to focus it on a spot that merits attention. A seat hidden behind a bend in a path adds the element of surprise. A dining ensemble creates a functional accent in the garden.

Protect your terra-cotta pots. Nothing is more disappointing than finding your valuable containers cracked or spalled at the end of winter. As freezing weather approaches, take terra-cotta containers into a frost-free spot. Another way to protect them is to empty the soil and invert the containers in a garage or other dry spot. If they are dry, freezing will not cause cracking.

Choose winter-proof containers. Outdoor art is meant to be enjoyed year-round. Terra-cotta is a natural, earthy material, a perfect foil for the lushness of foliage. Unfortunately, most terra-cotta pots do not hold up to frost. Choose a pot made of dense, high-fired clay or a waterproof, double-glazed container.

Garden focal points can be functional as well as beautiful. Among this complex planting, a vibrant Adirondack-style chair cries out to all who pass. If you linger against the bold backdrop of Mediterranean spurge (*Euphorbia characias* ssp. *wulfenii*) and Jerusalem sage (*Phlomis fruticosa*), you may enjoy the pots planted with coleus, black mondo grass (*Ophiopogon planiscapus* 'Nigrescens'), and 'Silver Queen' lemon thyme.

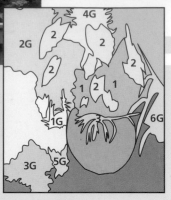

PHOTO KEY

In the Container

1. 'Zwartkop' aeonium (*Aeonium* 'Zwartkop'); Zones 9 to 11
2. Black stem elephant ear (*Colocasia esculenta* 'Fontanesii'); Zones 8 to 10
3. Mistletoe cactus (*Lepismium [Rhipsalis] cruciforme*); Zones 10 to 11

In the Ground

1. 'Beaujolais' loosestrife (*Lysimachia atropurpurea* 'Beaujolais'); biennial, Zones 4 to 9
2. 'Velvet Cloak' smokebush (*Cotinus coggygria* 'Velvet Cloak'); Zones 4 to 9
3. 'Obsidian' heuchera (*Heuchera* 'Obsidian'); Zones 4 to 8
4. Blue Spanish pin fir (*Abies pinsapo* 'Glauca'); Zones 6 to 9
5. 'Edge of Night' dwarf calla lily (*Zantedescia* 'Edge of Night'); Zones 8 to10
6. Soft soapwort (*Yucca recurviflolia*); Zones 5 to 10

Containers with Clout

The line between art and container is often blurred. Here black stem elephant ear is the sculptural standout in this colorful pot that echoes the blue theme of this garden. Against the indigo backdrop, dark moody foliage creates a minor chord in this narrow bed. Planted urns, washtubs, even old shoes are other decorative elements that expand the space for growing plants but also serve various other design purposes. As in this garden, drop them into a bed or spot in the garden wherever a bit of seasonal color or special drama is needed; when a spectacular plant finishes flowering or goes dormant, a carefully chosen potted specimen easily carries the spot for the remainder of the growing season.

Secrets of Successful Containers

❧ Choose the right potting mix. Success with containers depends on choosing the correct potting mix. Commercially prepared potting-media are easiest to use and can be augmented as needed. Bark, perlite, sand, and grit aerate the soil and help it drain freely. Sphagnum peat holds water. Choose a mix based on the water requirement of the plants you are growing. Plants combined in community containers should share the same soil, light, and moisture requirements.

❧ Try water-absorbing products. Containers are prone to drying out, and the more exuberant the plants are, the more water they demand. In high summer, you may have to water daily, unless you incorporate water-saving products into your mix. Polymer gels work by absorbing large quantities of water, in addition to beneficial nutrients, and then slowly releasing them through osmosis. Coir coconut fiber is organic; it does not absorb water but retains up to 300 percent moisture. Incorporated into potting mixes, these products make water and nutrients easily available to your plants. This allows for efficient use of water in your containers. In addition to storing water and reducing water use in your garden, water-absorbing products take up space in the soil, aiding soil aeration and soil porosity.

❧ Use polymer gels safely and effectively. Follow the application and disposal instructions carefully. Recent research has determined that these products may be neurotoxic. Wear gloves and a mask when mixing them. Thoroughly mix prehydrated gel into the soil before planting. To hydrate the crystals, start off with a teaspoonful in a cup of water (or a tablespoon in a pint). It takes anywhere from 30 minutes to several hours for the material to ab-

Exuberant containers take the place of foundation plantings in this narrow space fronting an urban cottage. Season-long color comes from tender perennials like flowering maple (*Abutilon*), lady's eardrops (*Fuchsia triphylla*), geraniums, and nasturtiums. Hardy coral bells along with tender sweet potato vine and 'Red Star' cordyline add foliage interest.

sorb all the water it can hold. Now mix 1 part hydrated gel to 8 parts soil mix (1 to 6 if containers are in full sun). Add the gel-soil mix to your container, and then add your plants.

❧ Put color in your containers. Color is a powerful design element. The color of your container is a major part of the color scheme of your bed. Why choose something drab when you can punch up a combination with a scintillating container? Glazed containers offer the widest range of colors and styles. Try a tile mosaic container for a unique accent. Or paint a terra-cotta pot with latex paint if you use a few coats to make sure it is sealed.

Bold Foliage Combinations

Ostrich Fern

Imperial Taro

Tattered Umbrellas

Blue Corydali

'Sulphureum Bicolor Barrenwort'

Plant Names	Bloom Color and Season	Height and Spread
'Sulphureum bicolor barrenwort'	Yellow flowers in early spring	1' tall, 2' to 3' wide
Tattered umbrellas	Ragged green foliage	2' to 4' tall, 1' to 2' wide
Ostrich fern	Bright green fronds	2' to 5' tall, 3' wide
Imperial taro	Black-stained green foliage	2' to 3' tall and wide
'Asahi' cast-iron plant	White-tipped green foliage	1' to 2½' tall, 2' to 3' wide
Blue corydalis	Electric blue spring flowers	6" to 12" tall, 1' to 2' wide

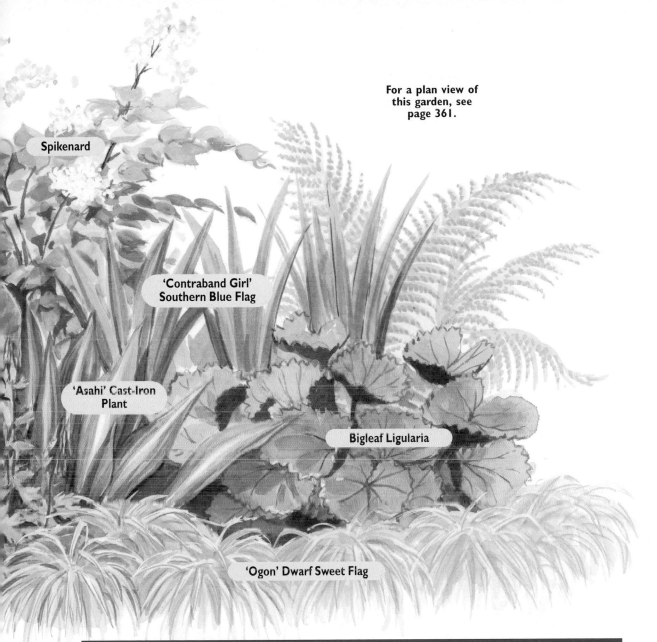

Spikenard

For a plan view of
this garden, see
page 361.

'Contraband Girl'
Southern Blue Flag

'Asahi' Cast-Iron
Plant

Bigleaf Ligularia

'Ogon' Dwarf Sweet Flag

Plant Names	Bloom Color and Season	Height and Spread
'Ogon' dwarf sweet flag	Gold-striped foliage	6" to 12" tall, 2' to 3' wide
'Contraband Girl' southern blue flag	Blue flowers in late spring	3' to 4' tall and wide
Spikenard	Green summer flowers/purple fruits	2' to 4' tall and wide
Bigleaf ligularia	Purple foliage, orange late-summer flowers	3' to 4' tall and wide

Bold and Colorful Flower Combinations

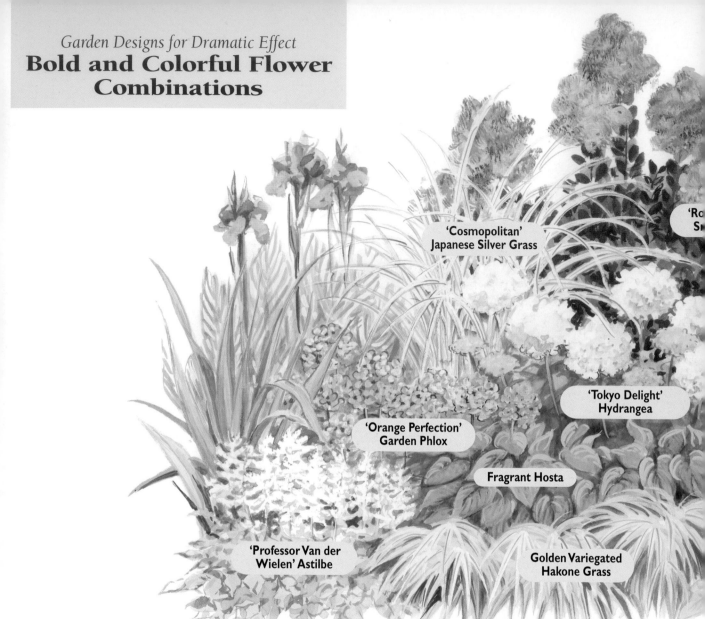

'Cosmopolitan' Japanese Silver Grass

'Ro S

'Tokyo Delight' Hydrangea

'Orange Perfection' Garden Phlox

Fragrant Hosta

'Professor Van der Wielen' Astilbe

Golden Variegated Hakone Grass

Plant Names	Bloom Color and Season	Height and Spread
'Professor Van der Wielen' astilbe	White flowers in early summer	2' to 3' tall and wide
'Maori Maiden' New Zealand flax	Pink and apricot-striped foliage	2' to 3' tall and wide
'Pretoria' canna	Yellow-striped foliage/orange summer flowers	4' to 5' tall, 3' wide
'Orange Perfection' garden phlox	Orange flowers in midsummer	2' to 2½' tall and wide
'Cosmopolitan' Japanese silver grass	White-striped foliage	4' to 6' tall and wide
Golden variegated hakone grass	Yellow-striped foliage	1' tall, 2' wide

For a plan view of
this garden, see
page 362.

'Pretoria' Canna

'Salmon Rays' Dahlia

'Maori Maiden'
New Zealand Flax

'Axminster Gold'
Giant Comfrey

'Marguerite' Sweet
Potato Vine

rple'
ush

Plant Names	Bloom Color and Season	Height and Spread
Fragrant hosta	Fragrant white flowers in late summer	2' to 2½' tall and wide
'Tokyo Delight' hydrangea	White flowers fade pink in summer	3' to 4' tall, 4' to 6' wide
'Marguerite' sweet potato vine	Chartreuse foliage	1' tall, 1' to 5' wide
'Salmon Rays' dahlia	Salmon-orange summer flowers	3' to 5' tall, 2' wide
'Axminster Gold' giant comfrey	Gold-edged foliage/blue spring flowers	2' to 4' tall and wide
'Royal Purple' smokebush	Purple foliage	10' to 15' tall and wide

Bold Accent Combinations

'Lavender Mist' Meadow Rue

Shaggy Shield Fern

Bigleaf Ligularia

Snakeweed

'Biokovo' Cambridge Cranesbill

Golden Variegated Hakone Grass

Plant Names	Bloom Color and Season	Height and Spread
'Biokovo' Cambridge cranesbill	White/pale pink flowers in early summer	6" to 8" tall, 8" to 12" wide
Golden variegated hakone grass	Yellow-striped foliage	1' tall, 2' wide
Snakeweed	Pink flowers in summer	1½' to 2½' tall and wide
Shaggy shield fern	Dark olive evergreen fronds	2' to 3' tall and wide
Bigleaf ligularia	Purple foliage, orange late-summer flowers	3' to 4' tall and wide
Fragrant hosta	Fragrant white flowers in late summer	2' to 2½' tall and wide

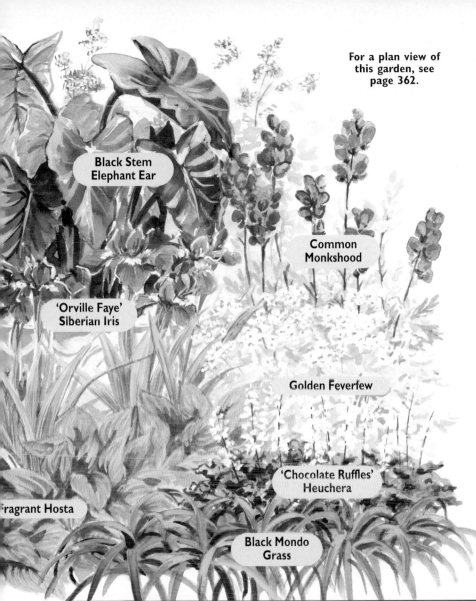

For a plan view of this garden, see page 362.

Black Stem Elephant Ear

Common Monkshood

'Orville Faye' Siberian Iris

Golden Feverfew

'Chocolate Ruffles' Heuchera

Fragrant Hosta

Black Mondo Grass

Plant Names	Bloom Color and Season	Height and Spread
Black mondo grass	Dark purple foliage/white summer flowers	2' to 6' tall, 8" to 12" wide
'Chocolate Ruffles' heuchera	Purple foliage/white flowers in late spring	1' to 3' tall, 18" wide
Golden feverfew	Gold foliage/white summer flowers	1' to 3' tall, 1' to 2' wide
'Lavender Mist' meadow rue	Lavender flowers in midsummer	4' to 6' tall, 2' to 3' wide
Common monkshood	Blue flowers in early to midsummer	3' to 4' tall, 1' to 2' wide
'Orville Faye' Siberian iris	Rich blue flowers in late spring/early summer	2' to 3' tall and wide
Black stem elephant ear	Deep lustrous green foliage	3' to 6' tall, 2' to 4' wide

Garden Plot Plans

A Garden for Wet Soil

Dimensions:
10 × 5 feet

Illustration:
page 228

Scale:
1 inch = 2½ feet

Hardiness:
Zones 3 to 8

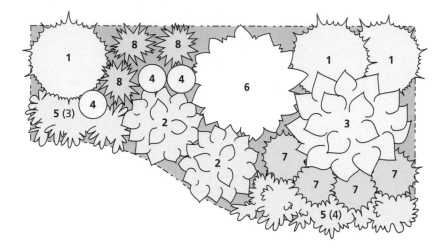

A Woodland Wildflower Garden

Dimensions:
6 × 3 feet

Illustration:
page 272

Scale:
1 inch = 1½ feet

Hardiness:
Zones 4 to 8

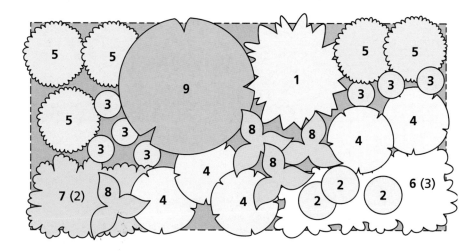

A Garden for Sandy Soil

Dimensions:
6 × 3 feet

Illustration:
page 226

Scale:
1 inch = 1¾ feet

Hardiness:
Zones 4 (with protection) or 5 to 8

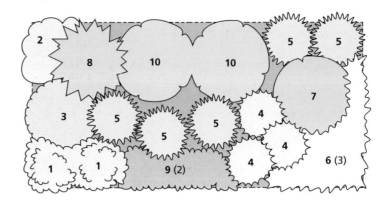

1. Common chives (*Allium schoenoprasum*)
2. Feverfew (*Chrysanthemum parthenium*)
3. Lavender (*Lavandula angustifolia*)
4. Lily leek (*Allium moly*)
5. Rocky mountain penstemon (*Penstemon strictus*)
6. Prairie smoke (*Geum triflorum*)
7. Autumn sage (*Salvia greggii*)
8. Spanish bayonet (*Yucca baccata*)
9. Mother-of-thyme (*Thymus serpyllum*)
10. 'Moonshine' yarrow (*Achillea* 'Moonshine')

A Garden for Clay Soil

Dimensions:
8 × 5 feet

Illustration:
page 224

Scale:
1 inch = 2¼ feet

Hardiness:
Zones 4 to 9

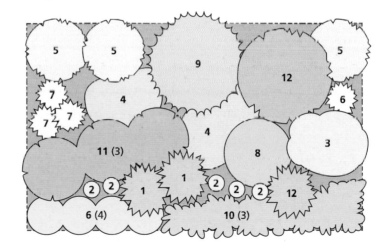

1. 'Golden Sword' Adam's-needle (*Yucca filamentosa* 'Golden Sword')
2. Hardy ageratum (*Eupatorium coelestinum*)
3. 'Violet Carpet' aster (*Aster* 'Violet Carpet')
4. 'Blue Stocking' bee balm (*Monarda* 'Blue Stocking')
5. 'Herbstsonne' shining coneflower (*Rudbeckia nitida* 'Herbstsonne', also offered as R. nitida 'Autumn Sun')
6. 'Zagreb' threadleaf coreopsis (*Coreopsis verticillata* 'Zagreb')
7. 'Lucifer' crocosmia (*Crocosmia* 'Lucifer')
8. Daylily (*Hemerocallis* species or hybrid)
9. 'Cabaret' Japanese silver grass (*Miscanthus sinensis* 'Cabaret')
10. Lamb's-ears (*Stachys byzantina*, also offered as S. lanata)
11. 'Autumn Joy' sedum (*Sedum* 'Autumn Joy')
12. Giant sunflower (*Helianthus giganteus*)

An Early-Summer Garden

Dimensions:
10 × 6 feet

Illustration:
page 138

Scale:
1 inch = 3 feet

Hardiness:
Zones 4 to 8

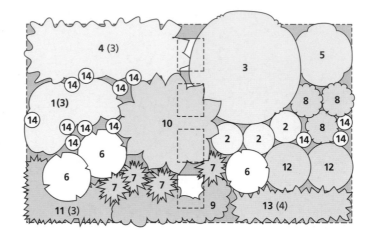

PLANT LIST

1. Big betony (*Stachys grandiflora*)
2. 'Souvenir d'Andre Chaudron' catmint (*Nepeta* 'Souvenir d'Andre Chaudron')
3. Heartleaf crambe (*Crambe cordifolia*)
4. Delphinium (*Delphinium* hybrid)
5. Blue false indigo (*Baptisia australis*)
6. Caucasus geranium (*Geranium ibericum*)
7. Variegated sweet iris (*Iris pallida* 'Variegata', also offered as *I. pallida* 'Aurea-variegata')
8. Knautia (*Knautia macedonica*)
9. Lady's-mantle (*Alchemilla mollis*)
10. 'Sea Shell' peony (*Paeonia lactiflora* 'Sea Shell')
11. 'Bath's Pink' pinks (*Dianthus* 'Bath's Pink'
12. 'May Night' salvia (*Salvia* × *sylvestris* 'May Night')
13. 'Vera Jameson' sedum (*Sedum* 'Vera Jameson')
14. Star of Persia (*Allium christophii*)

A Fall Garden

Dimensions:
4 × 2 feet

Illustration:
page 142

Scale:
1 inch = 1½ feet

Hardiness:
Zones 4 (with protection) or 5 to 8

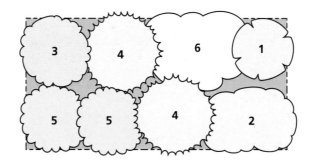

PLANT LIST

1. 'Prince Henry' Japanese anemone (*Anemone* × *hybrida* 'Prince Henry', also offered as *A.* × *hybrida* 'Prinz Heinric')
2. 'Blue King' Italian aster (*Aster amellus* 'Blue King')
3. 'Clara Curtis' hardy garden chrysanthemum (*Chrysanthemum zawadskii* var. *latilobum* 'Clara Curtis')
4. Prairie dropseed (*Sporobolus heterolepis*)
5. 'Golden Fleece' dwarf goldenrod (*Solidago sphacelata* 'Golden Fleece')
6. 'Autumn Joy' sedum (*Sedum* 'Autumn Joy')

A Sunny Perennial Garden

Dimensions:
6 × 3 feet

Illustration:
page 218

Scale:
1 inch = 1¾ feet

Hardiness:
Zones 4 to 8

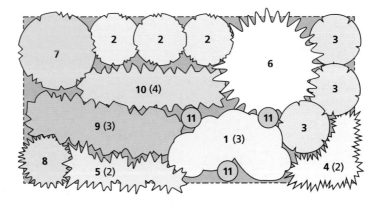

Illustration:
page 218

PLANT LIST

1. 'Silver Brocade' artemisia (*Artemisia stelleriana* 'Silver Brocade')
2. White purple coneflower (*Echinacea purpurea* 'Alba')
3. Jupiter's beard (*Centranthus ruber*)
4. 'Emerald Cushion Blue' moss phlox (*Phlox subulata* 'Emerald Cushion Blue')
5. Pinks (*Dianthus* pink-flowered species or cultivar)
6. Russian sage (*Perovskia atriplicifolia*)
7. Sea lavender (*Limonium latifolium*)
8. 'Vera Jameson' sedum (*Sedum* 'Vera Jameson')
9. 'Crater Lake Blue' Austrian speedwell (*Veronica austriaca* ssp. *teucrium* 'Crater Lake Blue')
10. Sundrops (*Oenothera pilosella*)
11. Winecups (*Callirhoe involucrata*)

A Spring Garden

Dimensions: 5 × 2 feet   **Illustration: page 136**   **Scale:** 1 inch = 1¼ feet   **Hardiness: Zones 4 to 9**

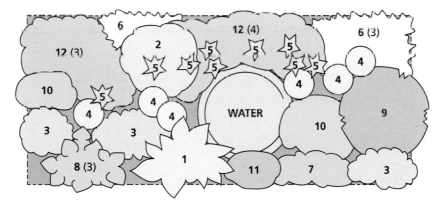

PLANT LIST

1. 'Mrs. Moon' Bethlehem sage (*Pulmonaria saccharata* 'Mrs. Moon')
2. Old-fashioned bleeding heart (*Dicentra spectabilis*)
3. Wild bleeding heart (*Dicentra eximia*)
4. Virginia bluebells (*Mertensia virginica*)
5. 'Peeping Tom' daffodil (*Narcissus* 'Peeping Tom')
6. Ostrich fern (*Matteuccia struthiopteris*)
7. Allegheny foamflower (*Tiarella cordifolia*)
8. Canada wild ginger (*Asarum canadense*)
9. Garden hybrid hellebore (*Helleborus* × *hybridus*)
10. Wild blue phlox (*Phlox divaricata*)
11. Woodland primrose (*Primula kisoana*)
12. Variegated Solomon's seal (*Polygonatum odoratum* 'Variegatum')

A Shady Perennial Garden

Dimensions:
8 × 4 feet

Illustration:
page 222

Scale:
1 inch = 2¼ feet

Hardiness:
Zones 3 (with snow cover) or 4 to 8

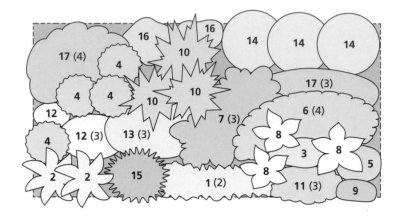

A Seaside Perennial Garden

Dimensions:
6 × 2 feet

Illustration:
page 276

Scale:
1 inch = 1¾ feet

Hardiness:
Zones 4 to 8

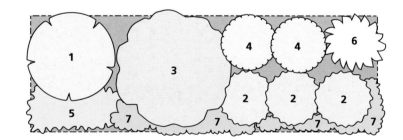

A Warm Color Garden

Dimensions:
4½ × 2½ feet

Illustration:
page 78

Scale:
1 inch = 1 foot

Hardiness:
Zones 4 to 8

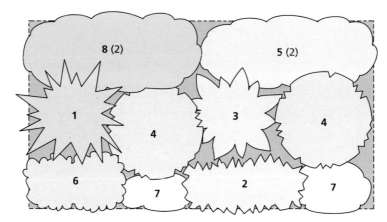

1. 'Bright Edge' Adam's-needle (*Yucca filamentosa* 'Bright Edge')
2. Blood-red cranesbill (*Geranium sanguineum*)
3. Daylily (*Hemerocallis* orange-flowered species or hybrid)
4. 'Husker Red' foxglove penstemon (*Penstemon digitalis* 'Husker Red')
5. 'Starfire' garden phlox (*Phlox paniculata* 'Starfire')
6. 'Purple Gem' rock cress (*Aubrieta deltoidea* 'Purple Gem')
7. 'Orange Bedder' Siberian wallflower (*Erysimum cheiri* 'Orange Bedder')
8. Fernleaf yarrow (*Achillea filipendulina*)

A Partial Shade Garden

Dimensions:
6 × 4 feet

Illustration:
page 220

Scale:
1 inch = 2 feet

Hardiness:
Zones 4 to 8

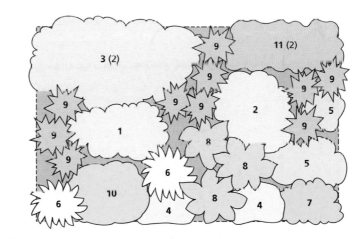

1. 'Deutschland' astilbe (*Astilbe* × *arendsii* 'Deutschland')
2. 'Superba' Chinese astilbe (*Astilbe chinensis* var. *taquetii* 'Superba')
3. 'Loddon Anna' milky bellflower (*Campanula lactiflora* 'Loddon Anna')
4. Serbian bellflower (*Campanula poscharskyana*)
5. 'Johnson's Blue' cranesbill (*Geranium* 'Johnson's Blue')
6. Japanese painted fern (*Athyrium niponicum* 'Pictum')
7. 'Dale's Strain' heuchera (*Heuchera americana* 'Dale's Strain')
8. 'Halcyon' hosta (*Hosta* × *tardiana* 'Halcyon')
9. 'Orville Fay' Siberian iris (*Iris siberica* 'Orville Fay')
10. Lady's-mantle (*Alchemilla mollis*)
11. 'David' garden phlox (*Phlox paniculata* 'David')

A Color Echo Garden

Dimensions:
6 × 4 feet

Illustration:
page 84

Scale:
1 inch = 1¾ feet

Hardiness:
Zones 4 (with protection) or 5 to 8

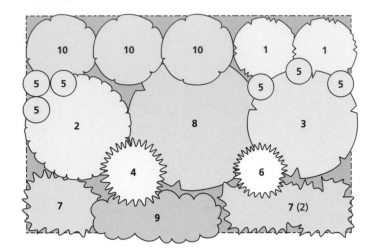

1. 'September Charm' Chinese anemone (*Anemone hupehensis* 'September Charm', also offered as *A. × hybrida* 'September Charm')
2. 'Patricia Ballard' New York aster (*Aster novi-belgii* 'Patricia Ballard')
3. 'Pink Fairy' baby's-breath (*Gypsophila paniculata* 'Pink Fairy')
4. 'Kobold' dense blazing-star (*Liatris spicata* 'Kobold')
5. Prairie blazing-star (*Liatris pycnostachya*)
6. 'Dawn to Dusk' Persian catmint (*Nepeta* 'Dawn to Dusk')
7. Common chives (*Allium schoenoprasum*)
8. Armenian cranesbill (*Geranium psilostemon*)
9. 'Wargrave Pink' Endress cranesbill (*Geranium endressii* 'Wargrave Pink')
10. 'Bright Eyes' garden phlox (*Phlox paniculata* 'Bright Eyes')

A Contrasting Color Garden

Dimensions:
5 × 3 feet

Illustration:
page 82

Scale:
1 inch = 1¾ feet

Hardiness:
Zones 4 to 8

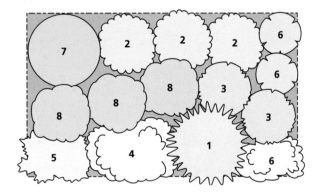

1. 'Bressingham Blue' agapanthus (*Agapanthus* 'Bressingham Blue')
2. 'Monch' Frikart's aster (*Aster × frikartii* 'Monch')
3. Black-eyed Susan (*Rudbeckia hirta*)
4. 'Blue Wonder' Persian catmint (*Nepeta × faassenii* 'Blue Wonder')
5. 'Mavis Simpson' cranesbill (*Geranium × riversleaianum* 'Mavis Simpson')
6. Jacob's ladder (*Polemonium caeruleum*)
7. 'May Night' salvia (*Salvia × sylvestris* 'May Night')
8. 'Moonshine' yarrow (*Achillea* 'Moonshine')

A Late-Summer Garden

Dimensions:
5 × 3½ feet

Illustration:
page 140

Scale:
1 inch = 1½ feet

Hardiness:
Zones 6 to 9

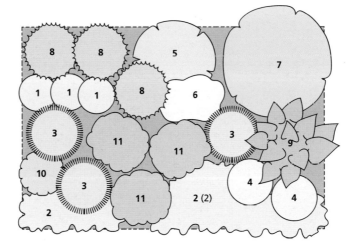

PLANT LIST

1. 'Pamina' Japanese anemone (*Anemone* × *hybrida* 'Pamina')
2. 'Monch' Frikart's aster (*Aster* × *frikartii* 'Monch')
3. Blue oat grass (*Helictotrichon sempervirens*)
4. Purple coneflower (*Echinacea purpurea*)
5. 'Herbstsonne' shining coneflower (*Rudbeckia nitida* 'Herbstsonne')
6. 'Fireworks' rough-stemmed goldenrod (*Solidago rugosa* 'Fireworks')
7. 'Atropurpureum' Joe-Pye weed (*Eupatorium maculatum* or *E. purpureum* 'Atropurpureum')
8. Feather reed grass (*Calamagrostis* × *acutiflora* 'Stricta')
9. Russian sage (*Perovskia atriplicifolia*)
10. Clary sage (*Salvia sclarea*)
11. Autumn sage (*Salvia greggii*)

A Cool Color Garden

Dimensions:
7 × 3 feet

Illustration:
page 80

Scale:
1 inch = 1¾ feet

Hardiness:
Zones 4 (with protection) or 5 to 8

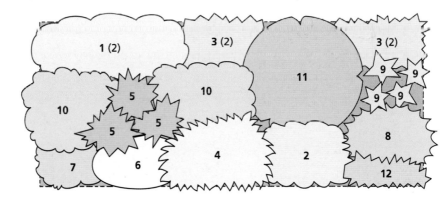

PLANT LIST

1. 'Pritchard's Variety' milky bellflower (*Campanula lactiflora* 'Pritchard's Variety')
2. 'Blue Wonder' Persian catmint (*Nepeta* × *faassenii* 'Blue Wonder')
3. 'A. T. Johnson' Endress cranesbill (*Geranium endressii* 'A. T. Johnson')
4. Common foxglove (*Digitalis purpurea*)
5. Golden variegated hakone grass (*Hakonechloa macra* 'Aureola')
6. Bearded iris (*Iris* blue-flowered bearded hybrid)
7. Lady's-mantle (*Alchemilla mollis*)
8. Lamb's-ears (*Stachys byzantina*, also offered as *S. lanata*)
9. 'Hidcote' lavender (*Lavandula angustifolia* 'Hidcote')
10. Miss Willmott's ghost (*Eryngium giganteum*)
11. 'Sea Shell' peony (*Paeonia lactiflora* 'Sea Shell')
12. Pinks (*Dianthus* spp.)

An All-White Garden for Partial Shade

Dimensions:
5 × 4 feet

Illustration:
page 76

Scale:
1 inch = 1½ feet

Hardiness:
Zones 4 to 8

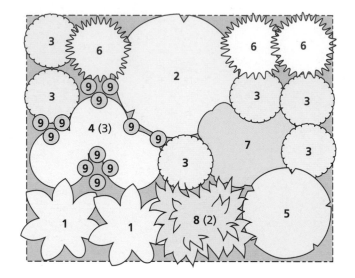

PLANT LIST

1. 'British Sterling' Bethlehem sage (*Pulmonaria saccharata* 'British Sterling')
2. White old-fashioned bleeding heart (*Dicentra spectabilis* 'Alba')
3. Maidenhair fern (*Adiantum pedatum*)
4. 'Kashmir White' Clark's geranium (*Geranium clarkei* 'Kashmir White')
5. 'Dale's Strain' heuchera (*Heuchera americana* 'Dale's Strain')
6. 'Fourfold White' Siberian iris (*Iris sibirica* 'Fourfold White')
7. 'Fuller's White' wild blue phlox (*Phlox divaricata* 'Fuller's White')
8. Creeping variegated broad-leaved sedge (*Carex siderostica* 'Variegata')
9. 'Mount Tacoma' tulip (*Tulipa* 'Mount Tacoma')

A Meadow and Prairie Perennial Garden

Dimensions:
15 × 5 feet

Illustration:
page 274

Scale:
1 inch = 3½ feet

Hardiness:
Zones 3 to 9

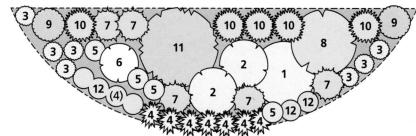

PLANT LIST

1. New England aster (*Aster novae-angliae*)
2. Wild bergamot (*Monarda fistulosa*)
3. Little bluestem (*Schizachyrium scoparium*)
4. Butterfly weed (*Asclepias tuberosa*)
5. Gray-headed coneflower (*Ratibida pinnata*)
6. Purple coneflower (*Echinacea purpurea*)
7. Culver's root (*Veronicastrum virginicum*)
8. Cup plant (*Silphium perfoliatum*)
9. Sunflower heliopsis (*Heliopsis helianthoides*)
10. Indian grass (*Sorghastrum nutans*)
11. Spotted Joe-Pye weed (*Eupatorium maculatum*)
12. Great blue lobelia (*Lobelia siphilitica*)

A Fragrant Garden for Evening Enjoyment

Dimensions:
10 × 5 feet

Illustration:
page 314

Scale:
1 inch = 2½ feet

Hardiness:
Zones 4 to 8

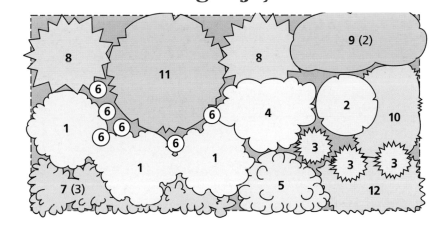

A Garden of Flowers for Cutting and Drying

Dimensions: 12 × 4 feet   **Illustration:** page 316   **Scale:** 1 inch = 3¼ feet   **Hardiness:** Zones 4 to 8

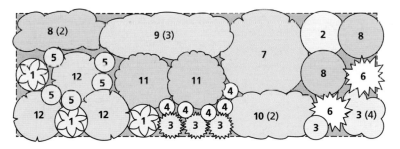

A Butterfly and Hummingbird Garden

Dimensions:
12 × 8 feet

Illustration:
page 312

Scale:
1 inch = 3¼ feet

Hardiness:
Zones 4 to 8

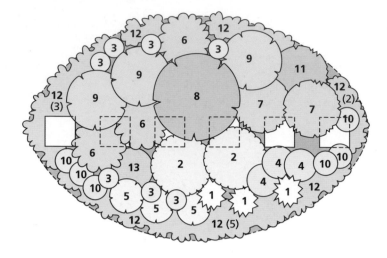

1. Allium (*Allium senescens*)
2. 'Marshall's Delight' bee balm (*Monarda* 'Marshall's Delight')
3. 'Kobold' dense blazing-star (*Liatris spicata* 'Kobold')
4. Butterfly weed (*Asclepias tuberosa*)
5. 'Zagreb' threadleaf coreopsis (*Coreopsis verticillata* 'Zagreb')
6. Globe thistle (*Echinops ritro*)
7. 'Karat' sunflower heliopsis (*Heliopsis helianthoides* 'Karat')
8. 'Atropurpureum' Joe-Pye weed (*Eupatorium maculatum* or *E. purpureum* 'Atropurpureum')
9. 'Rosalinde' early phlox (*Phlox maculata* 'Rosalinde')
10. Fire pink (*Silene virginica*)
11. 'Blue Charm' spike speedwell (*Veronica spicata* 'Blue Charm')
12. Rose verbena (*Verbena canadensis*)
13. Common yarrow (*Achillea millefolium*)

A Perennial Water Garden

Dimensions:
18 × 6 feet

Illustration:
page 278

Scale:
1 inch = 4½ feet

Hardiness:
Zones 5 to 8, except for Imperial taro

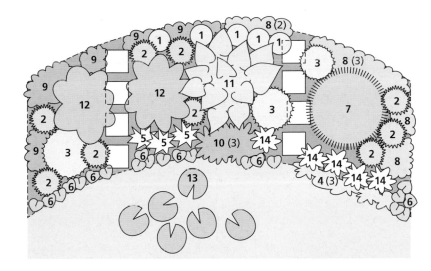

1. Cardinal flower (*Lobelia cardinalis*)
2. Lady fern (*Athyrium filix-femina*)
3. Royal fern (*Osmunda regalis*)
4. Golden club (*Orontium aquaticum*)
5. Variegated rabbit-ear iris (*Iris laevigata* 'Variegata')
6. Marsh marigold (*Caltha palustris*)
7. Evergreen miscanthus (*Miscanthus transmorrisonensis*)
8. Scarlet monkey flower (*Mimulus cardinalis*)
9. Yellow monkey flower (*Mimulus guttatus*)
10. Japanese primrose (*Primula japonica*)
11. Imperial taro (*Colocasia esculenta* 'Illustris')
12. Umbrella plant (*Darmera peltata*)
13. Fragrant water lily (*Nymphaea odorata*)
14. Variegated yellow flag (*Iris pseudacorus* 'Variegata')

Bold Foliage Combinations

Dimensions:
9 feet × 4 feet

Illustration:
page 344

Scale:
1 inch = 1 foot

Hardiness:
Zones 4 to 8. Numbers 4 and 5 are hardy to Zone 8.

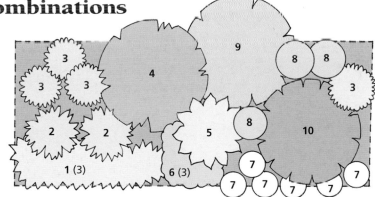

1. 'Sulphureum bicolor barrenwort' (*Epimedium × versicolor* 'Sulphureum')
2. Tattered umbrellas (*Syneilesis aconitifolia*)
3. Ostrich fern (*Matteuccia struthiopteris*)
4. Imperial taro (*Colocasia esculenta* 'Illustris')
5. 'Asahi' cast-iron plant (*Aspidistra elatior* 'Asahi')
6. Blue corydalis (*Corydalis flexuosa*)
7. 'Ogon' dwarf sweet flag (*Acorus gramineus* 'Ogon')
8. 'Contraband Girl' southern blue flag (*Iris virginica* 'Contraband Girl')
9. Spikenard (*Aralia racemosa*)
10. Bigleaf ligularia (*Ligularia dentata*)

Bold and Colorful Flower Combinations

Dimensions:
20 feet × 8 feet

Illustration:
page 346

Scale:
1 inch = 2 feet

Hardiness:
Zones 5 to 8. Numbers
2, 3, and 10 are hardy
to Zone 8. Number 9 is tender.

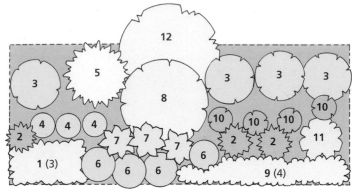

PLANT LIST

1. 'Professor Van der Wielen' astilbe (*Astilbe thunbergii* 'Professor Van der Wielen')
2. 'Maori Maiden' New Zealand flax (*Phormium tenax* 'Maori Maiden')
3. 'Pretoria' canna (*Canna* 'Pretoria')
4. 'Orange Perfection' garden phlox (*Phlox paniculata* 'Orange Perfection')
5. 'Cosmopolitan' Japanese silver grass (*Miscanthus sinensis* var *condensatus* 'Cosmopolitan')
6. Golden variegated hakone grass (*Hakonechloa macra* 'Aureola')
7. Fragrant hosta (*Hosta plantaginea*)
8. 'Tokyo Delight' hydrangea (*Hydrangea serrata* 'Tokyo Delight')
9. 'Marguerite' sweet potato vine (*Ipomoea batatas* 'Marguerite')
10. 'Salmon Rays' dahlia (*Dahlia* 'Salmon Rays')
11. 'Axminster Gold' giant comfrey (*Symphytum* × *uplandicum* 'Axminster Gold')
12. 'Royal Purple' smoke bush (*Cotinus coggygria* 'Royal Purple')

Bold Accent Combinations

Dimensions:
20 feet × 8½ feet

Illustration:
page 348

Scale:
1 inch = 2 feet

Hardiness:
Zones 5 to 8. Number 13 is tender.

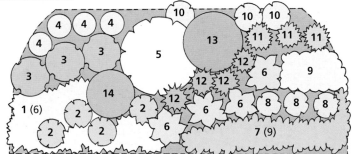

PLANT LIST

1. 'Biokovo' Cambridge cranesbill (*Geranium* × *cantabrigiense* 'Biokovo')
2. Golden variegated hakone grass (*Hakonechloa macra* 'Aureola')
3. Snakeweed (*Persicaria bistorta* 'Superba')
4. Shaggy shield fern (*Dryopteris cycadina*)
5. Bigleaf ligularia (*Ligularia dentata*)
6. Fragrant hosta (*Hosta plantaginea*)
7. Black mondo grass (*Ophiopogon planiscapus* 'Nigrescens')
8. 'Chocolate Ruffles' heuchera (*Heuchera* 'Chocolate Ruffles')
9. Golden feverfew (*Tanacetum parthenium* 'Aurem')
10. 'Lavender Mist' meadow rue (*Thalictrum rochebrunianum* 'Lavender Mist')
11. Common monkshood (*Aconitum napellus*)
12. 'Orville Faye' Siberian iris (*Iris sibirica* 'Orville Faye')
13. Decorative pot filled with black-stemmed elephant ear (*Colocasia esculenta* 'Fontanesii')
14. Water basin

Mail-Order Sources of Perennials

Ambergate Gardens
8730 County Road 43
Chaska, MN 55318-9358
Phone/fax: 952-443-2248
www.ambergategardens.com

**Andre Viette
Farm & Nursery**
PO Box 1109
Fishersville, VA 22939
Phone: 540-943-2315
Fax: 540-943-0782
www.viette.com

Arrowhead Alpines
PO Box 857
Fowlerville, MI 48836
Phone: 517-223-3581
Fax: 517-223-8750
www.arrowhead-alpines.com

Asiatica Nursery
PO Box 270
Lewisberry, PA 17339
Phone: 717-938-8677 (no phone
orders, please)
Fax: 717 938 0771
www.asiaticanursery.com

Avant Gardens
710 High Hill Road
Dartmouth, MA 02747
Phone: 508-998-8819
Toll-free fax: 866-442-8268
www.avantgardensne.com

**Bluestone
Perennials, Inc.**
7211 Middle Ridge Road
Madison, OH 44057-3096
Phone: 800-852-5243
Fax: 440-428-7198
www.bluestoneperennials.com

Brent and Becky's Bulbs
7900 Daffodil Lane
Gloucester, VA 23061
Phone: 804-693-3966
Fax: 804-693-9436
www.brentandbeckysbulbs.com

Canyon Creek Nursery
3527 Dry Creek Road
Oroville, CA 95965
Phone/fax: 530-533-2166
www.canyoncreeknursery.com

Carroll Gardens
444 East Main Street
Westminster, MD 21157
Phone: 800-638-6334
Fax: 410-857-4112
www.carrollgardens.com

Digging Dog Nursery
PO Box 471
Albion, CA 95410
Phone: 707-937-1130
Fax: 707-937-2480
www.diggingdog.com

Fairweather Gardens
PO Box 330
Greenwich, NJ 08323
Phone: 856-451-6261
Fax: 856 451-0303
www.fairweathergardens.com

Fancy Fronds
PO Box 1090
Gold Bar, WA 98251
Phone: 360-793-1472
www.fancyfronds.com

Foliage Gardens
2003 128th Avenue SE
Bellevue, WA 98005
Phone: 425-747-2998
www.foliagegardens.com/
index.html

Forestfarm
Ray and Peg Prag
990 Tetherow Road
Williams, OR 97544-9599
Phone: 541-846-7269
Fax: 541-846-6963
www.forestfarm.com

Fraser's Thimble Farms
175 Arbutus Road
Salt Spring Island, V8K 1A3 BC
Canada
Phone/fax: 250-537-5788
www.thimblefarms.com

Gossler Farms Nursery
1200 Weaver Road
Springfield OR 97478
Phone: 541-746-3922
Fax: 541-744-7924
www.gosslerfarms.com/home.php

High Country Gardens
2902 Rufina Street
Santa Fe, NM 87505-2929
Phone: 800-925-9387
Fax: 800-925-0097
www.highcountrygardens.com

Joy Creek Nursery
20300 Northwest Watson Road
Scappoose, OR 97056
Phone: 503-543-7474
Fax: 503-543-6933
www.joycreek.com

Kurt Bluemel, Inc.
2740 Greene Lane
Baldwin, MD 21013-9523
Phone: 410-557-7229
Fax: 410-557-9785
www.bluemel.com

Lazy S's Farm Nursery
2360 Spotswood Trail
Barboursville, VA 22923
www.lazyssfarm.com/index.html

Meadowbrook Nursery/ WeDu Natives
2055 Polly Spout Road
Marion, NC 28752
Phone: 828-738-8300
Fax: 828-287-9348
www.we-du.com

Munchkin Nursery
323 Woodside Drive NW
Depauw, IN 47115-9039
Phone: 812-633-4858
www.munchkinnursery.com

Native Gardens
5737 Fisher Lane
Greenback, TN 37742
Phone/fax: 423-856-0220
www.native-gardens.com

The Natural Garden
38W443 Highway 64
St. Charles, IL 60175
Phone: 630-584-0150
Fax: 630-584-0185
www.thenaturalgardeninc.com

Niche Gardens
1111 Dawson Road
Chapel Hill, NC 27516
Phone: 919-967-0078
Fax: 919-967-4026
www.nichegardens.com

Plant Delights
9241 Sauls Road
Raleigh, NC 27603
Phone: 919-772-4794
Fax: 919-662-0370
www.plantdel.com

Plants of the Southwest
Agua Fria Road
Route 6, Box 11A
Santa Fe, NM 87501
Phone: 505-471-2212
Fax: 505-438-8800
www.plantsofthesouthwest.com

Prairie Moon Nursery
31837 Bur Oak Lane
Winona, MN 55987-9515
Phone: 866-417-8156
Fax: 507-454-5238
www.prairiemoon.com

Prairie Nursery
PO Box 306
Westfield, WI 53964
Phone: 608-296-3679
Fax: 608-296-2741
www.prairie-nursery.com

Rare Find Nursery
957 Patterson Road
Jackson, NJ 08527
Phone: 732-833-0613
Fax: 732-833-1623
www.rarefindnursery.com

Russell Graham
Purveyor of Plants
4030 Eagle Crest Road, NW
Salem, OR 97304
Phone: 503-362-1135

Schreiner's Iris Gardens
3625 Quinaby Road NE
Salem, OR 97303
Phone: 503-393-3232
Fax: 503-393-5590
www.schreinersgardens.com

Seneca Hill Perennials
3712 County Route 57
Oswego, NY 13126
Phone: 315-342-5915
www.senecahill.com

Siskiyou Rare Plant Nursery
2115 Talent Avenue
Talent, Oregon 97540
Phone: 541-535-7103
Fax: 541-535-2113
www.srpn.net

Song Sparrow Perennial Farm
13101 East Rye Road
Avalon, Wisconsin 53505
Phone: 800-553-3715
Fax: 608-883-2257
www.songsparrow.com

Sunlight Gardens
174 Golden Lane
Andersonville, TN 37705
Phone: 865-494-8237
Fax: 865-494-7086
www.sunlightgardens.com

Wayside Gardens
1 Garden Lane
Hodges, SC 29695-0001
Phone: 800-845-1124
Fax: 800-457-9712
www.waysidegardens.com

White Flower Farm
PO Box 50, Route 63
Litchfield, CT 06759-0050
Phone: 800-411-6159
Fax: 860-496-1418
www.whiteflowerfarm.com

Woodlander's
1128 Colleton Avenue
Aiken, SC 29801
Phone/fax: 803-648-7522
www.woodlanders.net

Recommended Reading

Adams, Denise. *Restoring American Gardens.* Portland, OR: Timber Press, 2002.

Armitage, Allan. *Herbaceous Perennial Plants.* 2nd ed. Champaign, IL: Stipes Publishing, 1997.

Burrell, C. Colston. *A Gardener's Encyclopedia of Wildflowers.* Emmaus, PA: Rodale, 1997.

Chatto, Beth. *The Green Tapestry.* New York: Simon & Schuster Trade, 1989.

Cox, Jeff. *Perennial All-Stars.* Emmaus, PA: Rodale, 1998.

Cullina, William. *The New England Wild Flower Society Guide to Growing and Propagating Wildflowers of the United States and Canada.* Boston, MA: Houghton Mifflin Company, 2000.

DiSabato Aust, Tracy. *The Well-Tended Perennial Garden.* Portland, OR: Timber Press, 1998.

Druse, Ken. *The Natural Garden.* New York: Clarkson N. Potter, 1989.

———. *The Natural Shade Garden.* New York: Clarkson N. Potter, 1992.

Eddison, Sydney. *The Gardener's Pallette.* Chicago, IL: Contemporary Books, 2002.

Glattstein, Judy. *Consider the Leaf.* Portland, OR: Timber Press, 2003.

Harper, Pamela J. *Designing with Perennials.* New York, NY: Sterling, 2001.

Lacy, Allen. *The Garden in Autumn.* New York: Henry Holt & Co., 1995.

Lloyd, Christopher. *Succession Planting.* Portland, OR: Timber Press, 2005.

———. *Garden Flowers.* London: Cassell & Company, 2000.

———. *Foliage Plants.* New and rev. New York: Random House, 1985.

———. *The Well-Tempered Garden.* New York: Random House, 1985.

Lord, Tony, and Andrew Lawson. *The Encyclopedia of Planting Combinations.* London: Mitchell Beazley, 2003.

Lovejoy, Ann. *Ann Lovejoy's Organic Garden Design School.* Emmaus, PA: Rodale, 2001.

———. *The American Mixed Border.* New York: Macmillan Publishers Ltd., 1993.

Mickel, John. *Ferns for American Gardens.* New York, NY: Macmillan, 1994.

Phillips, Ellen, and C. Colston Burrell. *Rodale's Illustrated Encyclopedia of Perennials* 10th anniversary edition. Emmaus, PA: Rodale, 2004.

Phillips, Roger, and Martyn E. Rix. *The Random House Book of Perennials.* 2 vols. New York: Random House, 1991.

Roth, Susan, and Dennis Schrader. *Hot Plants for Cool Climates.* Portland, OR: Timber Press, 2005.

Schneck, Marcus. *Your Backyard Wildlife Garden.* Emmaus, PA: Rodale, 1992.

Speichert, Greg, and Sue Speichert. *Encyclopedia of Water Garden Plants.* Portland, OR: Timber Press, 2004.

Springer, Lauren. *The Undaunted Garden.* Golden, CO: Fulcrum Publishing, 1994.

Photo Credits

All photos are by C. Colston Burrell unless otherwise noted.

Gay Bumgarner, 127, 243, 280

©Karen Bussolini, 14, 27, 271

©David Cavagnaro, 113, 146, 155, 174, 182, 194, 195, 203, 230-231, 248, 285

©R. Todd Davis, 69, 128, 147, 215, 244, 245, 257, 283, 286, 308

©Alan & Linda Detrick, 44, 46, 120, 172

©Tracy DiSabato-Aust, 72, 165

©Galen Gates, 15, 26, 28, 32, 52, 71, 73, 130, 210, 211, 296, 299

Tom Gettings/Rodale Images, 15 (Buckwater Garden, Lancaster, PA); 54 (David Culp, garden designer, Downingtown PA); 88, 89, 134, 157, 160 (David Culp, garden designer, Downingtown PA); 293

©John Glover, 10, 12, 39, 49, 51, 55, 65, 67, 93, 95, 106, 151, 161, 173, 216, 261, 262, 289, 292, 295, 298, 301, 307

©David Goldberg/On Location, 90, 259

©Lucy Hardiman, 338

©Saxon Holt, 144–145, 184, 236, 263

Sydney Karp, 102, 234

©Charles Mann, cover (Julia Berman, designer, Santa Fe, NM), 19L, 19R, 21, 23, 48, 58, 63, 66, 101, 103, 156, 192, 193, 197, 202, 205, 207, 253, 260, 266, 287, 294, 305

©David McDonald/PhotoGarden, 45, 96, 175, 208

Clive Nichols, 37 (Sticky Wicket, Dorset); 60 (The Priory, Kemerton, Worcs); 64 (Eastgrove Cottage, Worcester); 74 (Sticky Wicket, Dorset); 86-87 (RHS Garden, Wisley); 108 (Eastgrove Cottage, Worcester); 112 (Butterstream, Eire); 119 (Picton Garden, Worcestershire); 126 (RHS Garden, Wisley); 135, 170 (Old Rectory, Berkshire); 183, 209 (Hadspen Garden, Somerset); 270 (Brook Cottage, Oxon); 302, 303 (Sticky Wicket, Dorset)

Jerry Pavia, 47, 38, 109, 114, 149, 179, 196, 204, 242, 245, 233, 264, 268, 284, 306, 311

©Pam Peirce/On Location, 61

©Susan A. Roth, 59, 92, 97, 110, 111 (Barbara Ashmun, garden designer; Katy McFadden, sculptor); 116, 122, 148, 176, 177 (Tom Pellett, garden designer); 206, 304

Richard Shiell, 42, 57, 100, 123 (Ed Sampson, garden designer/Mourning Cloak Ranch), 256, 280–281, 290, 291

©Brenda Skarphol, 125, 187, 190, 237, 250

©Spectrum Images/Kay Wheeler, 185

©David M. Stone, 265

©Aleksandra Szywala, 32, 33, 43, 50, 62, 168, 309, 310

©Paddy Wales, 16 (Kathy Leishman Garden, Vancouver BC), 40

Index

Boldface page references indicate photographs.

A

Abies pinsapo 'Glauca', 342
Abutilon, 343
Acanthus, 159
Acer palmatum, 268
Acer palmatum 'Dissectum Atropurpureum', 269
Achillea filipendulina, 36, 44, 307
Achillea filipendulina 'Cloth of Gold', 307
Achillea filipendulina 'Coronation Gold', 307
Achillea filipendulina 'Parker's Variety', 307
Achillea millefolium, 56, 283
Achillea 'Moonshine', 33, 58, 196, 306
Achillea taygetea, 110
Aconitum napellus, 340
Acorus gramineus 'Ogon', 192, 323
Actaea racemosa, 34, 168, 169, 169, 231
Actaea simplex 'Atropurpurea', 169
Actaea simplex 'White Pearl', 169
Adam's needle, 'Gold Sword', 45, 188, 189, 224
Adiantum capillus-veneris, 90
Adiantum pedatum, 91, 174
Aegopodium podagraria, 239
Aeonium, 'Zwartkop', 342
Agapanthus
    'Ben Hope', 289
    'Bressingham Blue', 82
    Headbourne hybrids, 56
Agastache barberi 'Tutti Frutti', 122
Agave americana, 326
Agave americana 'Marginata', 326
Ageratum, hardy, 189, 224
Agropyron, 297
Agropyron magellanicum, 296
Agropyron pubiferum, 297
Agropyron repens, 297
Ajuga, 172, 172, 173
Ajuga repens, 172
Ajuga reptans, 172
Alchemilla, 207
Alchemilla alpina, 207
Alchemilla erythropoda, 207

Alchemilla mollis, 32, 46, 168, 206, 207, 267
Alkaline soil, plants for, 49, 156–57, 156, 157
Allium, 18, 312
Allium afaltunense, 338
Allium cilicium, 289
Allium cristophii, 104
Allium 'Globemaster', 338
Allium moly, 110, 200
Allium schoenoprasum, 74, 196, 294, 299, 306
Allium sphaerocephalum, 37, 302
Allium tuberosum, 295
All-White Garden for Partial Shade, An
    illustration, 76–77
    plant list for, 76–77, 358
    plot plan for, 358
Amsonia hubrectii, 191
Amsonia tabernaemontana, 190
Anaphalis margaritacea, 242
Anchusa, 293
Anchusa azurea, 292
Andromeda, Japanese, 337
Andropogon gerardii, 245
Anemanthele lessoniana, 339
Anemone
    bloom time of, 115, 127
    buttercup, 321
    Chinese, 71
        'September Charm', 70, 84
    fall-blooming described, 127
    Japanese, 115, 334, 334
        'Bressingham Glow', 65
        'Pamina', 114, 141
        'Prince Henry' ('Prinz Heinrich'), 126, 127, 142
Anemone blanda, 95
Anemone hupehensis 'September Charm', 70
Anemone hupehensis var. japonica, 115
Anemone × hybrida, 115, 334
Anemone × hybrida 'Pamina', 114
Anemone × hybrida 'Prince Henry' ('Prinz Heinrich'), 126
Anemone ranunculoides, 321
Anemone tomentosa, 115
Angel's trumpet, 333
Anthemis frutescens, 309
Anthemis tinctoria, 203
Antirrhinum majus, 296

Ants, and wildflower seeds, 233, 235
Aquilegia canadensis, 236
Aquilegia flabellata 'Alba', 165
Aquilegia flabellata 'Nana Alba', 164
Aralia spinosa, 247
Arborvitae, Russian, 329
Armeria maritima, 260, 261
Aronia arbutifolia, 64
Arrhenatherum elatius var. bulbosum 'Variegatum', 48
Artemisia
    caring for, 157, 195
    growing conditions for, 29, 194, 298
    'Powis Castle', 28, 29, 73, 298, 299, 314
    'Silver Brocade', 195, 218
    'Silver King', 194
    'Silver Mound', 195
    'Valerie Finnis', 15
Artemisia absinthium, 195
Artemisia arborescens, 130
Artemisia canescens, 131
Artemisia lactiflora, 113
Artemisia ludoviciana, 296, 299
Artemisia ludoviciana 'Silver King', 194
Artemisia 'Powis Castle', 28, 298
Artemisia stelleriana 'Silver Brocade', 195
Artistic elements in gardens
    combinations for, 338–43, 338, 339, 340, 341, 342, 343
    garden design for, 348–49, 362
Arum italicum, 134, 170
Aruncus dioicus, 104, 163
Asarum caudatum, 90
Asarum europaeum, 266, 328
Asarum virginicum, 91
Asclepias incarnata, 153, 250, 285
Asclepias sullivantii, 242
Asclepias tuberosa, 242, 284
Aspidistra elatior 'Akebono', 323
Aspidistra elatior 'Amanogawa', 323
Aspidistra elatior 'Asahi', 323
Aspidistra elatior 'Hoshi Zora', 323
Aspidistra elatior 'Okame', 323
Aspidistra elatior 'Variegata', 323
Aspidistras, about, 323
Aster, 121, 249
    'Bluebird', 121
    'Dark Beauty', 121

USDA Plant Hardiness Zone Map

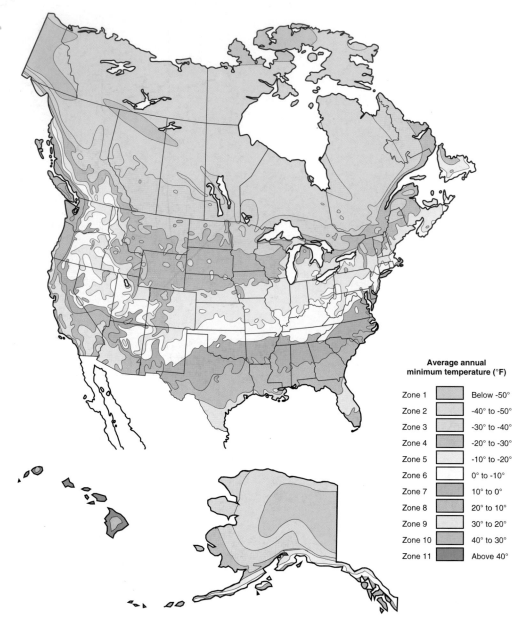

Average annual minimum temperature (°F)

Zone 1	Below -50°
Zone 2	-40° to -50°
Zone 3	-30° to -40°
Zone 4	-20° to -30°
Zone 5	-10° to -20°
Zone 6	0° to -10°
Zone 7	10° to 0°
Zone 8	20° to 10°
Zone 9	30° to 20°
Zone 10	40° to 30°
Zone 11	Above 40°

Revised in 1990 to reflect changes in climate, this map is now recognized as the best estimator of minimum temperatures available. Look at the map to find your area, then match its pattern to the key on the right. When you've found your pattern, the key will tell you what hardiness zone you live in. Remember that the map is a general guide; your particular conditions may vary.